Spelling
Workout

Phillip K. Trocki

Modern Curriculum Press
is an imprint of

Boston, Massachusetts

Chandler, Arizona

Glenview, Illinois

Upper Saddle River, New Jersey

COVER DESIGN: Pronk & Associates

ILLUSTRATIONS: Eric Larsen. 191: Jim Steck.

PHOTOGRAPHS: All photos © Pearson Learning unless otherwise noted.

Cover: *background dandelion* Andy Roberts/Stone. *t.l., m.l.* Artbase Inc.
b.l., b.r. Artbase Inc.
5: © Matteo Berlenga/Fotolia.com. 8: © Jason Reed. 9: © Kablonk Micro/Fotolia.com. 12: © Kathrin Hemkendreis/Fotolia.com.
13: © Duncan Noakes/Fotolia.com. 16: © PhotoDisc, Inc. 17: © Jupiterimages. 20: © Steve Gorton/Dorling Kindersley.
21: © Sean Prior/Fotolia.com. 24: © WITTY/Fotolia.com. 29: © Ryan McVay/PhotoDisc, Inc. 32: © Kelpfish/Fotolia.com.
33: © Dennis Donohue/Fotolia.com. 36: © Don Farrall/PhotoDisc, Inc. 37: © Tony Northrup/Fotolia.com. 40: © CMCD/PhotoDisc,
Inc. 41: © Patryssia. 44. Library of Congress. 53: © Steven Paine/Fotolia.com. 56: © NatUlrich/Fotolia.com. 57: © Georgios/
Crestock. 61: © Comstock. 64: © zimmytws/Fotolia.com. 65: © Chris White/Fotolia.com. 68: © Michal Kolodziejczyk/Fotolia.com.
69: © Yuri Timofeyev/Fotolia.com. 72: © Joanna Zielinsk/Fotolia.com. 77: © Elenathewise/Fotolia.com. 80: © Elenathewise/Fotolia.
com. 81: © Sebastien Windal/Fotolia.com. 85: © AlexQ/Fotolia.com. 88: © siberianmiracle/Fotolia.com. 89: © Elenathewise/
Fotolia.com. 92: © OMKAR A.V/Fotolia.com. 93: © gwimages/Fotolia.com. 96: © bat104/Fotolia.com. 105: © Andy Crawford/
Dorling Kindersley. 108: © Dave King/Dorling Kindersley. 109: © foodmaster/Fotolia.com. 112: © Ahmed Aboul-Seoud/Fotolia.com.
116: © Tim Ridley/Dorling Kindersley. 117: © Albertus/Fotolia.com. 120: © Stephen Coburn/Fotolia.com. 122: © Geostock/
PhotoDisc, Inc. 125: *b.* Library of Congress Prints and Photographs Division. *t.* New York World-Telegram and the Sun
Newspaper Photograph Collection (Library of Congress). 128: Library of Congress Prints and Photographs Division. 129: © AVAVA/
Fotolia.com. 132: © Ansja/Fotolia.com. 133: Library of Congress. 136: © SuperStock, Inc. 137: © fivespots/Fotolia.com.
140: © Natalia Bratslavsky/Fotolia.com. 141: © rook76/Fotolia.com. 144: © Photos.com. 145: © Justimagine/Fotolia.com.

Acknowledgments
ZB Font Method Copyright © 1996 Zaner-Bloser.

Some content in this product is based upon WEBSTER'S NEW WORLD DICTIONARY, 4/E. Copyright ©2013 by
Houghton Mifflin Harcourt Publishing Company. Reprinted by permission of Houghton Mifflin Harcourt Publishing
Company. All rights reserved.

NOTE: Every effort has been made to locate the copyright owner of material reprinted in this book. Omissions
brought to our attention will be corrected in subsequent editions.

Modern Curriculum Press
is an imprint of

ISBN–13: 978-0-7652-2484-2
ISBN–10: 0-7652-2484-4
35   19

Table of Contents

Learning to Spell a Word

1. Say the word.
   Look at the word and say the letters.

2. Print the word with your finger.

3. Close your eyes and think of the word.

4. Cover the word and print it on paper.

5. Check your spelling.

Keeping a Spelling Notebook
A spelling notebook will help you when you write.
Write the words you're having trouble with on a
separate sheet of paper or in the **Spelling Notebook**
at the back of the book.

Spelling Words in Action

What would you do if you felt an earthquake?

Earthquake

One moment it's **quiet**. The next, buildings **shake** and wobble. Dishes are **knocked** off shelves. Take cover **quickly**! It's an **earthquake**!

Though about a million quakes happen every year, most people have never felt one. This is because most tremors are small. Major earthquakes, big enough to knock buildings off their foundations, happen far less frequently. They can be very damaging, however, so schools in earthquake zones **require** students to know what to do in case of a quake. A **speaker** may talk to students about earthquake safety. Students might also practice taking shelter during earthquake drills.

Lots of people have **questions** about what to do if they feel a quake. **Knowing** a **sequence** of steps to follow can help people be safe during an earthquake. **Kneeling** under a strong piece of furniture or standing under a doorway gives some protection from falling objects. People should stay away from windows to avoid being hit by broken glass. People who are outside should go to an open space.

Families can work together to develop plans for earthquake safety at home. The best advice is to stay calm and to be prepared.

Say each boldfaced word in the selection. Which sounds are not spelled the way they are pronounced?

TIP

Sometimes a sound is not spelled the way you would expect. In the word <u>earthquake</u>, the sound for **kw** is spelled with the letters **qu**. The **n** sound in <u>knocked</u> is spelled with **kn**. The **k** sound can be spelled several ways: with **k**, as in <u>shake</u>; with **ch**, as in <u>mechanic</u>; and with **ck**, as in <u>quickly</u>.

LIST WORDS

1. quiet
2. aches
3. shake
4. knocked
5. jacket
6. quarter
7. quickly
8. knowing
9. quarrel
10. speaker
11. questions
12. kneeling
13. earthquake
14. mechanic
15. orchestra
16. knothole
17. inquire
18. sequence
19. require
20. character

Spelling Practice

Words with the Sound of k, kw, and n

Write each **list word** under the correct heading. You will use some words more than once.

kn spells the sound of n

1. _____ 2. _____

3. _____ 4. _____

k spells the sound of k

5. _____ 6. _____

7. _____

ch spells the sound of k

8. _____ 9. _____

10. _____ 11. _____

ck spells the sound of k

12. _____ 13. _____

14. _____

qu spells the sound of kw

15. _____ 16. _____

17. _____ 18. _____

19. _____ 20. _____

21. _____ 22. _____

23. _____

Puzzle

Read each clue. Write **list words** to complete the puzzle.

ACROSS

1. what we ask
4. twenty-five cents
8. short coat with sleeves
9. a group of musicians
10. silent
11. pains

DOWN

2. the person who is talking
3. tapped with your knuckles
4. in the fast way
5. a person who uses tools to work with machines
6. violent movement of the Earth's surface
7. order of things

Alphabetical Order

Write each group of **list words** in alphabetical order.

earthquake	1. _____		orchestra	9. _____
kneeling	2. _____		sequence	10. _____
character	3. _____		require	11. _____
aches	4. _____		shake	12. _____
knowing	5. _____		quarter	13. _____
jacket	6. _____		quickly	14. _____
knothole	7. _____		quarrel	15. _____
inquire	8. _____		questions	16. _____

Spelling and Writing

Proofreading

The following article has ten mistakes. Use the proofreading marks to fix the mistakes. Then write the misspelled **list words** correctly on the lines.

Proofreading Marks

⬭ spelling mistake

⌃ add something

Scientists have been trying foryears to accurately predict earthquakes. Nooowing as quikely as possible when an earthqwake will occur could save thousandsof lives. In California in 1989, special sensorsin a science lab picked up a rise in earth noise twelve days before a quake hit San Francisco. The noise, which increased greatly three hours before the earthquake hit, continued until power to the sensors was noacked out. Scientistsstill have quastons about these sensors. They think the sensors rekwire more testing to find out whether they can really help predict earthquakes.

1. _____

2. _____

3. _____

4. _____

5. _____

6. _____

Writing a Descriptive Paragraph

Special effects are used to create earthquakes and other disasters in the movies. What earthquake scenes can you imagine? Pretend that you are on a movie set watching a scene being filmed. Write a paragraph to describe what you see and hear. Try to use as many **list words** as you can. Remember to proofread your paragraph and fix any mistakes.

_____

_____

_____

_____

_____

_____

_____

BONUS WORDS

qualify

hammock

kindness

knob

leprechaun

Spelling Words in Action

How is training a dog at home like learning at school?

Your Dog, Your Student

You're a student all day at school. At home, your dog can be the student, and you can be the teacher!

Because dogs are pack animals, they love being told what to do. Just like people, dogs like **generous** praise when they do something right. Always make **certain** during training that you show your dog that you love it and that you are **grateful** for its efforts.

It is most important to teach your dog to come to you when called. This could save your dog from a **dangerous** situation someday. Call its name and use a hand **gesture** that signals the dog to come to you. Practice this a **couple** of times a day every day. Go easy, though! Training should be fun for the dog.

You can teach your dog to sit in a similar manner. With the dog on a leash, hold a treat just in front of its nose. Say "sit" and back the treat over its head, gently pushing its back end to the ground at the same time. When it sits, say "good dog" and give it the treat. Your dog deserves **credit** for working hard to learn a new skill.

Once your dog is a happy and well-behaved member of your family, both of you can **graduate** from dog training. **Celebrate** with something more than a **regular** treat. Training a dog can be a very rewarding experience for both you and your dog.

Look back at the boldfaced words. Say each word. What do you notice about the sounds that the letters <u>c</u> and <u>g</u> make?

9

Spelling Practice

TIP

The letter **c** can spell the hard sound heard at the beginning of <u>cow</u>. It can also spell the soft sound heard at the beginning of <u>cent</u>. The letter **g** can spell the hard sound in <u>garden</u> or the soft sound in <u>danger</u>.

When a **c** or **g** is followed by the vowel **e**, **i** or **y**, it usually spells its soft sound. When **c** or **g** is followed by **a**, **o**, or **u**, it usually spells its hard sound.

LIST WORDS

1. concert
2. certain
3. circus
4. couple
5. credit
6. celebrate
7. village
8. graduate
9. grateful
10. coupon
11. shortage
12. gesture
13. generous
14. garage
15. license
16. sausage
17. gadget
18. regular
19. dangerous
20. icicles

Words with Hard and Soft c and g

Write each **list word** under the correct heading. You will use some words more than once.

c as in <u>cent</u>

1. _____
2. _____
3. _____
4. _____
5. _____
6. _____

c as in <u>cow</u>

15. _____
16. _____
17. _____
18. _____
19. _____
20. _____

g as in <u>danger</u>

7. _____
8. _____
9. _____
10. _____
11. _____
12. _____
13. _____
14. _____

g as in <u>garden</u>

21. _____
22. _____
23. _____
24. _____
25. _____

Classification

Write the **list word** that belongs in each group.

1. snow, sleet, _____

2. barn, shed, _____

3. play, performance, _____

4. ticket, certificate, _____

5. hot dog, hamburger, _____

6. clown, ringmaster, _____

7. tool, invention, _____

8. scary, hurtful, _____

9. two, pair, _____

10. cash, funds, _____

11. need, lack, _____

12. thankful, appreciative, _____

Scrambled Words

Unscramble the words below to make these **list words**:
celebrate, certain, generous, gesture, graduate, license, regular, village. Then, write each **list word** on the line.

1. in crate _____

2. a dare tug _____

3. urge set _____

4. ice lens _____

5. give all _____

6. real rug _____

7. clear beet _____

8. user gone _____

Spelling and Writing

Proofreading

The following journal entry contains eleven mistakes. Use the proofreading marks to fix the mistakes. Then, write the misspelled **list words** correctly on the lines.

Proofreading Marks

⬭ spelling mistake

℘ take out something

Saturday, January 24

   My dog did an amazing thing today. I was taking it for a walk in the vilage when it stopped suddenly by a a mailbox. It wouldn't move. I looked behind the mailbox and saw a puppy whimpering. The day was so cold I was afraid its fur would turn turn to isicles! I was sertin it was lost. My dog went right up to it and licked its face. A cuple of minutes later we heard a woman call, "Rusty! Where are you?" I told her we had found a puppy that might be her lost Rusty, and it was! She was so happy to see Rusty. She thought it must have gone gone out the garaje door that morning. She was very gateful to us. She offered me a gift. I said that was a jenerous gestur, but I was just happy that I could help.

1. _____

2. _____

3. _____

4. _____

5. _____

6. _____

7. _____

8. _____

Writing a Narrative Paragraph

Many people love to talk about the funny or smart things their pets do. Write a paragraph about something special your pet or a pet you know did. Use any **list words** that you can. Remember to proofread your paragraph and fix any mistakes.

_____

_____

_____

_____

_____

_____

BONUS WORDS

sincere

gorge

concern

passage

casual

Words with the Sound of f

Spelling Words in Action

What would you find most fun to do if you were a dolphin?

Dolphin Play

Dolphins love to play. They leap out of the water and dance in the waves made by boats.

When dolphins jump out of the water, it's called breaching. Many smaller dolphins will perform one fast breach after another. Some dolphins make small jumps that look like belly flops. Others use more **physical effort** when they jump. Bottle-nosed dolphins can jump 16 feet out of the water. These dolphins can perform **flawless** acrobatics in the air.

Dolphins are friendly animals that live in groups. They whistle, squeak, and click to each other under the water. They're making a dolphin **symphony**. What do these sounds mean? No one knows **enough** about dolphins to be sure. Perhaps the sounds are **laughter**, **frightened** cries, or friendly talk.

Dolphins enjoy being with people who feed them or play games with them. Dolphins can **suffer** because of humans, however. Even though there are laws against hunting dolphins, many are caught in nets meant to catch tuna. People fear that water shows with dolphin stunts may be **tough** on the dolphins. That is why there are laws that protect dolphins from abuse.

Look back at the boldfaced words. Say each word. What do you notice about the way the sound of f is spelled?

13

TIP

The **f** sound can be spelled four ways:

f as in <u>frightened</u>
ff as in <u>suffer</u>
ph as in <u>paragraph</u>
gh as in <u>enough</u>

Spelling Practice

LIST WORDS

1. frightened
2. suffer
3. paragraph
4. effort
5. autographs
6. telephone
7. dolphins
8. enough
9. laughter
10. symphony
11. physical
12. photography
13. atmosphere
14. flawless
15. geography
16. triumph
17. typhoid
18. hyphen
19. typhoon
20. tough

Words with the Sound of f

Write each **list word** under the correct heading.

f spells the sound of f

1. _____

2. _____

ff spells the sound of f

3. _____

4. _____

gh spells the sound of f

5. _____

6. _____

7. _____

ph spells the sound of f

8. _____   9. _____

10. _____   11. _____

12. _____   13. _____

14. _____   15. _____

16. _____   17. _____

18. _____   19. _____

20. _____

Synonyms

Synonyms are words that have the same or nearly the same meanings. Write the **list word** that is a synonym for each word given.

1. perfect _____

2. strong _____

3. work _____

4. signatures _____

5. plenty _____

6. victory _____

7. scared _____

8. storm _____

9. dash _____

10. disease _____

Move the Words

Each underlined **list word** in the sentences below must be moved to a different sentence to make sense. Write the correct **list word** in the blank at the end of the sentence.

1. No one likes to see an animal <u>laughter</u>. _____

2. Learning <u>photography</u> helps you find places on maps. _____

3. For homework, write a <u>telephone</u> about dolphins. _____

4. There is concern about polluting the <u>symphony</u>. _____

5. It's fun to talk to friends on the <u>dolphins</u>. _____

6. A <u>physical</u> class teaches you how to use a camera. _____

7. <u>Atmosphere</u> usually swim and play in groups. _____

8. The baby's <u>geography</u> made everyone smile. _____

9. It takes a lot of <u>suffer</u> training to be a professional athlete. _____

10. The orchestra played a <u>paragraph</u> by Beethoven. _____

Spelling and Writing

Proofreading

The following poster has eleven mistakes. Use the proofreading marks to fix the mistakes. Then write the misspelled **list words** correctly on the lines.

Come one, come all!
Dont wait!
Afternoon shows at Tyfoon Bay!

See the dofins perform with flauless grace.

Watch the sailors triumh over the pirates in an exciting, noisy, and touf sea battle.

Join in with everyones laufter and cheers.

Hear the symfony play.

If you love fotography, be sure to bring your camera.

Telefone 555-3244 for more details.

1. _____

2. _____

3. _____

4. _____

5. _____

6. _____

7. _____

8. _____

9. _____

Writing a Letter

Pretend that you are a sea-animal photographer. Write a letter telling a friend about one of the pictures you've taken. What animal does the picture show? Was it difficult to get the shot? Use any **list words** that you can. Remember to proofread your letter and fix any mistakes.

_____

_____

_____

_____

_____

BONUS WORDS

waffle

festival

cough

telegraph

phonograph

Spelling Words in Action

What makes a Web page an efficient way to share information?

Web Pages

Computers have almost completely replaced **typewriters** as a way to create **written** messages. By typing on a computer connected to the Internet, a person can share a message with millions of people around the world.

One way to share information using the computer is with a page on the World Wide Web. A Web page can be set up for almost any reason. Many businesses have **designed** Web pages for selling things. Some businesses are big ones that people have **known** about for a long time, while others are brand-new. A Web page can help run a **campaign** for some cause, give helpful instructions, or just share ideas.

Making a Web page takes some knowledge. Some people think learning the computer language for creating Web pages, called HTML, is a lot like learning a **foreign** language. Books and classes can teach people the **correct** way to make a Web page. Of course, there are also Web pages about how to make a Web page! People don't have to **resign** themselves to learning HTML, though. Instead, they can **assign** the job to a Web master, an expert who designs Web pages for a living. For a more inviting Web page, a designer can **surround** the information with art. Adding sound and video can also help to make a Web page fun to visit.

Say each boldfaced word. Listen for the n sound or the r sound. What do you notice about how these sounds are spelled?

Spelling Practice

TIP

The **list words** contain either the **n** sound you hear in <u>n</u>ow or the **r** sound you hear in <u>r</u>ip. The **n** sound can sometimes be spelled **kn** as in <u>kn</u>own and **gn** as in assi<u>gn</u>. The **r** sound can sometimes be spelled **wr** as in <u>wr</u>itten and **rr** as in a<u>rr</u>ow.

LIST WORDS

1. wreath
2. known
3. typewriters
4. written
5. wrapper
6. arrow
7. correct
8. mirror
9. surround
10. knead
11. knotted
12. resign
13. designed
14. assign
15. wrinkled
16. foreign
17. wrestler
18. campaign
19. cologne
20. knuckles

Words with the Sound of n and r

Write each **list word** under the correct heading.

kn spells the sound of n

1. _____ 2. _____

3. _____ 4. _____

gn spells the sound of n

5. _____ 6. _____

7. _____ 8. _____

9. _____ 10. _____

rr spells the sound of r

11. _____ 12. _____

13. _____ 14. _____

wr spells the sound of r

15. _____

16. _____

17. _____

18. _____

19. _____

20. _____

Missing Words

Write the **list word** that best completes each sentence.

1. Carlos _____ the scenery for the class play.

2. Aunt Clara will _____ from her job.

3. The first _____ country I visited was Denmark.

4. The champion _____ entered the ring.

5. Robin Hood's _____ hit the center of the target.

6. She was wearing some _____ that smelled like roses.

7. One of Yellowstone National Park's most famous geysers is _____ as Old Faithful.

8. Mr. Hall will _____ the topics for our report.

9. Mrs. Blake saw her reflection in the _____.

10. The senator ran a successful _____.

11. Computers have replaced _____ in many offices.

12. Use the delete key to _____ your error.

Rhyming

Write the **list word** that rhymes with each word given.

1. feed _____

2. twinkled _____

3. teeth _____

4. spotted _____

5. around _____

6. buckles _____

7. bitten _____

8. trapper _____

Spelling and Writing

Proofreading

The following article has eight mistakes. Use the proofreading marks to fix the mistakes. Then, write the misspelled **list words** correctly on the lines.

Proofreading Marks

⬭ spelling mistake

⊙ add period

Across the Internet, any kind of writen message can be sent from one computer to another, even to those in forein countries The Internet was originally desiged for the military in the 1960's For years, it was hardly nown outside military and academic circles. Then, in 1989, the invention of the World Wide Web made the Internet useful for many purposes The popularity of the Web depends in part on the use of links to other Web sites. When you're looking for the corect answer to a question, links take you from one site to another with a single click of the mouse.

1._____   2._____   3._____

4._____   5._____

Writing an Informative Paragraph

Think of a topic for a Web site that would be helpful to others. It could provide directions, information, or a useful idea. Write a paragraph about your Web site. Try to use as many **list words** as you can. Remember to proofread your paragraph and fix any mistakes.

_____

_____

_____

_____

_____

_____

BONUS WORDS

knowledge

align

ferry

wrath

errand

Spelling Words in Action

Why is pizza such a popular food?

Pizza Pizzazz

Did you know that Americans eat billions of slices of pizza a year? On average, one person eats 23 pounds of pizza a year. That **equals** almost a half a pound of pizza a week.

Of all age groups in the United States, teenagers and college students eat the most pizza. Maybe they think pizza is the best **fuel** to help them study for **final** exams. Whatever the reason, pizza makers **scramble** to get spots near colleges to set up their shops.

The great thing about pizza is that you can put anything on it. You might like a **pickle** on your pizza or **double** cheese. You can choose whatever will **tickle** your fancy. Some people like broccoli or pineapple on their pizza. If you're like most people, however, you'll ask to **cancel** the anchovies.

Can pizza be improved? What if pizzas were **oval** instead of round? Or, what if pizza makers could twist the toppings, sauce, and crust into a **spiral**? What would you do to make an original pizza? How many toppings would it have? Would it have a thin crust or a thick one? Have a contest with your friends to see who can think of the best new pizza. Yum!

Look back at the boldfaced words. How is the last syllable in each word spelled? Say each word and listen to the sound made by the last syllable.

Spelling Practice

TIP

The sounds of **el** and **l** can be spelled in different ways. Listen to the sound made by the syllables spelled **le**, **el**, and **al** in the **list words**. The letters **le**, **el**, and **al** all spell the same sound in the last syllable of words such as <u>pickle</u>, <u>towels</u>, and <u>final</u>.

LIST WORDS

1. final
2. oval
3. fuel
4. equals
5. pickle
6. tickle
7. double
8. jungle
9. panel
10. towels
11. cancel
12. plural
13. mammal
14. sparkled
15. whistle
16. aisle
17. scramble
18. channel
19. spiral
20. jingle

Words with the Sound of <u>el</u> and <u>l</u>

Write each **list word** under the correct heading.

le spells the sound of **el** or **l**

1. _____ 2. _____

3. _____ 4. _____

5. _____ 6. _____

7. _____ 8. _____

9. _____

el spells the sound of **el** or **l**

10. _____

11. _____

12. _____

13. _____

14. _____

al spells the sound of **el** or **l**

15. _____ 16. _____

17. _____ 18. _____

19. _____ 20. _____

Definitions

Write a **list word** to match each definition clue. Find the answer to the riddle by reading down the letters in the shaded box.

1. shaped like an egg   __ __ __ __

2. is the same as   __ __ __ __ __

3. walkway between seats   __ __ __ __ __

4. last   __ __ __ __ __

5. end   __ __ __ __ __

6. twice as much   __ __ __ __ __

7. used for drying   __ __ __ __ __ __

8. used to supply heat or power   __ __ __

9. to cover a wall with wood   __ __ __ __ __

10. a noisemaker   __ __ __ __ __

11. to make ringing sounds   __ __ __ __ __ __

Riddle: What do most people order in a pizza shop? __ _____ ___ ____

Comparing Words

Study the relationship between the first two underlined words. Then, write a **list word** that has the same relationship with the third underlined word.

1. cold is to the Arctic as hot is to a _____

2. scream is to scare as laugh is to _____

3. pizza is to pepperoni as hamburger is to _____

4. fold is to half as twist is to _____

5. snake is to reptile as lion is to _____

6. cake is to bake as eggs are to _____

7. past is to present as single is to _____

8. radio is to station as TV is to _____

9. fire is to blazed as diamond is to _____

Spelling and Writing

Proofreading

Proofreading Marks

◯ spelling mistake

∧ add something

The following want ad has nine mistakes. Use the proofreading marks to fix the mistakes. Then, write the misspelled **list words** correctly on the lines.

Are you tired of the workday jungel Do you feel that life is a constant scamble? Do you have ideas that once sparkeld, but are now dull Then, you may be the person who fits the job of advertising manager for our pizza products. You will be responsible for writing a new jingel for our television commercials. Does all this tikel your fancy This is our finel offer! Call 555-1243 to set up an appointment.

1. _____   2. _____

3. _____   4. _____

5. _____   6. _____

Writing a Persuasive Paragraph

Think of a favorite healthy snack that you wish your school would serve. Write a paragraph to persuade your school to put the snack on the menu. Use any **list words** that you can. Remember to proofread your paragraph and fix any mistakes.

_____

_____

_____

_____

_____

_____

BONUS WORDS

general

dismal

muscle

noble

easel

In lessons 1 through 5, you learned different ways to spell words with the sounds **k**, **kw**, and **n**, as well as the sounds **f**, **r**, **el**, and **l**. You also learned to spell words with the soft and hard sounds for **c** and **g**.

Check Your Spelling Notebook

Look at the words in your spelling notebook. Which words for lessons 1 through 5 did you have the most trouble with? Write them here.

_____

_____

_____

Practice writing your troublesome words with a partner. Take turns writing each word as the other slowly spells it aloud.

Lesson 1

 Listen for the **kw** sound in quarrel. Notice how the **k** sound is spelled in <u>speaker</u>, <u>mechanic</u>, and <u>jacket</u>. The **n** sound can be spelled with **kn**, as in <u>knowing</u>.

Write a **list word** that belongs in each group. Not all the words will be used.

List Words

quiet
orchestra
aches
shake
knocked
jacket
quarter
mechanic
quickly
kneeling
sequence
character

1. events, order, _____

2. fast, rapidly, _____

3. shiver, rattle, _____

4. silent, calm, _____

5. nickel, dime, _____

6. plot, setting, _____

7. pains, sores, _____

8. coat, sweater, _____

9. standing, sitting, _____

10. rapped, tapped, _____

25

The letters **c** and **g** each have a soft sound and a hard sound. Listen for the sounds of **c** in <u>certain</u> and <u>coupon</u>. Listen for the sounds of **g** in <u>gadget</u>.

List Words

concert
sausage
circus
couple
village
celebrate
graduate
gesture
garage
license
dangerous
icicles

Write a **list word** that matches each clue. Not all the words will be used.

1. a sign of winter _____

2. a shelter for a car _____

3. finish high school _____

4. have a party _____

5. band performance _____

6. spicy meat _____

7. wave a hand _____

8. a pair _____

9. permits driving a car _____

10. has tents and clowns _____

 The **f** sound can be spelled four ways: **f**, **ff**, **ph**, and **gh**, as in <u>frightened</u>, <u>suffer</u>, <u>typhoon</u>, and <u>laughter</u>.

List Words

frightened
effort
autographs
symphony
dolphins
enough
atmosphere
flawless
triumph
laughter
hyphen
tough

Write the **list word** that is a synonym for the word given. Not all the words will be used.

1. dash _____

2. plenty _____

3. victory _____

4. signatures _____

5. hard _____

6. perfect _____

7. attempt _____

8. scared _____

9. air _____

10. giggles _____

The **r** sound can be spelled **wr** as in <u>wreath</u> and **rr** as in <u>mirror</u>. The **n** sound can be spelled **kn** as in <u>knotted</u> and **gn** as in <u>assign</u>.

List Words

wreath
typewriters
wrapper
correct
cologne
surround
knead
resign
mirror
foreign
campaign
knuckles

Write the **list word** next to its dictionary sound-spelling. Not all the words will be used.

1. (kam pān′) _____

2. (tīp′rīt′ərz) _____

3. (fôr′ in) _____

4. (nēd) _____

5. (rēth) _____

6. (rē zīn′) _____

7. (kə rekt′) _____

8. (sər round′) _____

9. (nuk′əlz) _____

10. (kə lōn′) _____

 The **l** or **el** sound in the last syllable of a word can be spelled **le**, **el**, or **al**, as in <u>tickle</u>, <u>fuel</u>, and <u>mammal</u>.

List Words

final
oval
equals
pickle
double
jungle
towels
plural
whistle
aisle
channel
sparkled

Write a **list word** to complete each sentence. Not all the words will be used.

1. This _____ has the best TV programs.

2. Hang the wet _____ on the line to dry.

3. The bride and groom walked down the _____.

4. That loud _____ hurts my ears.

5. This _____ is too sour for my taste.

6. The astronauts began the _____ countdown.

7. Four times four _____ sixteen.

8. Two frisky puppies are _____ trouble.

9. The _____ form of *child* is *children*.

10. The picture frame has an _____ shape.

Show What You Know

One word is misspelled in each set of **list words**. Fill in the circle next to the **list word** that is spelled incorrectly.

1. ○ aisle ○ resign ○ enoufh ○ generous ○ jacket
2. ○ wreth ○ scramble ○ knuckles ○ triumph ○ sausage
3. ○ quiet ○ couple ○ arrow ○ plural ○ gneeling
4. ○ inquire ○ garage ○ physical ○ knoted ○ towels
5. ○ symphony ○ quarrel ○ village ○ coupon ○ photograpy
6. ○ mirror ○ tickle ○ grateful ○ atmosphere ○ wistle
7. ○ laughter ○ sparkled ○ jungle ○ duble ○ correct
8. ○ speeker ○ spiral ○ channel ○ questions ○ shortage
9. ○ gesture ○ orkestra ○ flawless ○ surround ○ pickle
10. ○ desined ○ typhoid ○ gadget ○ sequence ○ aches
11. ○ concert ○ effort ○ nown ○ oval ○ equals
12. ○ knowing ○ celebrate ○ telephone ○ wrapper ○ cansel
13. ○ knothole ○ earthquake ○ cologn ○ campaign ○ mammal
14. ○ panle ○ knead ○ paragraph ○ circus ○ quarter
15. ○ dolphins ○ suffer ○ regular ○ lisense ○ wrinkled
16. ○ foreign ○ typhon ○ dangerous ○ knocked ○ jingle
17. ○ restler ○ hyphen ○ character ○ quickly ○ fuel
18. ○ written ○ autographs ○ credit ○ mechanic ○ finael
19. ○ asigne ○ frightened ○ certain ○ icicles ○ tough
20. ○ shake ○ requir ○ graduate ○ geography ○ typewriters

Spelling Words in Action

What are the pros and cons of bubble gum?

A Sticky Subject

Parents and teachers often **complain** about it. You might hear, "It's bad for your teeth!" or, "If anyone **swallows** it, it might become lodged in the throat!"

In case you haven't guessed, they're talking about chewing gum. You must admit, the complaints are well-founded. Gum is messy, and many people are careless with it. Instead of wrapping it after chewing, some people end up **throwing** it or dropping it. If you blow a bubble big enough to get stuck in your hair, removing the gum can be very **painful**.

Those who say that gum is bad for your teeth are also correct. We all know that too much sugar helps cause tooth **decay**. If you must chew, **borrow** some good advice and make the gum sugarless!

Americans can **boast** of chewing more gum than any other people in the world. The average American chews 300 sticks of gum a year. From **coast** to coast, Americans spend more than $2 billion a year on gum. Just for the record, Susan Montgomery Williams of Fresno, California, **gained** fame in 1979 by blowing the largest bubble ever. Using three pieces of gum, Susan blew a bubble that measured 19 inches in diameter. She went on to break that record three times. In 1994, she blew a 23-inch bubble. If you blew a bubble that big, would you have **fainted?**

Say the boldfaced words in the selection with the vowel pairs a<u>i</u> and a<u>y</u>. How are they alike? Say the boldfaced words with the vowel pairs <u>oa</u> and <u>ow</u>. How are they alike?

Spelling Practice

TIP

A vowel pair is made from two vowels that come together to make one long vowel sound. The first vowel in the pair usually stands for its long sound, and the second is silent. The vowel pairs **ai** and **ay** can spell the long **a** sound you hear in drains and decay. The vowel pairs **oa** and **ow** can spell the long **o** sound you hear in coast and borrow.

LIST WORDS

1. complain
2. braid
3. drains
4. coast
5. toasted
6. decay
7. roasting
8. throwing
9. tomorrow
10. borrow
11. boast
12. swallows
13. foamy
14. poach
15. cocoa
16. fainted
17. scarecrow
18. gained
19. hoax
20. painful

Words with the Sound of Long o and Long a

Write each **list word** under the correct heading.

long o sound

1. _____ 2. _____
3. _____ 4. _____
5. _____ 6. _____
7. _____ 8. _____
9. _____ 10. _____
11. _____ 12. _____
13. _____

long a sound

14. _____
15. _____
16. _____
17. _____
18. _____
19. _____
20. _____

Write a **list word** to match each definition clue. Then, use the numbered letters to solve the riddle. Copy each numbered letter onto the answer line with the same number.

1. tossing __ __ __ __ __ __ __
$\quad\quad\quad\quad$ 3 $\quad$ 4 $\quad$ 13

2. to rot or break down __ __ __ __ __
$\quad\quad\quad\quad\quad\quad\quad\quad$ 6 $\quad$ 1

3. the day after today __ __ __ __ __ __ __ __
$\quad\quad\quad\quad\quad\quad$ 10 $\;$ 5 $\quad\;$ 8 $\quad\quad\;$ 9

4. hot chocolate __ __ __ __ __
$\quad\quad\quad\quad\quad\quad$ 2

5. cook eggs in liquid __ __ __ __ __
$\quad\quad\quad\quad\quad\quad\;$ 12 $\;$ 7

6. to use for a time __ __ __ __ __ __
$\quad\quad\quad\quad\quad$ 11

7. becomes empty or dry __ __ __ __ __ __
$\quad\quad\quad\quad\quad\quad\quad\quad$ 14

Riddle: Where is the best place to have a gum-chewing contest?

Answer: __ __ __ __ __ __ __ __ __ __ __ __ __ __
$\quad\quad\;$ 1 $\quad$ 2 $\quad$ 3 $\quad$ 4 $\quad$ 5 $\quad\;$ 6 $\quad$ 7 $\quad$ 8 $\quad$ 9 $\quad\;$ 10 $\;$ 11 $\;$ 12 $\;$ 13 $\;$ 14

Add and subtract letters to form **list words**.

1. false – lse + into – o + flowed – flow _____

2. groan – gn + stinging – ing _____

3. compare – pare + apple – ape + rain – r _____

4. boat – t + rest – re _____

5. game – me + into – to + slowed – slow _____

6. swing – ing + balloon – boon + bellows – bell _____

7. scared – red + redo – do + crowd – d _____

8. space – sce + spin – sp + colorful – color _____

9. bring – ing + amid – m _____

10. come – me + base – be + t _____

11. house – use + beat - bet + x _____

12. fair – air + roam – r + stingy – sting _____

13. toad – ad + assign – sign + rented – ren _____

Spelling and Writing

Proofreading

The following article has ten mistakes. Use the proofreading marks to fix each mistake. Then, write the misspelled **list words** correctly on the lines.

Proofreading Marks

⬭ spelling mistake

≡ capital letter

∧ add something

Where do you think chewing gum came from It came from the dried sap of a jungle tree called sapodilla that was chewed by the aztecs. They called it *chictli*. chewing gum showed up on the east coost of the united States in 1871. Do you know what happened Many people loved the gum, but others began to complayn that chewing drayns moisture from the salivary glands; and if a person swalloes it, the stomach will be upset. It was not until the mid-1900s that people began to worry about tooth decai.

1. _____ 2. _____ 3. _____

4. _____ 5. _____

Writing a Problem-Solution Essay

Some people think that chewing gum is a bad habit. Do you have any ideas about how a bad habit, such as fingernail biting, might be broken? Write your ideas in a problem-solution essay that describes the problem and presents a possible solution. Use any **list words** that you can. Remember to proofread your paragraph and fix any mistakes.

BONUS WORDS

sorrow

stain

betray

toadstool

sparrow

_____

_____

_____

_____

_____

Spelling Words in Action

Why are feathers a bird's treasure?

On the Wing

It is said that birds of a **feather** flock together. Birds may not be in **agreement** with that statement. That's because no two feathers are exactly the same. Feathers come in a variety of shapes, colors, and sizes. One large bird alone can have as many as 25,000 feathers from head to tail.

Feathers are not only beautiful, but they also help a bird fly. Smaller feathers help streamline the **creature** so that it will not resist air. The larger wing and tail feathers help lift a bird into the sky.

Feathers help birds stay **healthy** by serving like a **sweater** to keep them warm and dry. Each quill has thousands of tiny shafts that lock together, **keeping** the bird dry **underneath**. Water simply rolls off the bird's back. In warmer weather, the feathers act to cool the bird.

The colors of a bird's feathers may be the same as the **meadows** or marshes in which it lives. This helps to protect the bird from enemies. Brightly colored feathers help a bird to **succeed** in finding a mate.

From the great condor to the tiny hummingbird, feathers are a bird's **treasure**.

Say the boldfaced words in the selection. Which vowels together make a long __e__ sound? Which vowels together make a long __e__ sound and a short __e__ sound?

Spelling Practice

TIP

In a vowel pair, the two vowels come together to make one long vowel sound. The vowel pair **ee** has the long **e** sound you hear in <u>speech</u>. The vowel pair **ea** also spells the long **e** sound, as in <u>underneath</u>. The vowels **ea** can also form a vowel digraph. A vowel digraph is two vowels together that can make a long or short sound, or have a special sound all their own. The vowel digraph **ea** can spell the short **e** sound, as in <u>steady</u>.

LIST WORDS

1. feather
2. sweater
3. underneath
4. agreement
5. meadows
6. speech
7. needles
8. keeping
9. treasure
10. northeast
11. steady
12. creature
13. breathe
14. pleasure
15. succeed
16. sweeter
17. healthy
18. preacher
19. leather
20. wealth

Words with Long and Short e Sounds

Write each **list word** under the correct heading.

ee spells the long **e** sound

1. _____   2. _____
3. _____   4. _____
5. _____   6. _____

ea spells the long **e** sound

7. _____
8. _____
9. _____
10. _____
11. _____

ea spells the short **e** sound

12. _____
13. _____
14. _____
15. _____
16. _____
17. _____
18. _____
19. _____
20. _____

Complete the Rhyme

Complete each rhyme with a **list word** that contains the vowel pair or digraph that is underlined.

1. The movie was a double fe<u>a</u>ture.

It starred a monster and a furry _____.

2. The pirate's map said, "Six feet down, me<u>a</u>sure.

There you will find my buried _____."

3. The sailboat captains got the sails r<u>ea</u>dy, now that

the wind was strong and _____.

4. People may wish to be w<u>ea</u>lthy, but to live a long life

you must be _____.

5. Here's advice you should h<u>ee</u>d: Always try to _____.

6. Birds of a _____ fly in all kinds of w<u>ea</u>ther.

Dictionary

Write the **list words** that would be found on dictionary pages between each pair of guide words shown. Be sure to write the **list words** in alphabetical order.

age/northwest	please/wear
1. _____	1. _____
2. _____	2. _____
3. _____	3. _____
4. _____	4. _____
5. _____	5. _____
6. _____	6. _____
7. _____	7. _____
8. _____	8. _____
9. _____	9. _____
10. _____	10. _____

Spelling and Writing

Proofreading

The following story summary has fourteen mistakes. Use the proofreading marks to fix each mistake. Then, write the misspelled **list words** correctly on the lines.

Proofreading Marks

⬭ spelling mistake

⊙ add period

↺ take out something

The Greek myth of Daedalus and Icarus tells of a father and son who are held prisoner by a king of great wealt After the the father sees a bird's fiether, he builds two pairs of wings made of feathers and wax In a a speich to his son, Daedalus says they will suced in escaping if they stay steadee and do not fly too close to the sun. At first, they fly over meadoews, keping low Excited by what he sees, Icarus forgets what his father told him. He flies too high over the sea His wings melt and and he falls into the ocean.

1. _____

2. _____

3. _____

4. _____

5. _____

6. _____

7. _____

Writing a Descriptive Paragraph

What is your favorite bird? Write a descriptive paragraph explaining why you like this bird. Be sure to use words that will create vivid images in a reader's mind. Try to use as many **list words** as you can. Remember to proofread your paragraph and fix any mistakes.

_____

_____

_____

_____

_____

_____

_____

BONUS WORDS

measure

heal

peasant

degree

seek

Spelling Words in Action

Money doesn't grow on trees, but where *does* it come from?

Making Money

A cashier takes a new roll of coins from a **drawer**. You **withdraw** brand-new bills from a bank. Where does the money come from?

The U.S. government makes all of our money. Every year, the U.S. Mint makes 14–20 billion coins. To make the coins, the Mint starts with 1,500-foot-long strips. Round **saucers** called blanks are punched out from the strips. A coining press stamps the designs and words on the coins. Then, the coins are counted, bagged, and stored in a **vault** before being **hauled** by truck to your local bank. After years of use, some money looks as if animals have been **gnawing** on it. No one wants to throw away money, so the U.S. Mint reshapes damaged coins.

To make paper money, the Bureau of Engraving and Printing goes through more than 65 steps. These steps include engraving steel plates by hand and stamping the plates on sheets of paper under 20 tons of pressure. Every bill is checked before it is given another stamp and number to make it official U.S. money.

It is **unlawful** for anyone but the U.S. government to make our money. The process is so complex that it is **awfully** difficult to copy. Even so, **caution** should be used when handling money. People should **pause** to look closely at the bills they receive to make sure the bills are real!

Say the boldfaced words in the selection. What do you notice about the vowel sounds made by the vowel digraphs au and aw?

TIP

The vowel digraphs **au** and **aw** sound alike. They spell the **aw** sound you hear in <u>hawk</u> and <u>pause</u>.

LIST WORDS

1. hawk
2. faucet
3. author
4. pause
5. daughter
6. withdraw
7. hauled
8. awfully
9. unlawful
10. lawyer
11. strawberries
12. squawk
13. saucers
14. drawer
15. caution
16. vault
17. naughty
18. gnawing
19. awkward
20. exhaust

Words with au and aw

Write each **list word** under the correct heading.

vowel digraph au

1. _____ 2. _____

3. _____ 4. _____

5. _____ 6. _____

7. _____ 8. _____

9. _____ 10. _____

vowel digraph aw

11. _____

12. _____

13. _____

14. _____

15. _____

16. _____

17. _____

18. _____

19. _____

20. _____

Classification

Write the **list word** that belongs in each group.

1. carried, dragged, _____

2. screech, scream, _____

3. illegal, wrong, _____

4. wall safe, piggy bank, _____

5. remove oneself, back out, _____

6. blueberries, raspberries, _____

7. closet, cupboard, _____

8. warning, advice, _____

9. robin, crow, _____

10. drain, sink, _____

11. cups, plates, _____

12. soot, smoke, _____

13. wait, rest, _____

14. child, son, _____

15. judge, juror, _____

Puzzle

Read each clue. Write **list words** to complete the puzzle.

ACROSS
2. chewing
3. terribly
4. warning
7. one who practices law

DOWN
1. safe storeroom
3. a published writer
5. not graceful
6. not behaving properly

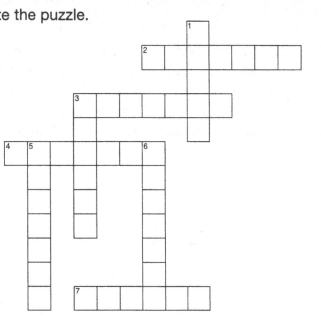

Spelling and Writing

Proofreading

This book review has thirteen mistakes. Use the proofreading marks to fix the mistakes. Then, write the misspelled **list words** correctly on the lines.

Proofreading Marks

⬭ spelling mistake

⌃ add something

The awthor of *Strauberries* has some funny ideas about what makes a goodmystery. His language is awkword ashe tells about the unlauful theft of prize fruit froma large volt. The fruit is hawled away by a store owner's daughter to stopits sale to a rival store in the next town. Clues are found on a fauset and in sawsers. Thisstory does not have a real ending either. It just stops.

1. _____   2. _____

3. _____   4. _____

5. _____   6. _____

7. _____   8. _____

Writing a Narrative Paragraph

Think about a time when you saved your money to buy something special. Write a paragraph that tells about how you saved your money and what you bought. Be sure to write in the first person, using *I* and *me*. Try to use as many **list words** as you can. Remember to proofread your paragraph and fix any mistakes.

_____

_____

_____

_____

_____

_____

BONUS WORDS

awe

thawed

sprawl

slaughter

audience

Spelling Words in Action

When do you not believe what you see?

Seeing Isn't Believing

Imagine you are walking down a street, and you see a door. You take a **brief** look and reach for the doorknob. You can't get your hand around it. The door won't open. Then, you realize you've been **deceived**! There is no door. There is no doorknob, **either**. It's just a wall painting, or a mural.

A painting this real proves that you can't always **believe** what you see. The French have a name for this kind of art. They call it *trompe l'oeil* (trawmp-loy). These words mean "fool the eye." Trompe l'oeil painting has been around since ancient times. It creates a look of great depth.

Many artists are turning blank walls into **pieces** of trompe l'oeil art. Any scene you could **conceive** of can be created. Three-foot-wide flowers painted on a hotel wall look so bright that you will **shield** your eyes. The people you see in the photo are actually painted on the building.

On another building, painter John Pugh worked hard to **achieve** the look of a decaying building, and he certainly succeeded. Someone who saw the mural even complained that the building's wall needed to be fixed! These mural painters also work indoors. A clever artist can turn a boring ceiling into a baseball **infield**. There's no end to the images these artists of **deceit** can create.

Say the boldfaced words in the selection. What vowel sounds do you hear? What do you notice about the vowel digraphs and vowel pair?

Spelling Practice

TIP

The vowels **ie** and **ei** can be vowel pairs as well as vowel digraphs. Vowel pair **ei** can spell the long **e** sound, as in the word <u>deceit</u>. The vowel digraph **ie** can also spell the long **e** sound (<u>believe</u>). Vowel digraph **ei** can spell the long **a** sound (<u>freight</u>). Here's a helpful rule:

"**I** before **E**, except after **C**, or when **ei** sounds like **A**, as in <u>eighty</u> and <u>freight</u>." The words <u>either</u> and <u>neither</u> are tricky! They do not follow this rule.

LIST WORDS

1. deceived
2. received
3. brief
4. believe
5. infield
6. review
7. freight
8. vein
9. shield
10. pieces
11. eighty
12. niece
13. yield
14. either
15. neither
16. deceit
17. grief
18. thief
19. achieve
20. conceive

Words with ie and ei

Write each **list word** under the correct heading.

ie

1. _____   2. _____

3. _____   4. _____

5. _____   6. _____

7. _____   8. _____

9. _____   10. _____

11. _____

ei after c

12. _____

13. _____

14. _____

15. _____

ei as in freight

16. _____

17. _____

18. _____

ei in "No Rule" words

19. _____

20. _____

Complete the Paragraph

Fill in the **list words** that best complete the sentences in the paragraph below.

While watching a baseball game on TV, an _____-year-

old woman could not _____ her eyes. The cameras

followed a fly ball over the _____ and into the stands.

Then, to her surprise, her youngest _____, Amy, held up

the ball. She couldn't _____ how an eight-year-old girl

could catch a fly ball. The woman wondered if her eyes had

_____ her. She called to her husband, who couldn't

believe his eyes _____. Then, for a _____

moment, they saw Amy again. This time, they noticed her enormous

baseball mitt. The mitt must have acted like a _____,

blocking others from catching the ball. It was an amazing thing for

an eight year old to _____.

Find these ten **list words** in the puzzle below: <u>deceit</u>, <u>freight</u>, <u>grief</u>, <u>neither</u>, <u>pieces</u>, <u>received</u>, <u>review</u>, <u>thief</u>, <u>vein</u>, <u>yield</u>. The words can go forward or backward, up, down, or diagonally. Then write the words on the lines below.

```
E  G  R  I  F  L  D  E  S  R
L  R  E  N  Q  F  E  I  H  T
S  E  C  E  I  P  R  I  Z  C
F  R  E  I  G  H  T  O  T  I
F  E  I  R  G  Y  P  A  I  H
L  V  V  N  E  I  T  H  E  R
T  R  E  V  I  E  W  I  C  L
N  E  D  I  S  L  B  I  E  Y
E  V  R  L  N  D  N  I  D  Y
```

1. _____ 6. _____

2. _____ 7. _____

3. _____ 8. _____

4. _____ 9. _____

5. _____ 10. _____

Spelling and Writing

Proofreading

Proofreading Marks

 spelling mistake

∧ add something

This article has twelve mistakes. Use the proofreading marks to fix the mistakes. Then, rewrite the misspelled **list words** correctly on the lines.

One of the greatest mural artists to achieeve fame was Diego Rivera. He was born in Guanajuato Mexico, on December 8 1886. A reveiw of his work shows that he had great respect for the common people. He also showed the greef he felt at how poorer people were treated by the government. He did not beleeve that people should yeild to those who wanted to rule them unfairly. His murals appeared on walls of government buildings schools and palaces. He traveled to Detroit New York City and San Francisco to paint. He recieved many honors while he was alive.

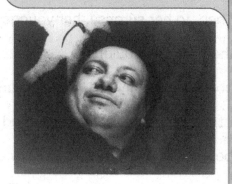

1. _____ 2. _____ 3. _____

4. _____ 5. _____ 6. _____

Writing a Narrative Paragraph

Have you ever thought you saw something that turned out to be something else? Write about your experience or make one up. Try to use as many **list words** as you can. Remember to proofread your paragraph and fix any mistakes.

_____

_____

_____

_____

_____

_____

BONUS WORDS

disbelief

relieved

grieve

eighteen

leisure

Diphthongs <u>ou</u>, <u>ow</u>, <u>oi</u>, and <u>oy</u>

Spelling Words in Action

How does the wind make a cold day colder?

The Big Chill

How many times have you **counted** on a thermometer to tell you how warmly to dress, then when you got outside it seemed much colder? What was different? Was it the **moisture** in the air? Perhaps, but if the wind was blowing, it was probably the windchill factor.

Does that mean that the wind has **joined** the cold to make things worse? Not really. When the air is still, your body heat forms a shield that acts like a **boundary** between you and the cold air. When the wind blows, however, that shield is broken. As a result, you feel much colder.

Here is a chart to find out what the temperature feels like when there's wind. Check the temperature on a thermometer, then find out the wind speed from a weather report.

Whether you're headed off on an ocean **voyage** or hoping to ski in some fresh **powder** snow falling in a **mountainous** area, consider the wind. Knowing the effect of the windchill could make your trip a lot more **enjoyable**. If you find yourself shivering on the way to school, try walking in **crowded** areas to keep warm. **Avoid** windy streets, and wear that windbreaker!

Windchill Chart

MPH	Temperature									
CALM	35	30	25	20	15	10	5	0	-5	-10
Wind Speed (Miles per hour)	Equivalent Chill Temperature									
5	30	25	20	15	10	5	0	-5	-10	-15
10	20	15	10	5	0	-10	-15	-20	-25	-35
15	15	10	0	-5	-10	-20	-25	-30	-40	-45
20	10	5	0	-10	-15	-25	-30	-35	-40	-50
25	10	0	-5	-15	-20	-30	-35	-45	-50	-60
30	5	0	-10	-20	-25	-30	-40	-50	-55	-65
35	5	-5	-10	-20	-30	-35	-40	-50	-60	-65
40	0	-5	-15	-20	-30	-35	-45	-55	-60	-70

Say the boldfaced words with <u>ou</u> and <u>ow</u> in the selection. What difference is there in the vowel sound you hear in these words? Say the boldfaced words with <u>oi</u> and <u>oy</u> in the selection. What difference is there in the vowel sound you hear in these words?

Spelling Practice

TIP

A diphthong is two letters blended together to make one vowel sound. The diphthongs **ou** and **ow** spell the **ow** sound you hear in <u>boundary</u> and <u>crowded</u>. The diphthongs **oi** and **oy** spell the **oy** sound you hear in <u>poise</u> and <u>loyalty</u>. Notice that the words <u>choir</u> and <u>courageous</u> and the last syllables in <u>mountainous</u> and <u>poisonous</u> do not have diphthong sounds.

LIST WORDS

1. crowded
2. joined
3. voyage
4. soiled
5. enjoyable
6. counted
7. powder
8. oyster
9. poise
10. boundary
11. loyalty
12. moisture
13. poisonous
14. mountainous
15. courageous
16. choir
17. toiled
18. broiled
19. avoid
20. joint

Words with <u>ou</u>, <u>ow</u>, <u>oi</u>, and <u>oy</u>

Write each **list word** under the correct heading. You will use some words more than once.

ou and ow spell the sound in <u>loud</u>

1. _____
2. _____
3. _____
4. _____
5. _____

ou spells the sound in <u>famous</u>

6. _____   7. _____

8. _____

oi spells the long i sound

9. _____

oi and oy spell the sound in <u>oil</u>

10. _____   11. _____

12. _____   13. _____

14. _____   15. _____

16. _____   17. _____

18. _____   19. _____

20. _____   21. _____

22. _____

Comparing Words

Study the relationship between the first two underlined words or phrases.
Then, write a **list word** that has the same relationship with the third underlined word.

1. <u>patience</u> is to <u>calmness</u> as <u>confidence</u> is to _____

2. <u>hive</u> is to <u>bee</u> as <u>shell</u> is to _____

3. <u>went</u> is to <u>returned</u> as <u>separated</u> is to _____

4. <u>player</u> is to <u>team</u> as <u>singer</u> is to _____

5. <u>soap</u> is to <u>clean</u> as <u>dirt</u> is to _____

6. <u>flying</u> is to <u>flight</u> as <u>sailing</u> is to _____

7. <u>mutual</u> is to <u>common</u> as <u>shared</u> is to _____

8. <u>empty</u> is to <u>full</u> as <u>unoccupied</u> is to _____

9. <u>heat</u> is to <u>warmth</u> as <u>water</u> is to _____

10. <u>do</u> is to <u>don't</u> as <u>try</u> is to _____

11. <u>enemy</u> is to <u>treachery</u> as <u>friend</u> is to _____

12. <u>ladybug</u> is to <u>harmless</u> as <u>rattlesnake</u> is to _____

Scrambled Words

Unscramble the words below to make eight **list words**. Then, write
each **list word** on the line.

1. I led to   _____

2. aim noun to us   _____

3. you brand   _____

4. go our cause   _____

5. enable joy   _____

6. cot dune   _____

7. we drop   _____

8. red boil   _____

boundary
broiled
counted
courageous
enjoyable
mountainous
powder
toiled

Spelling and Writing

Proofreading Marks

○ spelling mistake

≡ capital letter

↙ add apostrophe

This science article has eleven mistakes. Use the proofreading marks to fix the mistakes. Then, write the misspelled words correctly on the lines.

Its true that mowtainous areas can affect the weather far away. they form a bowndary that breaks up clouds and releases moistchure. as a result, one side might have cool, enjoiable rains, while the other side is broyled by the sun. thats why many people live on one side of mountains and avoud the other side.

1. _____   2. _____

3. _____   4. _____

5. _____   6. _____

Writing a Poem

Has there ever been a time when you felt really cold? Recall or imagine how you would feel. Then write a short poem about the experience, using any **list words** that you can. Remember to proofread your poem and fix any mistakes.

_____

_____

_____

_____

_____

_____

_____

_____

BONUS WORDS

powerful

outrageous

destroyed

spoiled

snout

Lesson 12

In lessons 7 through 11, you learned how to spell words with vowels that work together to make one sound. These vowels are called vowel pairs, vowel digraphs, and diphthongs.

Check Your Spelling Notebook

Look at the words in your spelling notebook. Which words for lessons 7 through 11 did you have the most trouble with? Write them here.

_____

_____

Practice writing your troublesome words with a partner. Take turns saying each word and then saying the vowel sound made by the vowel pair, vowel digraph, or diphthong. Write the words.

Lesson 7

  A vowel pair is made from two vowels that come together to make one long vowel sound. The vowel pairs **ai** and **ay** can spell the long **a** sound you hear in <u>fainted</u> and <u>decay</u>. The vowel pairs **oa** and **ow** can spell the long **o** sound you hear in <u>cocoa</u> and <u>tomorrow</u>.

List Words

complain
decay
boast
scarecrow
braid
throwing
foamy
gained
fainted
coast
hoax
painful

Write a **list word** that is a synonym for the word given. Not all the words will be used.

1. straw man _____

2. increased _____

3. sudsy _____

4. aching _____

5. brag _____

6. grumble _____

7. pitching _____

8. rot _____

9. trick _____

10. shore _____

The vowel pairs **ee** and **ea** make the long **e** sound you hear in the words <u>sweeter</u> and <u>underneath</u>. The vowel digraph **ea** can spell the short **e** sound, as in the word <u>wealth</u>.

List Words

feather
underneath
meadows
speech
needles
northeast
pleasure
healthy
leather
preacher
steady
succeed

Study the relationship between the first two underlined words. Then, write a **list word** that has the same relationship with the third underlined word. Not all the words will be used.

1. <u>concrete</u> is to <u>sidewalks</u> as <u>grass</u> is to _____

2. <u>human</u> is to <u>skin</u> as <u>bird</u> is to _____

3. <u>hand</u> is to <u>touch</u> as <u>voice</u> is to _____

4. <u>bad</u> is to <u>good</u> as <u>sick</u> is to _____

5. <u>constant</u> is to <u>unchanging</u> as <u>balanced</u> is to _____

6. <u>out</u> is to <u>in</u> as <u>above</u> is to _____

7. <u>sadness</u> is to <u>sorrow</u> as <u>joy</u> is to _____

8. <u>carpentry</u> is to <u>hammers</u> as <u>sewing</u> is to _____

9. <u>dress</u> is to <u>fabric</u> as <u>belt</u> is to _____

10. <u>New Mexico</u> is to <u>southwest</u> as <u>Maine</u> is to _____

 The vowel digraphs **au** and **aw** both make the same vowel sound. Listen for the same vowel sound in <u>vault</u> and <u>unlawful</u>.

List Words

hawk
withdraw
strawberries
faucet
squawk
author
awkward
exhaust
saucers
pause
unlawful
caution

Write the **list words** that fit each description. Not all the words will be used.

1. What the people do who leave a burning house:

_____ with _____

2. What small plates of red fruit are: _____

of _____

3. What an illegal stop is: an _____ _____

4. What a mother bird is when her baby is threatened:

a _____ that will _____

5. What you call a clumsy writer: an _____

_____

The vowel pair **ei** can spell the long **e** sound, as in deceit. The vowel digraph **ie** can also spell the long **e** sound, as in believe. Vowel digraph **ei** can spell the long **a** sound, as in freight.

List Words

received
brief
believe
freight
infield
vein
pieces
niece
neither
review
grief
thief

Write five **list words** that could be found listed between each set of the dictionary guide words given. Write the words in alphabetical order. Not all the words will be used.

achieve/interest   **nebula/rushed**

1. _____   6. _____

2. _____   7. _____

3. _____   8. _____

4. _____   9. _____

5. _____   10. _____

 The diphthongs **ow** and **ou** spell the **ow** sound you hear in the words powder and counted. The diphthongs **oi** and **oy** spell the **oy** sound you hear in the words broiled and oyster.

List Words

voyage
enjoyable
oyster
boundary
loyalty
mountainous
crowded
courageous
choir
joined
toiled
broiled

Write a **list word** that belongs in each group. Not all t
be used.

1. brave, daring, _____

2. boiled, baked, _____

3. fun, pleasant, _____

4. worked, labored, _____

5. shell, pearl, _____

6. border, edge, _____

7. music, conductor, _____

8. devotion, faithfulness, _____

9. journey, trip, _____

10. rocky, hilly, _____

Show What You Know

One word is misspelled in each set of **list words**. Fill in the circle next to the **list word** that is spelled incorrectly.

1. ○ complain ○ meadows ○ lawyer ○ neither ○ tosted
2. ○ joint ○ braid ○ speech ○ straberries ○ northeast
3. ○ deceit ○ croded ○ drains ○ keeping ○ caution
4. ○ saucers ○ thief ○ joined ○ coast ○ conceve
5. ○ treasure ○ drawer ○ achive ○ voyage ○ soiled
6. ○ decay ○ stedy ○ vault ○ deceived ○ enjoyable
7. ○ roasting ○ creature ○ naghty ○ received ○ counted
8. ○ powder ○ brief ○ gnaing ○ breathe ○ throwing
9. ○ tomorow ○ boast ○ pleasure ○ sweeter ○ awkward
10. ○ hawk ○ believe ○ review ○ oyster ○ bondary
11. ○ poise ○ infeeld ○ exhaust ○ succeed ○ borrow
12. ○ swallows ○ grief ○ poach ○ squak ○ loyalty
13. ○ freit ○ vein ○ faucet ○ author ○ healthy
14. ○ preacher ○ lether ○ pause ○ shield ○ moisture
15. ○ poisonous ○ mountainous ○ pieces ○ eighty ○ fomy
16. ○ scarecrow ○ wealth ○ feather ○ daghter ○ withdraw
17. ○ hauled ○ niece ○ corageous ○ cocoa ○ fainted
18. ○ gained ○ sweater ○ awfully ○ unlawful ○ yeld
19. ○ choir ○ toiled ○ either ○ needles ○ underneth
20. ○ hoax ○ painful ○ agreement ○ avoyd ○ broiled

Spelling Words in Action

How can a person fly without using any kind of an engine?

Bird People

Many people have discovered the **unusual** sport of hang gliding. Perhaps it's the birds that **inspire** people to strap themselves to giant wings and soar with the wind. "Sometimes we fly in formation with the eagles and hawks," one pilot said. One might think that this would **disturb** the birds, but the pilot insisted that the birds don't mind.

A pilot holds on to the frame of a hang glider. On a day with 5 to 20 miles-per-hour winds, a pilot can run down a steep, open slope and launch into the air. To fly up, a pilot looks for areas where air rises to **transport** a glider upwards. To steer, a pilot shifts from one side of a glider to the other. The **transfer** of weight makes a hang glider turn toward that side. To end a flight, any flat, open area that a pilot has **discovered** can serve as a landing pad.

How high can a hang glider fly? Heights of 20,000 feet above the Earth have been reported. People who fly at such chilly altitudes don't want to leave their hands or head **uncovered**. These "high fliers" also **include** a parachute—just in case. How far do hang gliders go? Pilots often fly a **distance** of 100 miles or more.

Anyone just starting out in the sport should take lessons from a certified teacher. Students can **increase** their skill level by taking more lessons. For experienced and well-trained pilots, the sky's the limit!

Say the boldfaced words in the selection. These words have word parts called prefixes. Prefixes are added to the front of base words or roots to make new words. What prefixes can you find in the boldfaced words?

53

A prefix is a word part that is added to the beginning of a base word or a root to make a new word. The prefix **trans** means <u>across</u> or <u>over</u>, as in trans<u>plant</u>. The prefixes **un** and **dis** mean <u>not</u>, as in <u>unselfish</u> and <u>disgrace</u>. The prefix **dis** can also mean <u>away</u> or <u>opposite of</u>, as in <u>distance</u> and <u>discovered</u>. The prefix **in** can mean <u>into</u> or <u>not</u>, as in <u>inexpensive</u>. It can also mean <u>to cause to become</u>, as in <u>increase</u>.

Spelling Practice

LIST WORDS

1. transport
2. transfer
3. increase
4. disgrace
5. uncovered
6. discontinue
7. uncooked
8. discovered
9. include
10. inhale
11. disturb
12. incomplete
13. unjust
14. transplant
15. unusual
16. unselfish
17. insecure
18. distance
19. inspire
20. inexpensive

Words with <u>in</u>, <u>dis</u>, <u>trans</u>, or <u>un</u>

Write each **list word** under the correct heading.

words with the prefix **in**

1. _____   2. _____

3. _____   4. _____

5. _____   6. _____

7. _____

words with the prefix **dis**

8. _____

9. _____

10. _____

11. _____

12. _____

words with the prefix **trans**

13. _____

14. _____

15. _____

words with the prefix **un**

16. _____   17. _____

18. _____   19. _____

20. _____

Antonyms

Write the **list word** that is an antonym for each word given.

1. complete _____

2. secure _____

3. usual _____

4. continue _____

5. expensive _____

6. decrease _____

7. just _____

8. selfish _____

9. cooked _____

Definitions

Write a **list word** to match each definition clue. Then, use the numbered letters to solve the riddle. Copy each numbered letter onto the line below with the same number.

1. to change from one bus or train to another
___ ___ ___ ___ ___ ___ ___ ___
　　　　　　　　3

2. to cause or influence to do something ___ ___ ___ ___ ___ ___ ___ ___
　　　　　　　　　　　　　　　　　1

3. contain ___ ___ ___ ___ ___ ___ ___
　　　　　　　　　　4

4. came upon; found out about ___ ___ ___ ___ ___ ___ ___ ___ ___ ___
　　　　　　　　　　　　　6

5. carry from one place to another ___ ___ ___ ___ ___ ___ ___ ___ ___
　　　　　　　　　　　　　　　　5

6. loss of honor ___ ___ ___ ___ ___ ___ ___ ___
　　　　　　　12　　　　　　10

7. to plant in another place ___ ___ ___ ___ ___ ___ ___ ___ ___ ___ ___
　　　　　　　　　　　　　　　　　　　　8

8. exposed to view ___ ___ ___ ___ ___ ___ ___ ___ ___ ___
　　　　　　　7　　　　　　　13

9. amount of separation between two points ___ ___ ___ ___ ___ ___ ___ ___
　　　　　　　　　　　　　　　　　　　11

10. breathe in ___ ___ ___ ___ ___ ___ ___
　　　　　　　9

11. bother ___ ___ ___ ___ ___ ___ ___
　　　　　　　2

Riddle: Where is the hang glider going next?

Answer: __ __ __ __ __ __ __ __ __ __ __ __ __ .
　　　　　1　2　3　　4　5　　6　7　　8　9　10　　11　12　13

Spelling and Writing

Proofreading

Proofreading Marks

⬭ spelling mistake

⌃ add something

The following editorial has twelve mistakes. Use the proofreading marks to fix the mistakes. Then, write the misspelled **list words** correctly on the lines.

The way some dune-buggy riders treat the land is a dissgrase. Why dothey have to ride such a great destanc through the desert Don't they realize they disturb avery fragile environment? I don't mean to be unjust tothose riders who are careful. However, in the past few weeks, people have diskovered greatareas of wild land torn up by dune buggies and noted an increese in noise. The reports are incompleete now, but there will soon be enough evidence to take action. Isn't it time to inspyre others to help protect our land

1. _____ 2. _____ 3. _____

4. _____ 5. _____ 6. _____

Writing an Advertisement

Think of an exciting or unusual sport. Write copy for a poster that advertises the sport. Use any **list words** that you can. Remember to proofread your advertising copy and fix any mistakes.

_____

_____

_____

_____

_____

_____

BONUS WORDS

transparent

transmit

display

unavailable

invisible

Spelling Words in Action

How would your behavior have been regarded in the days of colonial America?

Minding Your Manners

Have you ever listed all the behaviors you've been told are **impolite** or **improper**? George Washington did. As a teenager, he wrote out a list of over 100 rules that describe how not to **misbehave**.

It must have been **impossible** to behave in colonial times! Here are just a few of the rules George wrote:

- Do not sit when others are standing.
- Do not **encourage** your friends to discover a secret.
- When around others, do not **engage** in singing or humming to yourself. Also, do not drum your fingers or feet.
- When you sit down, keep your feet **immobile** and flat on the floor. Do not put one foot on the other.
- It is a **mistake** either to run or to move too slowly in the streets. Do not walk with your mouth open.
- Think before you speak, and do not **mispronounce** your words.
- If you must criticize someone, do it as sweetly as you can.

Do you think you could **endure** these rules?

Say the boldfaced words in the selection. These words are made up of a base word or a root and a prefix. What prefixes do you find in the boldfaced words?

Spelling Practice

The prefix **en** usually means <u>cause</u> to be or <u>make</u>, as in <u>enable</u>. The prefix **im** usually means <u>not</u>, as in <u>impossible</u>. The prefix **im** can also mean <u>more</u>, as in <u>improve</u>. The prefix **mis** usually means <u>wrong</u> or <u>wrongly</u>, as in <u>misjudge</u>. The prefix **mis** can also mean <u>bad</u> or <u>badly</u>, as in <u>misbehave</u>.

LIST WORDS

1. engage
2. encourage
3. impolite
4. improve
5. enable
6. enforce
7. improper
8. misjudge
9. mistrust
10. mistake
11. misplaced
12. endanger
13. impossible
14. misunderstand
15. misbehave
16. endure
17. immerse
18. immobile
19. mistook
20. mispronounce

Words with en, im, or mis

Write each **list word** under the correct heading.

words with the prefix **en**

1. _____   2. _____
3. _____   4. _____
5. _____   6. _____

words with the prefix **im**

7. _____   8. _____
9. _____   10. _____
11. _____   12. _____

words with the prefix **mis**

13. _____
14. _____
15. _____
16. _____
17. _____
18. _____
19. _____
20. _____

Word Parts

Add a prefix from the box to each base word or root to form a **list word**. Write the **list words** on the lines.

en	im	mis

1. take _____

2. danger _____

3. able _____

4. merse _____

5. force _____

6. prove _____

7. judge _____

8. courage _____

9. took _____

10. gage _____

11. behave _____

12. placed _____

13. trust _____

14. possible _____

15. dure _____

16. polite _____

17. proper _____

18. mobile _____

19. understand _____

20. pronounce _____

Puzzle

Read each clue. Write **list words** to complete the puzzle.

ACROSS

2. dip into a liquid

4. say incorrectly

6. promise to marry

7. put up with

DOWN

1. cannot be done

2. rude

3. judge unfairly

5. make possible

Spelling and Writing

Proofreading

Proofreading Marks

⬭ spelling mistake

≡ capital letter

The following advice article has eleven mistakes. Use the proofreading marks to fix the mistakes. Then, rewrite the misspelled **list words** correctly on the lines.

   If you are planning to visit japan, you need to fully imerse yourself in the culture. Table manners can be very different there. For example, it would be a mistak to use your chopsticks to point to somebody. If you did this, your japanese host might misjuge you as immpolite. but, whereas it is considered impropper for americans to drink soup from the bowl, this is polite in Japan. your Japanese host might also encorage you to make slurping sounds when you eat noodles—so they will taste better!

1. _____   2. _____

3. _____   4. _____

5. _____   6. _____

Writing a Descriptive Paragraph

Think about going to a new place for the first time. The place and experience can be real or imaginary. How did you know how to act? Write a paragraph about the experience. Use any **list words** that you can. Remember to proofread your paragraph and fix any mistakes.

_____

_____

_____

_____

_____

_____

BONUS WORDS

mislead

enrich

impure

misfortune

impose

Spelling Words in Action

How were baseball teams before 1947 different from sports teams today?

Jackie Robinson, an American Hero

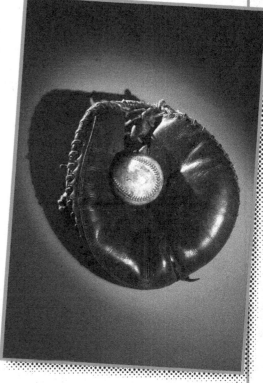

Today, African-American athletes are the stars of many **professional** sports teams. However, before 1947, integration did not **exist** in major-league baseball Then, the Brooklyn Dodgers hired a ballplayer named Jackie Robinson.

Known for his hitting, his fielding, and his stolen bases, Robinson quickly proved himself to be a great player. He was named Rookie of the Year in 1947, a great **reward** for his playing. Two years later, he was the National League's Most Valuable Player. Despite Robinson's record, there were people who would **protest** loudly that an African-American should not play on a team with white players. At first, Robinson had to **pretend** that he did not hear their insults.

The Dodgers' manager, Branch Rickey, was often asked to **explain** why he hired Robinson. Rickey believed that Robinson would **prepare** the way for other African-Americans in the major leagues. Rickey also wanted the best team possible. Teams had to rely on ticket sales to **provide** money. Rickey thought Robinson could help him **produce** the best and most profitable team.

After Robinson's ten-year career with the Dodgers, he would **reappear** in the news as an active member of organizations known to **promote** the rights of African-Americans. He was a great civil rights leader as well as one of the best athletes baseball has ever seen.

Look at the boldfaced words in the selection. How many different prefixes can you find? What do you notice about the meaning of the base words or roots when a prefix is added?

Spelling Practice

TIP

The prefix **pre** usually means <u>before</u>, as in <u>pre</u>pare.

The prefix **pro** usually means <u>for</u>, <u>in favor of</u>, or <u>forward</u>, as in <u>pro</u>pose.

The prefix **re** usually means <u>again</u> or <u>back</u>, as in <u>re</u>turning.

The prefix **ex** usually means <u>out of</u> or <u>from</u>, as in <u>ex</u>port.

LIST WORDS

1. explain
2. exactly
3. reappear
4. pretend
5. reward
6. returning
7. exchange
8. export
9. provide
10. promote
11. protest
12. preserve
13. prepare
14. reflect
15. professional
16. rearrange
17. exist
18. exclaim
19. produce
20. propose

Words with pre, pro, re, and ex

Write each **list word** under the correct heading.

words with the prefix ex

1. _____ 2. _____
3. _____ 4. _____
5. _____ 6. _____

words with the prefix pro

7. _____ 8. _____
9. _____ 10. _____
11. _____ 12. _____

words with the prefix pre

13. _____
14. _____
15. _____

words with the prefix re

16. _____
17. _____
18. _____
19. _____
20. _____

Word Parts

Add the prefix **pre**, **pro**, **re**, or **ex** to each base word or root to form a **list word**. Then, write the **list word** on the line. It should match the definition given.

1. _____ plain   _____ make understandable

2. _____ port   _____ to send goods from one country to sell in another

3. _____ arrange   _____ to arrange in a different way

4. _____ actly   _____ precisely the same

5. _____ fessional   _____ a person in a profession

6. _____ claim   _____ to cry out

7. _____ ward   _____ something that is given in return for a good deed

8. _____ pare   _____ to make or get ready

9. _____ turning   _____ going back again

10. _____ test   _____ to argue against

11. _____ serve   _____ to save or protect

12. _____ appear   _____ to appear again

Rhyming

Write the **list word** that rhymes with each word given.

1. defend   _____

2. divide   _____

3. shortchange   _____

4. insist   _____

5. suspect   _____

6. compose   _____

7. devote   _____

8. reduce   _____

Spelling and Writing

Proofreading

This biographical article has eleven mistakes. Use the proofreading marks to fix the mistakes. Then, write the misspelled **list words** correctly on the lines.

Sammy Sosa gained his fame a as a profesional ballplayer in 1998 by hitting the second highest number of home runs in one season For his 66 homers, he was named the National League's Most Valuable Player in 1998. His greatest rewward, though, was the opportunity he had to previde relief to the his home country, the Dominican Republic, after it suffered a devastating hurricane in September of 1998 After the storm, money from fans and major-league baseball came pouring into the Sammy Sosa Foundation. With this, Sosa was able to esport food and medicine to give the people of his country the relief they needed Upon reterning to his his homeland, Sosa received a great hero's welcome.

Proofreading Marks

⬭ spelling mistake

⊙ add period

‿ take out something

1. _____

2. _____

3. _____

4. _____

5. _____

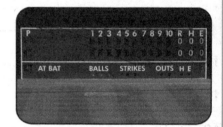

Writing a Letter

Think of someone you admire because of what he or she has accomplished. Write a letter to this person telling why you admire him or her. Use any **list words** that you can. Remember to proofread your letter and fix any mistakes.

_____

_____

_____

_____

_____

_____

BONUS WORDS

prevent

proceed

reprint

extend

exceed

Lesson 16

Spelling Words in Action

How does anyone know when a tornado is about to hit?

Spinning Out of Control

Tornadoes are considered the most violent storms on Earth. They create the fastest winds, which can exceed 300 miles per hour. Tornadoes can move across the land at speeds up to 70 miles per hour. Unfortunately, it's hard to **foresee** exactly when and where a tornado will hit.

Tornadoes form in particular weather **conditions**. Most form where air that is cold and dry meets air that is warm and moist. These air masses **compete** with each other. The cold, dry air pushes up the warm, moist air. This causes strong updrafts and spiraling winds that become tornadoes. The dust and debris picked up off the ground by tornadoes **contribute** to their gray or brown color.

Storm spotters help to **forewarn** people of tornadoes. Storm spotters are people who form a **committee** in a place where tornadoes occur. They look for warning signs such as a greenish sky or hail. Local radio and television news stations **cooperate** with the storm spotters to broadcast tornado warnings quickly.

Some people **overreact** in fearing tornadoes. What can people do to **overcome** their fears? Most importantly, they should be alert. When storms approach, people should tune into a weather **forecast**. If a tornado warning has been issued, they should **postpone** whatever they are doing and get to a safe shelter right away.

Everyone should **commend** the work of storm spotters. In the last fifty years, storm spotters and advanced technology have reduced the number of people killed by tornadoes.

Look at the boldfaced words. How are their prefixes alike? What do you notice about the word parts in overreact?

The prefix **fore** means in front of or before, as in forewarn. The prefix **post** means after, as in postwar. The prefix **over** means above or too much, as in overreact. The prefixes **co, com,** and **con** mean with or together, as in cooperate.

Spelling Practice

LIST WORDS

1. postpone
2. postwar
3. overlooked
4. overboard
5. forecast
6. forearm
7. overreact
8. conserve
9. conditions
10. consoled
11. compete
12. forewarn
13. overcome
14. company
15. cooperate
16. conquer
17. foresee
18. contribute
19. commend
20. committee

Words with fore, post, over, co, com, and con

For each **list word**, find the meaning of its prefix. Write the **list word** under the correct heading.

above or too much

1. _____ 2. _____

3. _____ 4. _____

after

5. _____ 6. _____

in front of or before

7. _____ 8. _____

9. _____ 10. _____

with or together

11. _____

12. _____

13. _____

14. _____

15. _____

16. _____

17. _____

18. _____

19. _____

20. _____

Replace the Words

Choose the **list word** that best replaces the underlined word or words.

1. During the hot, dry summer, people were asked to <u>save</u> water. _____

2. He could not <u>put off</u> his chores any longer. _____

3. When working with a group, it's important to <u>get along</u> with the others. _____

4. Sally could not be <u>comforted</u> after the death of her hamster. _____

5. In overtime, the Warriors were finally able to <u>defeat</u> the Panthers. _____

6. People often <u>give</u> copies of their favorite books to libraries. _____

7. The sailors wore life vests to protect themselves just in case

anyone went <u>into the water</u>. _____

8. The mistakes in the story were <u>not noticed</u> because the

writer proofread it too quickly. _____

9. Some people <u>get over</u> their fear of water by taking swimming lessons. _____

10. We had to clean the house before <u>a group of friends</u> arrived. _____

Word Building

Add and subtract letters to form **list words**.

1. comedy – edy + petal – al + e _____

2. before – be + armor – or _____

3. discover – disc + rest – st + faced – fed + t _____

4. foam – am + rewarding – ding + nail – ail _____

5. become – bee + meal – al + lend – le _____

6. posting – ing + warring – ring _____

7. combed – bed + mitten – ten + tease – as _____

8. cone – e + dire – re + time – me + ons _____

9. forest – rest + restore – store + seem – m _____

10. face – ace + lore – l + casting – ing _____

Spelling and Writing

Proofreading

The following weather report has ten mistakes. Use the proofreading marks to fix the mistakes. Then, write the misspelled **list words** correctly on the lines.

Proofreading Marks

⬭ spelling mistake

≡ capital letter

⊙ add period

The forcast for the weekend does not look promising Extremely windy and wet comditions will exist for the next two days. a cold front moving in from the north will bring lots of moisture. Gale-force winds may contribute to air-traffic delays A warning has been issued for sailors to pospone their plans for the weekend. people may be concoled, however, by knowing that we foresey a warming trend by the middle of the week.

1. _____   2. _____

3. _____   4. _____

5. _____   6. _____

Writing a Descriptive Paragraph

Remember or imagine a day with extreme weather conditions, such as a blizzard, a flood, or a really hot day. Write a paragraph describing that day's weather. Try to use as many **list words** as you can. Remember to proofread your paragraph and fix any mistakes.

_____

_____

_____

_____

_____

_____

BONUS WORDS

postgame

connect

foresight

overdue

commence

Spelling Words in Action

What do you get when you combine a bicycle with a motorcycle?

BMX

To some bikers, **bicycles** are for flying. They call their sport BMX. The letters stand for Bicycle Motocross. A motocross is a race for motorcycles, but BMX racers **substitute** bicycles for motorcycles.

A BMX race takes place on a dirt track. Riders pedal around steep, banked turns. They make double and **triple** jumps. A good jump can send a rider into **midair**! It's important for racers to get a good start out of the gate. It's easy for them to crash when they are in the **middle** of a crowd.

Besides racing, BMX riders do freestyle tricks. "Dirt riders" focus on jumping over obstacles in dirt trails. "Flatlanders" stay on the ground. Their tricks include different ways of riding the bike without touching the pedals. "Street riders" are **subject** to the most danger. They jump gaps in roads and sidewalks. With so many variations in the sport, interest in BMX is not likely to **subside** anytime soon.

BMX riders have to **submit** to hard training and perhaps a few bumps and bruises. While bicycle racers usually have strong leg muscles, BMX riders also need strong **biceps** to pull the bike into the air. The sport can be dangerous, so riders reduce risks by wearing helmets and checking that their bikes are in safe condition. If you think you're interested in BMX riding, watch a BMX race or **subscribe** to a magazine to learn more first.

Look at the boldfaced words in the selection. How many different prefixes can you find? How do the base words or roots change meaning when the prefixes are added?

69

Spelling Practice

LIST WORDS

1. trio
2. subject
3. midwinter
4. submit
5. midnight
6. triangle
7. midstream
8. triple
9. middle
10. bicycles
11. bisect
12. subscribe
13. midair
14. substitute
15. subtract
16. biceps
17. tripod
18. midday
19. subdue
20. subside

Words with sub, mid, bi, and tri

Write each **list word** under the correct heading.

words with the prefix tri

1. _____ 2. _____
3. _____ 4. _____

words with the prefix mid

5. _____ 6. _____
7. _____ 8. _____
9. _____ 10. _____

words with the prefix bi

11. _____
12. _____
13. _____

words with the prefix sub

14. _____
15. _____
16. _____
17. _____
18. _____
19. _____
20. _____

Definitions

Write a **list word** to match each definition clue.

1. take away _____

2. three times as much _____

3. three-sided figure _____

4. arm muscles _____

5. 12:00 A.M. _____

6. middle of the winter _____

7. three people who play music _____

8. 12:00 P.M. _____

9. a course of study _____

10. to conquer or overcome _____

11. the center _____

12. person or thing that replaces another _____

Riddles

Answer each pair of riddles with a **list word**. Write the word on the line.

1. My prefix usually means <u>three</u>. Peas grow in my base word. _____

2. You could order my prefix in a deli, but it also means <u>not quite</u>. My root is something that a triangle has three of. _____

3. My prefix can mean <u>under</u>. My root rhymes with <u>tribe</u>. _____

4. My prefix usually means <u>two</u>. My root means <u>wheels</u>. _____

5. My prefix means <u>two</u>. My root can be found in the word <u>section</u>. _____

6. My prefix can mean <u>below</u>. My root sounds like another name for a baseball glove. _____

7. My prefix means <u>in the middle part</u>. My base word means a <u>small river</u>. _____

8. My prefix rhymes with <u>bid</u>. You breathe my base word. _____

Spelling and Writing

Proofreading

This article has twelve mistakes. Use the proofreading marks to fix the mistakes. Then, write the misspelled **list words** correctly on the lines.

In 1896 bicickles filled Americas streets. People were quick to subskribe to the new craze and subbstitue horses with two-wheeled vehicles. Young people enjoyed midaye rides in the country while others rode to work. Orville and Wilbur Wrights bicycle shop was busy. However new ideas would subdoo the craze. The automobile would become the subjek of great interest, and the Wright brothers would soon be flying in middair in an airplane.

1. _____   2. _____   3. _____

4. _____   5. _____   6. _____

7. _____

Writing a Poem

People use all kinds of wheels to get around. Bicycles, wheelchairs, and in-line skates are just a few examples. Recall an experience you have had on wheels. Then, write a poem about the experience and your feelings. Use any **list words** that you can. Remember to proofread your poem and fix any mistakes.

_____

_____

_____

_____

_____

_____

BONUS WORDS

submarine

midway

bifocals

triplets

submerge

Lesson 18

In lessons 13 through 17, you learned that a prefix is added to a base word or root to make a new word. Look again at the **list words**. Think about what the prefixes mean.

Check Your Spelling Notebook

Look at the words in your spelling notebook. Which words for lessons 13 through 17 did you have the most trouble with? Write them here.

_____

_____

_____

With a partner, write each prefix on a slip of paper. Take turns writing a prefix, giving its meaning, and writing a word with the prefix.

Lesson 13

 TIP in = not, into, or to cause to be   dis = not, away, or opposite of
un = not   trans = across or over

List Words

transport
transfer
increase
discontinue
discovered
disturb
incomplete
uncooked
unjust
unusual
insecure
disgrace

Write the **list word** that completes each sentence. Not all the words will be used.

1. The office building had an _____ design.

2. Flatbed trucks are used to _____ heavy lumber.

3. With only eleven eggs, the dozen was _____.

4. Don't _____ her when she's concentrating.

5. If the medicine causes a rash, _____ its use.

6. Buy these on sale, before they _____ the price.

7. Let's encourage him; he's feeling somewhat _____.

8. Some students feel that certain rules are _____.

9. More ruins have been _____ in Peru.

10. Take the train and then _____ to the bus.

en = cause to be or make, as in en<u>courage</u>
im = <u>not</u>, as in <u>im</u>polite; <u>more</u>, as in <u>im</u>prove
mis = <u>bad</u> or <u>badly</u>, as in <u>mis</u>behave; <u>wrong</u> or <u>wrongly</u>, as in <u>mis</u>take

List Words

encourage
impolite
improve
enable
endanger
improper
mistrust
misplaced
impossible
misbehave
immobile
endure

Write a **list word** that is an antonym for each word given. Not all the words will be used.

1. obey _____

2. ruin _____

3. likely _____

4. mannerly _____

5. located _____

6. believe _____

7. prevent _____

8. discourage _____

9. movable _____

10. correct _____

 pre = before, as in <u>pre</u>pare   **re** = again or back, as in <u>re</u>arrange
pro = for, as in <u>pro</u>mote   **ex** = out of or from, as in <u>ex</u>port

List Words

explain
returning
protest
exchange
preserve
exist
exactly
reappear
pretend
reward
promote
professional

Write a **list word** to complete each sentence. Not all the words will be used.

1. If it doesn't fit, _____ it for another.

2. If she does well, we'll _____ her to manager.

3. If you want to be seen again, you _____.

4. If you live, you _____.

5. If he's coming back, he's _____.

6. If you like to make-believe, you _____.

7. If it's complicated, _____ it.

8. If you think it's unfair, you should _____.

9. If you want to save it, _____ it.

10. If he finds the dog, give him a _____.

TIP **fore** = in front of or before, as in forecast
post = after, as in postwar
over = above or too much, as in overcome
co, **com**, and **con** = with or together, as in contribute

List Words

postpone
overboard
forecast
conserve
consoled
compete
overcome
cooperate
foresee
committee

Write a **list word** to match each definition.

1. over a ship's side _____

2. to put off until later _____

3. comforted _____

4. to enter into a contest _____

5. to predict the weather _____

6. to save _____

7. a group organized to support a cause _____

8. to get the best of _____

9. to work together for a common purpose _____

10. to know beforehand _____

TIP **sub** = under, as in subtract   **bi** = two, as in biceps
mid = in the middle part, as in midnight   **tri** = three, as in triangle

List Words

trio
triangle
bisect
subject
subside
triple
midair
midwinter
middle
midnight
bicycles
subtract

Write a **list word** that belongs in each group. Not all the words will be used.

1. duo, quartet, _____

2. single, double, _____

3. lessen, decrease, _____

4. midyear, midsummer, _____

5. beginning, end, _____

6. course, class, _____

7. add, multiply, _____

8. square, circle, _____

9. unicycles, tricycles, _____

10. morning, noon, _____

Show What You Know

One word is misspelled in each set of **list words**. Fill in the circle next to the **list word** that is spelled incorrectly.

1. ○ coperate   ○ prepare   ○ discontinue   ○ trio   ○ endanger

2. ○ transport   ○ protest   ○ condisions   ○ submit   ○ rearrange

3. ○ endure   ○ uncooked   ○ midnight   ○ compete   ○ inexpencive

4. ○ inspire   ○ imposible   ○ preserve   ○ substitute   ○ conserve

5. ○ enhale   ○ improper   ○ subscribe   ○ middle   ○ disturb

6. ○ mistake   ○ provide   ○ miday   ○ tripod   ○ postwar

7. ○ reappear   ○ promote   ○ misjudge   ○ discovered   ○ forarm

8. ○ bicycles   ○ consolled   ○ company   ○ exist   ○ immerse

9. ○ immobile   ○ forewarn   ○ bisect   ○ overcome   ○ disgrase

10. ○ impolite   ○ explain   ○ overreact   ○ misplaced   ○ midstream

11. ○ midair   ○ conquer   ○ mistook   ○ exclame   ○ include

12. ○ incompleat   ○ improve   ○ returning   ○ subtract   ○ produce

13. ○ mispronounce   ○ transpher   ○ increase   ○ foresee   ○ biceps

14. ○ reflect   ○ misunderstand   ○ transplant   ○ exaktly   ○ enable

15. ○ uncovered   ○ triple   ○ subgect   ○ subdue   ○ unjust

16. ○ unusual   ○ misbehave   ○ professional   ○ reward   ○ engaige

17. ○ postpone   ○ unselfish   ○ insecure   ○ triangel   ○ exchange

18. ○ forecast   ○ inforce   ○ midwinter   ○ distance   ○ propose

19. ○ pretend   ○ encourage   ○ subside   ○ comend   ○ mistrust

20. ○ committee   ○ export   ○ overboerd   ○ overlooked   ○ contribute

Spelling Words in Action

Why is Mary-Jo's boat ride both fun and scary?

Yours Till Niagara Falls

Dear Amy,

Guess what? I'm writing to you from the bottom of Niagara Falls! The falls are on the border of Canada and New York State in the United States. I'm on a boat that tours the gorge below the falls.

It's so exciting! I've chewed away at least one **fingernail**. I can feel one **kneecap** hit the other as I look nervously over the side of the boat. I need all my **self-control** not to pull back when we approach the roaring water. It seems as if we'll end up as a **shipwreck** for divers to find **underwater** someday. I shouldn't worry, though. Boats like this one have been making this cruise for over 150 years.

I bought the **paperback** book you suggested, but I am too **spellbound** by the view to read. The **sunshine** through the mist makes the most beautiful **rainbows**, and the water has an unusual **blue-green** color. The mist comes from the water breaking over the crest of the waterfall and dropping over 100 feet to the gorge. Our tour guide told us that more than 6 million cubic feet of water go over the crest every minute.

We had a big breakfast of **grapefruit** and **pancakes** at the hotel this morning. Still, I know I'll be hungry again soon after this!

Your friend,
Mary-Jo

Say the boldfaced words in the selection. What do you notice about the way these words are formed?

Spelling Practice

LIST WORDS

1. shoelaces
2. paperback
3. haircut
4. jellyfish
5. underwater
6. shipwreck
7. sunshine
8. fingernail
9. cornbread
10. snowdrift
11. hallway
12. kneecap
13. pancakes
14. rainbows
15. blue-green
16. self-control
17. spellbound
18. countdown
19. grapefruit
20. forty-six

Compound Words

Write the **list words** on the lines below. Make sure you remember to use hyphens correctly. Then, circle the words that make each compound word.

1. _____   13. _____

2. _____   14. _____

3. _____   15. _____

4. _____   16. _____

5. _____   17. _____

6. _____   18. _____

7. _____   19. _____

8. _____   20. _____

9. _____

10. _____

11. _____

12. _____

Missing Words

Write the **list word** that completes each sentence.

1. The astronauts anxiously awaited the _____ before the launch.

2. The ocean turns a beautiful shade of _____ in the sunshine.

3. It takes _____ to practice an instrument regularly.

4. The divers searched the _____ in hopes of finding lost treasure.

5. A _____ is rich in vitamin C.

6. She needs a _____ to keep her hair out of her eyes.

7. During the blizzard, Mom's car was stuck in a _____.

8. If you don't tie your _____, you could trip and fall.

9. My favorite breakfast is _____ with maple syrup.

10. We celebrated the fact that Dad had turned _____.

11. At the campout, we made _____ with cornmeal.

12. The movie was so interesting that we were _____ by it.

Riddles

Answer each riddle with a **list word**.

1. What kind of a nail should you never pound? a _____

2. What's a whale's favorite kind of sandwich? peanut butter and _____

3. Which way will take you from your classroom to the gym? the _____

4. What kind of cap do you always take with you but can never put on your head?

   a _____

5. Name a book that's often read but never found between hard covers. a _____

6. Why are goldfish orange? They get rusty _____.

7. What did the leprechaun wear in her hair? a _____

8. What does a mother star call her son? _____

Spelling and Writing

Proofreading

The following story has eleven mistakes. Fix the mistakes by using the proofreading marks. Then, write the misspelled **list words** correctly on the lines.

Proofreading Marks

⬭ spelling mistake

⌃ add something

Our canoe trip began with a bang We watched the splash of the blugrean water make raynbows in the sunshine. When we saw the huge rock underwater it was too late. What a crash It was an instant shipwreack. Our corn-bred and my paprebak book fell into the water. My kneekap was scraped and one fingernail was torn. What a mess However we still had enough food to make some pancakes.

1. _____   2. _____

3. _____   4. _____

5. _____   6. _____

Writing a Descriptive Paragraph

Have you ever seen or heard about a shipwreck? Recall what you saw or imagine what you might see. Describe or make up how the accident might have occurred. Use any **list words** that you can. Remember to proofread your paragraph and fix any mistakes.

_____

_____

_____

_____

_____

_____

BONUS WORDS

undersea

broadcast

railway

self-preservation

sixty-four

Spelling Words in Action

Why is controlling kudzu so important?

Kudzu

The vine that Americans call kudzu was originally one of **Japan's** and China's native plants. In the 1930s, the U.S. government began planting kudzu to keep topsoil in place. Then, things got a little out of hand.

It seems that the plant liked the climate of the American South, especially Alabama's and **Georgia's** warmth. It began to grow and grow, spreading at the rate of as much as a foot a day. It spread across thousands of acres, covering **farmers'** land. The strong vines pulled down telephone wires. In fact, **they've** completely covered forests. Kudzu isn't just in the South, either. Though it hasn't yet reached **Canada's** borders, the plant can be found as far north as Connecticut.

It has become some men and **women's** goal to find uses for kudzu. There are some people who make baskets from the vine and others **who'll** make deep-fried kudzu leaves. A **class's** task might be to study ways to use the kudzu that surrounds them.

Kudzu is a very real concern. It now covers about 7 million acres of land in **America's** Southeast. Anyone who could find a safe way to control the growth of kudzu would surely receive a **champion's** reward. In the meantime, southerners hold kudzu festivals to celebrate the "plant that ate the South."

Look back at the boldfaced words in the selection. Each word is spelled with an apostrophe. How are the words alike? How are they different?

Spelling Practice

TIP

To show possession:
add **'s** to a singular noun, as in Japan's
add **'s** to a plural noun not ending in **s**, as in women's
add **'** to a plural noun ending in s, as in farmers'
add **'** to some proper nouns ending with the **s** sound, as in Texas'
In a contraction, an apostrophe stands for the missing letter or letters as in who'll.

LIST WORDS

1. Georgia's
2. class's
3. America's
4. Canada's
5. who'll
6. champion's
7. Japan's
8. women's
9. parent's
10. farmers'
11. college's
12. you'd
13. Kansas'
14. Montreal's
15. governor's
16. senator's
17. mayor's
18. Mexico's
19. they've
20. Texas'

Possessives and Contractions

Write each **list word** under the correct heading. You will write two words more than once.

singular possessives

1. _____
2. _____
3. _____
4. _____
5. _____
6. _____
7. _____
8. _____
9. _____
10. _____
11. _____
12. _____
13. _____
14. _____
15. _____

plural possessives

16. _____
17. _____

contractions

18. _____
19. _____
20. _____

Write the two **list words** that add only an apostrophe to form their singular possessives.

21. _____
22. _____

Missing Words

Write the **list word** that best completes each sentence.

1. The trophy of the champion is the _____ trophy.

2. The stories of the women are the _____ stories.

3. The peaches of Georgia are _____ peaches.

4. They have means the same as the contraction _____.

5. You would means the same as the contraction _____.

6. The history of Mexico is _____ history.

7. The vote of the senator is the _____ vote.

8. The mansion of the governor is the _____ mansion.

9. The hockey players of Canada are _____ hockey players.

10. The flag of Texas is _____ flag.

11. The citizens of Japan are _____ citizens.

12. The cornfields of Kansas are _____ cornfields.

Move the Words

Each underlined **list word** in the sentences below must be moved to a different sentence to make sense. Write the correct **list word** in the blank at the end of the sentence.

1. Have you seen the size of some of the who'll potatoes this season? _____

2. It's a Montreal's purpose to continue educating students after high school. _____

3. Mayor's take a turn passing out papers next? _____

4. It's a America's job to take care of a town. _____

5. Parent's winter festival is filled with beautiful ice sculptures. _____

6. Our farmer's art projects are on display in the hallway. _____

7. My college's name is Mrs. Rita Lewis. _____

8. Class's flag is red, white, and blue. _____

Spelling and Writing

Proofreading

The following movie review has ten words that need apostrophes. Use the proofreading mark to fix the mistakes. Write the **list words** correctly on the lines.

Americas film industry has surpassed even Japans epic monster movies with "Youd Better Hide." The movie features Canadas best actor, a womens softball team, and Georgias beautiful scenery. The giant, green, and hairy monster wipes out farms, towns, and forests, even though the governors orders try to stop it. Wholl save the people from this menace? Theyve kept the ending a closely guarded secret, but someone does turn out to be a hero. It's a parents decision whether or not to allow a child to see this film.

Proofreading Marks

ˇ add apostrophe

1. _____

2. _____

3. _____

4. _____

5. _____

6. _____

7. _____

8. _____

9. _____

10. _____

Writing a News Story

Do you think a plant could ever become overgrown and take over the world? Using your imagination, write the lead paragraph for a news story telling about what happens. Use any **list words** that you can. Remember to proofread your story and fix any mistakes.

_____

_____

_____

_____

_____

_____

BONUS WORDS

you've

she'll

Oregon's

geese's

ladies'

Spelling Words in Action

In what kind of race do dogs compete?

Mush!

It's the day of the big race. The competitors are outside in the snow, jumping about . . . and barking. These competitors are sled dogs, trained to pull sleds in races over the snow. They can't wait to **perform**. It is a **challenge** for the trainers to hold them at the starting line. Then, the **signal** is given. The teams, groups of muscle-bound dogs, pull together. This race is a short sprint, but the most famous dogsled race, Alaska's Iditarod, is over 1,000 miles long.

A **normal** sled-racing team has from four to ten dogs. The most intelligent, alert dog is the "lead." He or she is considered the **expert** racer. In a "double lead," a dog and a **partner** lead the team side by side. Though several breeds are popular in dogsled racing, the Siberian husky is probably the best-known **symbol** of a sled dog.

The driver uses a few basic **command** words. *Gee* means "turn right," and *haw* means "left." It's rare for a driver to shout "mush!" to his team. It's too hard to **forbid** the excited crowds on the sidelines from yelling out "mush!" as the racing team passes. The lead dog could get confused, causing a **problem**. The sled drivers do use one form of the word, though. They call themselves "mushers."

Say the boldfaced words in the selection slowly. Notice how many separate sounds make up each word. Do the words have as many vowel sounds as they do syllables?

Spelling Practice

TIP

Words have as many syllables as they do vowel sounds. When you spell a word, think about how each syllable is spelled. When two consonants come between two vowels in a word, the word is usually divided between the two consonants: <u>sug</u>•<u>gest</u>   <u>per</u>•<u>form</u>

LIST WORDS

1. normal
2. problem
3. shallow
4. manners
5. symbol
6. perform
7. suggest
8. fossil
9. scanner
10. expert
11. collect
12. mental
13. forbid
14. signal
15. command
16. cassette
17. rescue
18. challenge
19. partner
20. support

Syllables

Write the **list words** on the lines. Put a • between the two syllables in each word. Look in your dictionary if you need help.

1. _____ 2. _____

3. _____ 4. _____

5. _____ 6. _____

7. _____ 8. _____

9. _____ 10. _____

11. _____ 12. _____

13. _____ 14. _____

15. _____ 16. _____

17. _____ 18. _____

19. _____ 20. _____

Classification

Write the **list word** that belongs in each group.

1. tell, direct, _____

2. average, satisfactory, _____

3. difficulty, error, _____

4. sign, announcement, _____

5. prohibit, not allow, _____

6. save, get back, _____

7. record, CD, _____

8. hold up, carry, _____

9. physical, emotional, _____

10. printer, copier, _____

Word Search

Find these eleven **list words** in the puzzle. The words can go forward or backward, up or down. Write the **list words** on the lines below.

fossil	
shallow	
manners	
collect	
partner	
suggest	
symbol	
challenge	
perform	
expert	
cassette	

```
C Y M A L C R M A P N R D
O S Y M B O L A C X F E R
I C H A L L E N G E B N Z
F O S S I L X N O R W T E
O T W E M E P E R F O R M
L N G N U C E R W L L A M
G Z G D P T R S P T L P N
S U G G E S T P I R A L D
C U K J E F D O H C H Q X
L M Y I T E T T E S S A C
```

1. _____ 2. _____ 3. _____

4. _____ 5. _____ 6. _____

7. _____ 8. _____ 9. _____

10. _____ 11. _____

Spelling and Writing

Proofreading

The following article has thirteen mistakes. Use the proofreading marks to fix the mistakes. Then, write the misspelled **list words** correctly on the lines.

Proofreading Marks

⬭ spelling mistake
≡ capital letter
ℒ take out something

The great sled dogs are a cymbol of the far far north. Some of of the breeds who meet the chalenge are the alaskan malamute and the siberian husky. in the past, these dogs worked with a human parner to rezcue people and and collect supplies. Sled dogs respond well to every comand and and signal. It's wonderful to watch them purform.

1. _____ 2. _____

3. _____ 4. _____

5. _____ 6. _____

Writing a Letter

Think about a personal challenge that you have experienced. What aspects of the experience made it seem difficult? Write a letter to a friend describing the challenge. Try to use as many **list words** as you can. Remember to proofread your letter and fix any mistakes.

_____

_____

_____

_____

_____

_____

_____

BONUS WORDS

guilty

advance

sherbet

adhere

mammoth

Syllables

Spelling Words in Action

Why do people sneeze?

achOO!

There's nothing like a sneeze to break a **silence**. Some people don't like to sneeze, because their **posture** might become contorted. Long ago, though, a sneeze was considered a **splendid** thing. Ancient Greeks believed that a person couldn't sneeze if he or she was lying.

Modern science looks at a sneeze as a reflex action. When a person's nose has an irritant of some sort, the body responds with a sneeze. A single sneeze doesn't contain just a **dozen** or so germs. One sneeze can send 100,000 bacteria into the air. If people **cover** their noses and mouths, they spread fewer germs.

One of the **major** causes of sneezing is hay fever. People with hay fever often use medication to **reduce** the amount of sneezing. Hay fever sufferers are allergic to the pollen produced by grasses, trees, and weeds. One of the most common pollen-producing weeds is ragweed. Some communities have tried to come up with **answers** as to how to get rid of ragweed. However, because the wind can carry pollen great distances, removing ragweed has not been a **success**.

Hay fever isn't the only thing that causes sneezing. Some people sneeze when they are in bright sunlight. Others sneeze after they eat a big meal!

Say the boldfaced words in the selection. Each word has two syllables. How many vowel sounds do you hear in each syllable? Which group of letters form each syllable?

89

TIP

When a single consonant comes between two vowels in a word, the word is usually divided after the consonant if the first vowel is short, and before the consonant if the vowel is long.

short first vowel: <u>mod</u> • <u>ern</u>

long first vowel: <u>ma</u> • <u>jor</u>

There are exceptions to the rule, as in <u>wa</u> • ter.

Divide a compound word into two words before dividing it into syllables.

Spelling Practice

LIST WORDS

1. unit
2. plastic
3. helmet
4. mission
5. rubble
6. splendid
7. cover
8. dozen
9. closet
10. divide
11. major
12. modern
13. grandparents
14. watermelon
15. fingerprints
16. posture
17. silence
18. reduce
19. answers
20. success

Syllables

Write each **list word** under the correct heading. Put a • between the syllables in each word. Use your dictionary for help. Two words will be used more than once.

more than one consonant between two vowels

1. _____
2. _____
3. _____
4. _____
5. _____
6. _____
7. _____
8. _____
9. _____
10. _____
11. _____

single consonant between two vowels

12. _____
13. _____
14. _____
15. _____
16. _____
17. _____
18. _____
19. _____
20. _____
21. _____
22. _____

Answer the Questions

Write the **list word** that answers each question. Write the **list word** on the line.

1. What material might a shower curtain or a soda bottle be made of? _____

2. Where are clothes and shoes kept? _____

3. Who are your parents' parents? your _____

4. What do detectives hope to find when trying to solve a crime? _____

5. What's left when there's no sound? _____

6. What must a bike rider wear on his or her head? _____

7. What does a big earthquake leave behind? _____

8. What's a large fruit that's green on the outside and pink and juicy on the inside?

   _____

9. What usually follows questions? _____

10. What's the opposite of failure? _____

Mixed-Up Syllables

The syllables in the nonsense words below have become mixed up. Put them back in their proper order to form **list words**. Write the words on the lines below.

1. u • sion   mis • nit   _____   _____

2. ma • zen   do • jor   _____   _____

3. splen • vide   di • did   _____   _____

4. mod • ture   pos • ern   _____   _____

5. re • ver   co • duce   _____   _____

Spelling and Writing

Proofreading

This script for an allergy medicine ad has ten mistakes. Use the proofreading marks to fix the mistakes. Then, write the misspelled **list words** correctly on the lines.

Proofreading Marks

⬭ spelling mistake

⌃ add something

⊙ add period

Sniffles: Achoo! Doctor, is there a cure for my allergies I sneeze more than a duzen times in an hour My parents and grandparrents all have the same problem.

Doctor: Please, covere your mouth Yours is a magor problem, indeed. Unfortunately, there is no cure for your allergies, but medicine might reduse the problem and silents some of your sneezes.

Sniffles: Oh, I hope so! Achoo

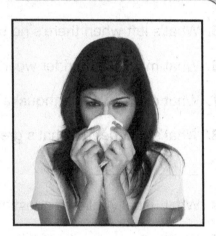

1. _____   2. _____   3. _____

4. _____   5. _____   6. _____

Writing an Advertisement

Write an advertisement for a new cure for hay fever. The ad could be a script for TV or radio, or a print ad for a newspaper or magazine. Use any **list words** that you can. Remember to proofread your ad and fix any mistakes.

_____

_____

_____

_____

_____

_____

BONUS WORDS

radar

granite

satin

bookkeeper

spoken

Spelling Words in Action

What game did Alice play with the Queen of Hearts in *Alice in Wonderland*?

Don't Lose Your Head!

If you have ever read Lewis Carroll's *Alice in Wonderland*, you may **remember** Alice playing croquet with the **horrible** Queen of Hearts. Poor Alice had to put up with flamingos for mallets, hedgehogs for croquet balls, and a queen who kept crying, "Off with her head!" In spite of Caroll's **unlikely** portrayal, croquet has been a **popular** game throughout its **history**.

The game is thought to have begun in France. It was enjoyed in England and Ireland during the 1800s, and was probably brought to the United States around 1870. To play, you need two competing sides with one or two players each, a lawn, and, of course, a croquet set. A croquet set contains mallets, balls, and narrow wire arches called wickets. The object is to knock the ball in a course through the wickets. You must knock your ball to the **opposite** side of the course and back in as few "strokes" as possible. Sound too easy? With **serious** players, the game can be very hard. One of the rules allows a player to knock another player's ball off course!

Some people have the **impression** that croquet is a game for the wealthy. However, it can be enjoyed by anyone. It's a game that people of different **athletic** abilities can play as equals. Playing on **beautiful** lawns adds to its appeal!

Say the boldfaced words in the selection. Say each syllable slowly. What do you notice about the spelling of each syllable?

Spelling Practice

TIP

When a vowel is sounded alone in a word, it usually forms a syllable by itself, as in <u>an</u> • <u>i</u> • <u>mal</u>. When a word ends in a consonant **+ le**, divide the word before that consonant, as in <u>ve</u> • <u>hi</u> • cle. These syllabication rules, and those you have already learned, will help you to spell and pronounce the **list words**.

LIST WORDS

1. history
2. unlikely
3. remember
4. athletic
5. religion
6. citizen
7. animal
8. magazine
9. popular
10. artistic
11. yesterday
12. stadium
13. horrible
14. beautiful
15. serious
16. vehicle
17. opposite
18. impression
19. electric
20. chocolate

Syllables

Write the **list words** on the lines. Put a • between the syllables, as in <u>hol</u> • <u>i</u> • <u>day</u>. Look in your dictionary if you need help.

1. _____
2. _____
3. _____
4. _____
5. _____
6. _____
7. _____
8. _____
9. _____
10. _____
11. _____
12. _____
13. _____
14. _____
15. _____
16. _____
17. _____
18. _____
19. _____
20. _____

Classification

Write the **list word** that belongs in each group.

1. vanilla, strawberry, _____
2. voter, taxpayer, _____
3. newspaper, book, _____
4. dog, cat, _____
5. car, truck, _____
6. strong, active, _____
7. gym, field, _____
8. biology, math, _____
9. today, tomorrow, _____
10. pretty, stunning, _____

Missing Syllables

A syllable has escaped from each of the following **list words**. Capture the syllable and put it in the blank. Then, write the words on the lines.

1. _____ • i • ous

   _____

2. re • _____ • ber

   _____

3. un • like • _____

   _____

4. pop • ____• lar

   _____

5. re • _____ • gion

   _____

6. _____ • tis • tic

   _____

7. op • _____ • site

   _____

8. hor • _____ • ble

   _____

9. im • _____ • sion

   _____

10. _____ • lec • tric

   _____

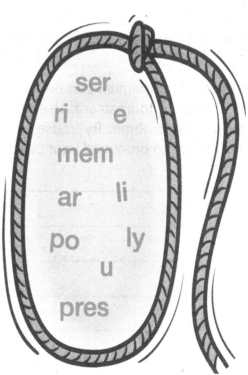

ser
ri   e
mem
ar   li
po   ly
u
pres

Spelling and Writing

Proofreading

The following poem has ten mistakes. Use the proofreading marks to fix the mistakes. Then, write the misspelled **list words** correctly on the lines.

Isnt ita beutiful day,

To stroll on the lawn and play croquet?

Its really quite artistik,

To see a ball go through a wicket.

You can feel the electrik force,

As you hit your opponents ball off course.

All the players look so serius,

While the spectators look so curious.

Another game is about tostart—

Rememmber, the game of croquet is an art!

1. _____   2. _____   3. _____

4. _____   5. _____

Writing a Poster

A croquet tournament can be an enjoyable event. Create a poster for an upcoming tournament. Use attention-getting headlines and copy to get people to come. Try to use as many **list words** as you can. Remember to proofread your poster and fix any mistakes.

_____

_____

_____

_____

_____

_____

_____

BONUS WORDS

electronic

hamburger

medical

mantle

manager

Lesson
24

In lessons 19 through 23, you learned how to form compound words, how to divide words into syllables, and how to use an apostrophe to write possessive nouns and contractions.

Check Your Spelling Notebook

Look at the words in your spelling notebook. Which words for lessons 19 through 23 did you have the most trouble with? Write them here.

_____

_____

_____

Practice writing your troublesome words with a partner. Take turns dividing the words into syllables as the other spells them aloud.

Lesson 19

TIP Compound words are made by combining two words, as in **snowdrift** (**snow** + **drift**) and **self-control** (**self** + **control**).

Two words in each sentence below form a compound **list word**. Circle the words, and write the compound word on the line. Not all the words will be used.

List Words

paperback
haircut
jellyfish
shipwreck
cornbread
sunshine
snowdrift
hallway
self-control
blue-green
countdown
forty-six

1. He will cut my hair. _____

2. The paper is at the back door. _____

3. Show me the way to the hall. _____

4. Six waiters served forty people. _____

5. Tiny fish swam in the jelly jar. _____

6. Snow will drift in the wind. _____

7. The sun will shine tomorrow. _____

8. The house is blue and green. _____

9. A storm could wreck the ship. _____

10. Sit down and count to ten. _____

To form a singular or plural possessive, add **'s**; to form the possessive of a plural noun ending in **s**, just add **'**. Only add **'** if adding **'s** to a proper noun ending with the **s** sound makes the word difficult to pronounce, as in <u>Texas</u>' or <u>Kansas</u>'. Use an apostrophe to stand for letters left out of contractions.

Write a **list word** to complete each sentence. Not all the words will be used.

America's
Canada's
who'll
Japan's
women's
champion's
farmers'
you'd
Kansas'
senator's
Mexico's
class's

1. The people of Japan are _____ people.

2. The farms of Kansas are _____ farms.

3. <u>Who will</u> can also be written _____.

4. The flag of America is _____ flag.

5. The letter of the senator is the _____ letter.

6. The food of Mexico is _____ food.

7. <u>You would</u> can also be written _____.

8. The ideas of women are _____ ideas.

9. The rivers of Canada are _____ rivers.

10. The crops of the farmers are the _____ crops.

 When two consonants come between two vowels in a word, the word is usually divided between the two consonants, as in <u>scan</u> • <u>ner</u>.

Combine two syllables from the box to make a **list word**. Write the words on the lines. Not all the words will be used.

problem
command
perform
suggest
expert
collect
forbid
normal
cassette
challenge
partner
support

sug	form	for	gest	col	sette	sup	lenge	prob	ner
chal	lem	part	pert	per	lect	cas	port	ex	bid

1. _____   2. _____

3. _____   4. _____

5. _____   6. _____

7. _____   8. _____

9. _____   10. _____

When a single consonant comes between two vowels in a word, usually divide the word after the consonant if the first vowel is short, as in cov • er. Usually divide before the consonant if the vowel is long, as in re • duce. There are exceptions, as in wa • ter.

List Words

helmet
rubble
dozen
cover
closet
major
unit
watermelon
fingerprints
silence
answers
success

Write a **list word** to match each clue. Not all the words will be used.

1. result of hard work _____

2. left by an earthquake _____

3. opposite of minor _____

4. a juicy fruit _____

5. opposite of noise _____

6. protects your head _____

7. useful to a detective _____

8. where you put your coat _____

9. result of questions _____

10. top of a jar _____

 A vowel can form its own syllable in a word, as in pop • u • lar. When **le** precedes the last consonant in a word, the word is divided before that consonant, as in hor • ri • ble.

Write the **list words** that fit each description. Two of the words will not be used.

List Words

history
unlikely
remember
athletic
beautiful
animal
artistic
yesterday
serious
horrible
vehicle
chocolate

1. What people do who recall the day before today:

_____ _____

2. What a jogger who paints is:

_____ and _____

3. What a peacock is: a

_____ _____

4. What the story of cocoa is:

_____ _____

5. What a car with wings is: an

_____ _____

Show What You Know

One word is misspelled in each set of **list words**. Fill in the circle next to the **list word** that is spelled incorrectly.

1. ○ popular ○ Canada's ○ divide ○ cornbred ○ snowdrift

2. ○ fosil ○ history ○ unit ○ normal ○ you'd

3. ○ rainbows ○ silense ○ closet ○ shoelaces ○ partner

4. ○ spellbound ○ parent's ○ yesterday ○ moddern ○ fingerprints

5. ○ pancakes ○ mental ○ reduce ○ choclate ○ major

6. ○ Kansas' ○ hallway ○ shallow ○ grandparents ○ religon

7. ○ covver ○ scanner ○ countdown ○ answers ○ Texas'

8. ○ Georgia's ○ citizen ○ collect ○ watermellon ○ grapefruit

9. ○ electric ○ harcut ○ animal ○ manners ○ helmet

10. ○ class's ○ atheletic ○ mission ○ stadium ○ success

11. ○ remember ○ rubble ○ suggest ○ rescue ○ forty six

12. ○ Japan's ○ artistic ○ women's ○ plastic ○ cassett

13. ○ blue-green ○ jelly-fish ○ perform ○ serious ○ posture

14. ○ champion's ○ college's ○ support ○ splendid ○ neecap

15. ○ self-control ○ mayor's ○ veicle ○ farmers' ○ magazine

16. ○ dozzen ○ command ○ signal ○ Montreal's ○ shipwreck

17. ○ sunshine ○ forbid ○ horrible ○ Mexico's ○ impresion

18. ○ unlikley ○ problem ○ underwater ○ beautiful ○ challenge

19. ○ simbol ○ paperback ○ fingernail ○ opposite ○ governor's

20. ○ they've ○ expert ○ senator's ○ wholl ○ America's

Spelling Words in Action

What kind of a job would you like to have when you're an adult?

Choosing a Career

Some people know exactly what career they want to choose. Others don't have the **slightest** idea. Choosing a career doesn't have to be your **scariest** experience. Thinking about your personal interests and learning about different jobs will help you figure out a good career choice.

For instance, if you love both science and the ocean, you could consider a career as a **scientist** in the field of marine biology. A love of science and writing, on the other hand, could lead to a career as a science-fiction **novelist**. If you love to sing but don't like to perform onstage, you could consider being a **vocalist** for radio advertisements. If you enjoy history and foreign languages, you might want to work as an **interpreter** for

tourists visiting historical sites. If you are concerned about health and safety, you could be a very good health **inspector**. If you love to draw and have thought about being a **cartoonist**, you could consider starting out as an artist in advertising.

A lot of schools have a career day. That's a day when adults working in different careers visit the school to tell students about their jobs. Many high schools and colleges have a career **counselor** to help students choose a career. Someone who knows about a lot of careers and who likes working with people would be a great career counselor!

Say the boldfaced words in the selection. What suffixes do you find at the end of the words? How are they different?

Spelling Practice

LIST WORDS

1. louder
2. scientist
3. warrior
4. director
5. scariest
6. slightest
7. prisoner
8. sweeper
9. novelist
10. greater
11. emperor
12. busiest
13. tourist
14. drearier
15. interpreter
16. hungrier
17. counselor
18. inspector
19. cartoonist
20. vocalist

Words with Suffixes

Write each **list word** under the correct heading.

suffix shows comparison

1. _____

2. _____

3. _____

4. _____

5. _____

6. _____

7. _____

suffix means something or someone <u>who does something</u>

8. _____

9. _____

10. _____

11. _____

12. _____

13. _____

14. _____

15. _____

16. _____

17. _____

18. _____

19. _____

20. _____

Synonyms

Write a **list word** that is a synonym for each word given.

1. artist _____   **2.** advisor _____

3. singer _____   **4.** smallest _____

5. ruler _____   **6.** captive _____

7. duller _____   **8.** noisier _____

9. translator _____   **10.** fighter _____

11. writer _____   **12.** traveler _____

13. larger _____   **14.** most frightening _____

Definitions

Write a **list word** to match each definition clue. Then, use the numbered letters to solve the riddle. Copy each numbered letter onto the line below with the same number.

1. person who directs __ __ __ __ __ __ __ __
                              15   1   7

2. one who sweeps __ __ __ __ __ __ __
                        3   8   16

3. most active __ __ __ __ __ __ __
                          14 12

4. detective __ __ __ __ __ __ __ __ __
                                    2

5. least __ __ __ __ __ __ __ __
            9   13   5

6. more in need of food __ __ __ __ __ __ __ __
                             6   10 11

7. expert in science __ __ __ __ __ __ __ __ __ __
                                4   17

Riddle: Why did the girl sleep with a ruler next to her bed?

Answer: She wanted __ __   __ __ __   __ __ __   __ __ __ __
                        1 2   3 4 5   6 7 8   9 2 10 11

__ __ __   __ __ __ __ __ __ .
12 13 14   12 9 15 16 17

Spelling and Writing

Proofreading

The poster below has ten mistakes. Use the proofreading marks to fix the mistakes. Then, write the misspelled **list words** correctly on the lines.

Career Day Fair
April 12th
9:00–12:00 in the Cafeteria

Come meet a movie directer, a cartonist, a nuclear sientist, and more. whether you know exactly what you want to do as a career, or don't have the slightist idea, there's no greator opportunity to learn about different career choices

this exciting day may leave you hungryer than usual, so a special lunch is planned for immediately after the fair

1. _____
2. _____
3. _____
4. _____
5. _____
6. _____

Writing an Interview

Imagine that you're a reporter for a local TV news show. Your assignment is to interview people who are speaking at a school's career day. Write a list of questions that you would ask. Use any **list words** that you can. Remember to proofread your interview and fix any mistakes.

_____

_____

_____

_____

_____

BONUS WORDS

realist

aviator

fanciest

harsher

voter

Spelling Words in Action

What is the secret of magic?

Abracadabra

The **dominant** theme in magic is the idea of creating an illusion. In other words, magicians want to make people think they are watching something happen that really isn't taking place. If you're interested in learning magic tricks, a book on the subject is an **excellent** place to begin.

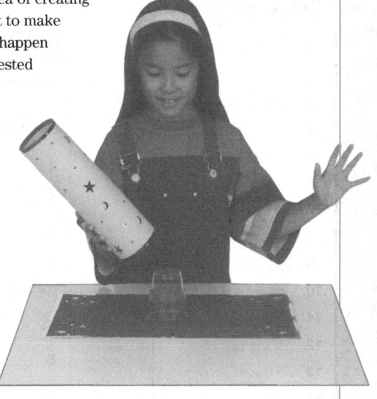

Know what card a person chose from a deck and people will think you're a genius. Make an object disappear and reappear and people won't believe their eyes. Of course, the secret to your magic tricks is fast work with your hands. It also helps if you can distract the audience by talking as you perform your tricks.

It usually takes a magician **abundant** practice in order to appear **competent**. Once you feel that you've mastered a few tricks, try putting on a magic show. You could become the first **resident** magician in your neighborhood. Some magicians are **reliant** on an **assistant**. You can have a friend do the show with you, or you can choose a **pleasant volunteer** from the audience to be a **participant** in your tricks. Wear a top hat and a cape to look like a real professional!

Say the boldfaced words in the selection. How many suffixes can you find? What pattern do you see in the way words end?

105

TIP

The suffixes **ee**, **eer**, **ent**, and **ant** usually mean <u>one who</u>. For example: absentee means <u>one who</u> is absent; mountaineer means <u>one who climbs mountains</u>;
resident means <u>one who resides</u>; assistant means <u>one who assists</u>.

The suffixes **ent** and **ant** can also mean <u>that which</u>. For example: excellent means <u>that which excels</u>; abundant means <u>that which abounds</u>.

LIST WORDS

1. employee
2. mountaineer
3. absentee
4. excellent
5. reliant
6. volunteer
7. puppeteer
8. engineer
9. payee
10. participant
11. resident
12. pleasant
13. competent
14. violent
15. assistant
16. accountant
17. repellent
18. abundant
19. dominant
20. applicant

Spelling Practice

Words with Suffixes

Write each **list word** under the correct heading.

words with the suffix ee

1. _____
2. _____
3. _____

words with the suffix ent

4. _____
5. _____
6. _____
7. _____
8. _____

words with the suffix eer

9. _____
10. _____
11. _____
12. _____

words with the suffix ant

13. _____
14. _____
15. _____
16. _____
17. _____
18. _____
19. _____
20. _____

Definitions

Write the **list word** that matches each definition.

1. one who is absent _____

2. one who is employed _____

3. one who is paid _____

4. one who assists _____

5. that which is characterized by strong force _____

6. that which dominates _____

7. one who works for free _____

8. one who does accounting _____

9. one who is capable _____

10. one who resides _____

11. that which repels _____

12. one who applies _____

Riddles

Use the **list words** in the box to answer these riddles.

pleasant	reliant	puppeteer	mountaineer
excellent	engineer	participant	abundant

1. What do you call a mountain climber who shows up every day?

A _____ _____

2. What do you call someone who operates a train extremely well?

An _____ _____

3. What do you call a pleasing puppet-maker? A _____ _____

4. What do you call a student who loves to take part in every school activity?

An _____ _____

Spelling and Writing

Proofreading

The following how-to directions for a coin trick have ten mistakes. Use the proofreading marks to fix the mistakes. Then, write the misspelled **list words** correctly on the lines.

Proofreading Marks

⬯ spelling mistake

✗ take out something

/ make small letter

Here's a simple trick you can do with a coin. You don't need a an asistant or a volunter. It's an exellent trick for passing time as you sit with friends at a Restaurant or cafeteria.

Show your audience a Coin. Tell them you're going to make it disappear. Put your hand over the coin and slowly drag your hand and the coin toward to the edge of the table. Let the coin drop to your lap silently. Pretend to try to pick up the coin from the table and find that it has it disappeared!

This one doesn't take abundent practice—with just a little work you'll be compatent!

1. _____ 2. _____ 3. _____

4. _____ 5. _____

Writing a Letter

How would you like to be a magician's assistant? Write a letter convincing a magician that you should be hired. Describe any experience or qualifications you have that would make you a good choice. Try to use as many **list words** as you can. Remember to proofread your letter and fix any mistakes.

_____

_____

_____

_____

_____

BONUS WORDS

appointee

auctioneer

absorbent

occupant

persistent

Spelling Words in Action

Which animal is the shyest animal in the ocean?

Shy Guy

The octopus is thought of as the most bashful inhabitant of the ocean **wilderness**. The octopus's **shyness** shows. When an octopus spies another animal—even another octopus—it hides. When frightened, it will squirt a cloud of ink to confuse its enemy. **Afterward**, it will scoot away to some dark place. It might even **darken** or lighten its color, or camouflage itself, so that no animal can **recognize** it.

An octopus is a **delightful** animal to watch— if you can get a glimpse of one! Rather than swimming **forward** like most fish, it can swim **backward** in a very unusual manner. First, it draws water into its body. Then, it forces the water out in a strong gush.

An octopus has eight strong arms called tentacles. Each tentacle has two **plentiful** rows of suckers. With these suckers, the octopus can pull itself along the ocean floor. It also uses the suckers to catch its food, such as crabs, clams, and snails.

An octopus is very smart. Tests have shown that an octopus can **memorize** the solution to a problem it has figured out. It can even remove a cork from a jar to get food!

Say the boldfaced words in the selection. Notice how each word ends. Can you find the five different suffixes? How are they different?

TIP

The suffix **ward** means in the direction of, as in forward. The suffixes **en** and **ize** can mean to make, to become, or to cause to be, as in darken or alphabetize. The suffix **ful** means full of or having a tendency to, as in peaceful. The suffix **ness** means the quality or condition of being, as in politeness.

Spelling Practice

LIST WORDS

1. shyness
2. peaceful
3. forward
4. cheerful
5. afterward
6. darken
7. plentiful
8. loudness
9. backward
10. tighten
11. politeness
12. sharpen
13. memorize
14. wonderful
15. recognize
16. shameful
17. friendliness
18. alphabetize
19. delightful
20. wilderness

Words with Suffixes

Write each **list word** under the correct heading.

words with the suffix ward

1. _____
2. _____
3. _____

words with the suffix en

4. _____
5. _____
6. _____

words with the suffix ize

7. _____
8. _____
9. _____

words with the suffix ful

10. _____
11. _____
12. _____
13. _____
14. _____
15. _____

words with the suffix ness

16. _____
17. _____
18. _____
19. _____
20. _____

Synonyms and Antonyms

In the first column, write the **list word** that is a synonym for each word or phrase given. In the second column, write the **list word** that is an antonym for each word given. For number **14**, write both of the **list words** that are antonyms for the word given.

Synonyms

1. calm _____
2. later _____
3. disgraceful _____
4. deepen in color _____
5. identify _____
6. bashfulness _____
7. ahead _____

Antonyms

8. loosen _____
9. rudeness _____
10. sad _____
11. quietness _____
12. lacking _____
13. forward _____
14. terrible _____

_____

Puzzle

Read each clue. Write **list words** to complete the puzzle.

Across

4. full of pleasure
5. a wild region
7. meekness
8. remember

Down

1. kindness
2. noisiness
3. to put in A,B,C order
6. put an edge on

Spelling and Writing

Proofreading

The following TV listing has ten mistakes. Use the proofreading marks to fix the mistakes. Then, write the misspelled **list words** correctly on the lines.

8:00 P.M. Channel 89: Wonnarfull Ocean Willderniss

The Host, Shirley Chin, takes a delitefull underwater tour suitable for the whole family. Time-lapse Photography lets the viewer see some unusual sights. You can actually see how a Shark's reserve teeth move foreword to replace lost ones. You'll see a starfish lose an arm, and afterword, grow a new one. You'll watch camouflage in action as Fish darkin their colors to blend in with their backgrounds.

1. _____   2. _____

3. _____   4. _____

5. _____   6. _____

Proofreading Marks

⬭ spelling mistake

/ make a small letter

Writing a Tall Tale

Make yourself the superhero of a <u>delightful</u> tall tale that you write. It takes place in the sea. Exaggerate the <u>wonderful</u> feats that you accomplish. Try to use as many **list words** as you can. Remember to proofread your tall tale and fix any mistakes.

_____

_____

_____

_____

_____

BONUS WORDS

shoreward

thicken

minimize

resourceful

stiffness

Spelling Words in Action

Why is it so fun to watch someone juggle?

A Juggling Act

Did you know that it's **possible** to learn to juggle in just a few easy steps? Most beginners start by juggling balls. It helps if they are **dependable** and **durable**.

You begin with one ball in each hand. First, you toss the ball in your right hand in an arc toward the left hand. When this ball is at the high point of its arc, that's the signal to throw the second ball from your left hand to the right. First, you catch the ball heading toward your left hand. Then, you catch the ball heading toward your right hand. When you are **comfortable** with this, repeat the exercise, but start by tossing the ball in your left hand toward the right. Eventually, you will add a third ball to begin juggling.

Experienced jugglers may juggle rings, clubs, or other objects and might use four or five objects at a time. For a first-time juggler, however, learning to juggle just three balls is more **sensible** and will give you a greater **likelihood** of success. If juggling is **agreeable** to you, you might consider **membership** in a juggling club.

There are lots of clubs in towns and cities across the country for all different ages. Even if you don't win a championship, you can create a lot of **excitement** by putting on your own **neighborhood** juggling act.

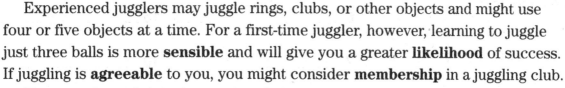

Say the boldfaced words in the selection. Notice how each word ends. Can you find the five different suffixes? How are they different?

Spelling Practice

The suffixes, **hood**, **ship**, and **ment** mean the state or condition of being, as in <u>motherhood</u>, <u>leadership</u>, and <u>statement</u>.
The suffixes **able** and **ible** usually mean able to be or full of, as in <u>agreeable</u> and <u>sensible</u>.

LIST WORDS

1. possible
2. excitement
3. terrible
4. neighborhood
5. leadership
6. membership
7. equipment
8. profitable
9. ownership
10. falsehood
11. championship
12. statement
13. sensible
14. motherhood
15. dependable
16. comfortable
17. visible
18. likelihood
19. agreeable
20. durable

Words with Suffixes

Write each **list word** under the correct heading. Then, circle the suffix in each word.

words with the suffixes **able** or **ible**

1. _____
2. _____
3. _____
4. _____
5. _____
6. _____
7. _____
8. _____
9. _____

words with the suffixes **hood**, **ship**, or **ment**

10. _____
11. _____
12. _____
13. _____
14. _____
15. _____
16. _____
17. _____
18. _____
19. _____
20. _____

Definitions

Write the **list word** that matches each definition.

1. lasting in spite of hard wear _____

2. able to be seen _____

3. fearful; frightful; dreadful _____

4. legal right of possession _____

5. the position of being the one who guides or shows the way _____

6. at ease in body or mind _____

7. having or showing sound judgment _____

8. able to happen or be done _____

9. all the things needed for some purpose _____

10. chance of something happening _____

Mixed-Up Suffixes

The words below have mixed-up suffixes. Draw a line from the word on the left that goes with a word on the right. Put the suffixes back in place to form two **list words**. Then, write the correct pair of words on the lines. One line has been drawn for you.

excitehood   dependment

neighborship   agreehood

profitship   falsement

stateable   memberable

motherable   championhood

agreeable
championship
dependable
excitement
falsehood
membership
motherhood
neighborhood
profitable
statement

1. _____   _____

2. _____   _____

3. _____   _____

4. _____   _____

5. _____   _____

Spelling and Writing

Proofreading

Proofreading Marks

⬯ spelling mistake

⌃ add something

The following Web site's home page about a juggling festival has eleven mistakes. Use the proofreading marks to fix the mistakes. Then, write the misspelled **list words** correctly on the lines.

Martinsville Juggling Festival—February 28th

Join the exitement!

Watch champeonship jugglers, and learn their tricks.

Buynew equiptment—balls rings, batons, and more.

Consider membershipp in our clubs for children teenagers, and adults. Ledership positions are always available for those who want totake charge of a club.

Wear comfotable clothes, andplan to spend the day.

1. _____   2. _____

3. _____   4. _____

5. _____   6. _____

Writing a Journal Entry

Think of a sport or hobby that you enjoy. Write a brief journal entry describing a day that you spent pursuing your sport or hobby. Use any **list words** that you can. Remember to proofread your journal and fix any mistakes.

_____

_____

_____

_____

_____

BONUS WORDS

brotherhood

scholarship

settlement

washable

legible

Lesson 29

Spelling Words in Action

What would it be like to be blind and go skiing?

Brave and Bold

A ski instructor is describing snow conditions to a student. "The surface is powdery, and it's a wide, easy slope with no bumps. Try to get up some speed. Go for it!" The student reaches the bottom of the hill, beaming over her demonstration of **independence**.

These two skiers are part of a group called BOLD. The letters stand for "Blind Outdoor Leisure Development." The young instructor is a volunteer. It's his job to help the blind student experience the thrill of skiing on her winter **vacation**. Guides are carefully trained to give each **direction** clearly. For **protection**, they also ski closely to the students. They know the **importance** of winning a student's **confidence**.

BOLD was begun by Jean Eymere, who learned to ski again after he became blind. He realized that other blind people could also learn to ski. He believed that a program such as BOLD would help the blind **population** to be less **selective** about sports in which they participate.

What is a blind skier's **opinion** of the program? Participants in BOLD feel an **equality** with other athletes. In addition, they discover they can do something they never thought was possible.

Look back at the boldfaced words in the selection. Notice how each word ends. How are the suffixes alike? How are they different?

Spelling Practice

LIST WORDS

1. direction
2. protection
3. allowance
4. equality
5. selective
6. population
7. massive
8. captive
9. humidity
10. vacation
11. importance
12. opinion
13. election
14. humanity
15. objection
16. confidence
17. imitation
18. attendance
19. originality
20. independence

Words with Suffixes

Write each **list word** under the correct heading.

words with the suffix **ive**

1. _____
2. _____
3. _____

words with the suffix **tion** or **ion**

4. _____
5. _____
6. _____
7. _____
8. _____
9. _____
10. _____
11. _____

words with the suffix **ence**

12. _____
13. _____

words with the suffix **ity**

14. _____
15. _____
16. _____
17. _____

words with the suffix **ance**

18. _____
19. _____
20. _____

Missing Words

Write the **list word** that best completes each sentence.

1. People who are not dependent show _____.

2. People who select carefully are _____.

3. People who direct give a lot of _____.

4. A person who objects has an _____.

5. People who protect give _____.

6. If you confide, or trust, in people, you have _____ in them.

7. People who elect officials vote in an _____.

8. A person who opines, or thinks, has an _____.

9. People who are equal have _____.

10. People are humans and are part of _____.

11. People call objects that are large and have a lot of mass _____.

12. People who are original and creative show _____.

13. People vacate, or leave, home to go on a _____.

14. What people notice about humid, or damp, weather is the _____.

15. A person who imitates shows an _____.

Hidden Words

Each word in the box is hidden in a **list word**. Pull a word out of the box. On the lines, write the hidden word and the **list word** that contains it.

cap	pin
pop	confide
mass	allow
man	tend
port	depend

1. _____   _____

2. _____   _____

3. _____   _____

4. _____   _____

5. _____   _____

6. _____   _____

7. _____   _____

8. _____   _____

9. _____   _____

10. _____   _____

Spelling and Writing

Proofreading

The certificate below honoring a local BOLD organization has ten mistakes. Use the proofreading marks to fix the mistakes. Then, write the misspelled **list words** correctly on the lines.

The Mayor's Helping Huminaty Award

Under the direcshion of capable volunteers, our local chapter of BOLD has helped further the indipendanse and confidance of others. our citizens recognize the importince of one person reaching out to help another, and, therefore, the city of lynbrook awards this certificate. in our upinion, BOLD instructors are heroes.

mayor Juan Daquino

Proofreading Marks

⬭ spelling mistake

≡ capital letter

1. _____

2. _____

3. _____

4. _____

5. _____

6. _____

Writing a Dialogue

Imagine that you are an instructor trying to convince a student to try a new sport. Write the dialogue that might take place between you and that student. Use any **list words** that you can. Remember to proofread your dialogue and fix any mistakes.

_____

_____

_____

_____

_____

_____

_____

_____

BONUS WORDS

adoption

violence

acceptance

sincerity

relative

In lessons 25 through 29, you learned about suffixes and their meanings. Look again at the suffixes in these lessons. How do they change the meaning of base words and roots?

Check Your Spelling Notebook

Look at the words in your spelling notebook. Which words for lessons 25 through 29 did you have the most trouble with? Write them here.

_____

_____

_____

Practice writing your troublesome words with a partner. Circle the suffix in each word and tell its meaning.

Lesson 25

TIP The suffixes **er**, **or**, and **ist** mean something or someone who does something, as in counselor. The suffixes **er** and **est** can be added to adjectives to show comparison, as in hungrier and scariest.

List Words

louder
warrior
scariest
slightest
novelist
greater
sweeper
emperor
busiest
tourist
inspector
vocalist

Write the two **list words** that fit each description. Not all the words will be used.

1. a better writer of books:

the _____ _____

2. the detective with the most to do:

the _____ _____

3. the most frightening fighter:

the _____ _____

4. the least important ruler:

the _____ _____

5. the singer who can be heard farther away:

the _____ _____

ee, **eer**, **ent**, and **ant** = <u>one who</u>
ent and **ant** = <u>that which</u>

Write the **list word** that relates best to the word or words given. Not all the words will be used.

List Words

employee
mountaineer
engineer
participant
resident
competent
violent
assistant
accountant
repellent
abundant
puppeteer

1. helper _____

2. occupant _____

3. conductor _____

4. hiker _____

5. member _____

6. bug spray _____

7. capable _____

8. plenty _____

9. counting _____

10. worker _____

 ward = <u>in the direction of</u>   **ful** = <u>full of or having a tendency to</u>
en and **ize** = <u>to make,</u>   **ness** = <u>the quality or condition</u>
<u>to become, to cause to be</u>   <u>of being</u>

Write a **list word** to complete each sentence. Not all the words will be used.

List Words

peaceful
forward
shyness
cheerful
afterward
darken
plentiful
loudness
politeness
sharpen
memorize
recognize

1. You _____ a friend you know.

2. You _____ a pencil.

3. You _____ a poem to recite it.

4. You are_____ when you sleep.

5. You arrive _____ when you're late.

6. You are _____ when you're happy.

7. You _____ the room to go to sleep.

8. Your _____ shows you have manners.

9. You move _____ to get ahead.

10. You cover your ears because of the band's _____.

Lesson 28

 hood, ship, and **ment** = <u>the state or condition of being</u>
able and **ible** = <u>able to be</u> or <u>full of</u>

Write five **list words** that could be found listed between each set of the dictionary guide words given. Write the **list words** in alphabetical order. Not all the words will be used.

List Words

possible
excitement
agreeable
membership
equipment
statement
sensible
visible
dependable
comfortable
likelihood
durable

clasp/falsehood

1. _____
2. _____
3. _____
4. _____
5. _____

leadership/terrible

6. _____
7. _____
8. _____
9. _____
10. _____

Lesson 29

 ion and **tion** = <u>the act of</u> or <u>the condition of being</u>
ive = <u>likely</u> or <u>having to do with</u>
ance, ence, and **ity** = <u>the quality or state of being</u>

Write the **list word** that means the same as the word given. Not all the words will be used.

List Words

direction
allowance
equality
selective
population
objection
vacation
confidence
imitation
massive
attendance
originality

1. creativity _____
2. particular _____
3. inhabitants _____
4. way _____
5. payment _____
6. sameness _____
7. disapproval _____
8. fake _____
9. sureness _____
10. presence _____

Show What You Know

One word is misspelled in each set of **list words**. Fill in the circle next to the **list word** that is spelled incorrectly.

1. ○ profitable ○ elektion ○ backward ○ payee ○ greater

2. ○ drearier ○ direction ○ politness ○ falsehood ○ pleasant

3. ○ reliunt ○ cartoonist ○ wonderful ○ imitation ○ engineer

4. ○ terrible ○ novelist ○ peaceful ○ mountaneer ○ captive

5. ○ darken ○ prisoner ○ louder ○ humannity ○ visible

6. ○ possible ○ loudness ○ hungrier ○ puppeter ○ scariest

7. ○ cheerful ○ asisstant ○ tighten ○ massive ○ statement

8. ○ importance ○ participant ○ motherhood ○ equality ○ warior

9. ○ likelihood ○ attendence ○ repellent ○ sharpen ○ objection

10. ○ busiest ○ absentie ○ allowance ○ humidity ○ plentiful

11. ○ abundent ○ ownership ○ emperor ○ vacation ○ durable

12. ○ selective ○ population ○ employee ○ shiness ○ protection

13. ○ independance ○ wilderness ○ agreeable ○ applicant ○ vocalist

14. ○ scientist ○ exellent ○ forward ○ excitement ○ opinion

15. ○ confidence ○ neghborhood ○ afterward ○ resident ○ director

16. ○ inspector ○ slightest ○ competent ○ domminant ○ delightful

17. ○ originality ○ councelor ○ accountant ○ alphabetize ○ comfortable

18. ○ sweaper ○ leadership ○ memorize ○ violent ○ tourist

19. ○ interpreter ○ recognize ○ shamefull ○ friendliness ○ membership

20. ○ equiptment ○ championship ○ sensible ○ dependable ○ volunteer

Lesson 31

Spelling Words in Action

Who really discovered the North Pole?

The Race to the North Pole

In September 1909, an American doctor and explorer named Frederick Cook made an **amazing** announcement. He said that in 1908, he had discovered the North Pole! Bad weather had prevented him from returning any earlier. There was just one problem. A few days later, explorer Robert E. Peary returned from the Arctic and said *he* had discovered the North Pole in April 1909.

The North Pole had long captured the world's **imagination**. Peary had been **hoping** to find it on two previous trips that he had **planned**. However, the trip to the far north by ship and dogsled was a very difficult one.

A bitter argument arose. Photographs, diaries, and records of navigation methods were the only proof available. Eventually, people became **persuaded** that Cook never reached the pole. But had Peary reached his goal? Some said yes and some said no.

In 1989, the National Geographic Society **pledged** to settle the question. They looked at every **usable** clue, even analyzing the shadows cast by the people in Peary's photos. They **decided** that the pictures were taken "very close" to the pole—within about five miles. The news was **pleasing** to supporters of Peary. The argument has been settled—unless modern science invents even more **valuable** ways to unlock the secrets of the past.

Robert E. Peary

Frederick Cook

Look back at the boldfaced words in the selection. Find the base word in each boldfaced word. What happened to the base word when the suffixes or endings were added?

Spelling Practice

TIP

Some short-vowel words end in a single consonant. If you add a suffix or ending beginning with a vowel to them, first double the final consonant: spin + **ing** = spinning; shred + **ed** = shredded.
Some words end in a silent **e**. If you add a suffix or ending beginning with a vowel to them, first drop the silent e: imagine + **ation** = imagination.

LIST WORDS

1. shredded
2. planned
3. pledged
4. throbbing
5. spinning
6. hoping
7. decided
8. strangest
9. shipping
10. usable
11. valuable
12. pleasing
13. scraping
14. skidded
15. imagination
16. introducing
17. disapproved
18. unforgivable
19. persuaded
20. amazing

Adding Suffixes, Endings, and Prefixes

Add a suffix or ending, or a prefix and a suffix or ending, to each word given to make a **list word**.

1. amaze

_____

2. value

_____

3. strange

_____

4. skid

_____

5. forgive

_____

6. plan

_____

7. approve

_____

8. ship

_____

9. decide

_____

10. hope

_____

11. imagine

_____

12. throb

_____

13. introduce

_____

14. spin

_____

15. persuade

_____

16. shred

_____

17. please

_____

18. scrape

_____

19. use

_____

20. pledge

_____

Replace the Words

Find the **list word** that best replaces the underlined word or words in each sentence. Write the **list word** on the line.

1. The company plans on <u>sending</u> its merchandise overseas. _____

2. The car <u>slipped</u> on the snowy road. _____

3. My teacher <u>did not accept</u> my project choice. _____

4. The witness <u>promised</u> to be honest when answering questions. _____

5. My friends <u>convinced</u> me to try mountain-bike riding. _____

6. I saw an <u>astonishing</u> movie on television last night. _____

7. My friend wore the <u>weirdest</u> costume for Halloween. _____

8. I wonder if the old coin I found is <u>worth a lot</u>. _____

9. I was <u>anticipating</u> that the turn-out for the show would be good. _____

10. Artists are known for their <u>creativity</u>. _____

11. Thank you for <u>presenting</u> us to our new neighbors. _____

12. Handing in the assignment a month late is <u>inexcusable</u>. _____

Rhyming Words

Fill in the blank with the **list word** that makes sense in the sentence and rhymes with the underlined word.

1. As the roller coaster was weaving and <u>bobbing</u>, I could feel my head

   _____.

2. We went to hear the <u>band</u>, just as we had _____.

3. The hole was <u>gaping</u> where the dog had been_____.

4. It will be <u>inexcusable</u> if that train ticket is not

   _____.

5. To hear my cat <u>sneezing</u>

   was not at all _____.

6. The skater with the best chance of <u>winning</u> was the one who did the most

   _____.

7. It was the sight I had <u>dreaded</u>: my homework had been

   _____.

8. Because the votes were <u>divided</u>,

   nothing could be _____.

Spelling and Writing

The following biography of explorer Matthew Henson has eight mistakes. Use the proofreading marks to correct them. Then, write the **list words** correctly on the lines.

Matthew Hensons life was truly amazeing. He was orphaned at an early age and went to sea when he was twelve. Henson became an expert sailor and mapmaker. By the stranjest coincidence, he met Robert Peary. Impressed with Hensons skills, Peary disided to bring him on his expeditions. On Pearys 1909 trip to the North Pole, it was Henson who made friends with the Inuit guides and learned their ways of survival. Henson, who was an African American, experienced racism during his lifetime, and it took many years for the public to recognize his valable achievements. Today, he is known as one of Americas true heroes.

1. _____

2. _____

3. _____

4. _____

Writing an Editorial

Write a short editorial to convince readers that one of your personal heroes deserves a medal. Give examples to support your argument. Use as many **list words** as you can. Remember to proofread your editorial and fix any mistakes.

_____

_____

_____

_____

_____

_____

strutted

rotting

observation

advanced

forgivable

Lesson 32

Spelling Words in Action

Why do some speeches capture an audience's attention better than others?

Stand and Deliver

How do you feel about making a speech? Do you approach the task **angrily** or **merrily**? Do you spend the night before **worrying** about what you'll say? Perhaps, like a lot of people, you've **envied** those who seem to make a speech as easily as they talk to a friend. **Obeying** a few helpful rules can help you make great speeches.

A common concern is being heard. Think about the size of the room and practice in it if you can to judge how loudly you need to speak. Speak slowly and clearly, not **hastily**. It's also a good idea to vary your tone of voice. The speeches that can make listeners the **sleepiest** are those in which the speaker has used the same tone throughout! Look over your speech for places where a **friendlier** tone or a more serious one might be appropriate. Think about **magnifying** your voice when you reach the most important parts.

Most importantly, be sure you are **supplying** your audience with news, entertainment, or information about something that matters to them. You're **occupying** their time, so you want them to feel it's worthwhile to listen carefully. If you're like most people, you'll find that the more speeches you give, the easier they become!

Look back at the boldfaced words in the selection. Say the base word for each boldfaced word. What happens to base words that end in *y* when a suffix is added?

129

TIP

When a final **y** follows a consonant, change the **y** to **i** before adding a suffix or ending, *unless* adding the ending **ing**.

wor**ry**   wor**ri**ed   wor**ri**er   worr**y**ing

When a final **y** follows a vowel, just add the suffix or ending.

ob**ey**   obe**y**ed   obe**y**ing

LIST WORDS

1. envied
2. worrying
3. friendlier
4. obeying
5. sunniest
6. readily
7. stickiest
8. hastily
9. heavier
10. noisily
11. sturdier
12. greedily
13. sleepiest
14. merrily
15. occupying
16. supplying
17. classified
18. magnifying
19. angrily
20. cheerily

Adding Suffixes and Endings

Write each **list word** below its base word. Circle the suffix or ending in each **list word**.

1. greedy

_____

2. angry

_____

3. sunny

_____

4. sturdy

_____

5. noisy

_____

6. ready

_____

7. envy

_____

8. worry

_____

9. cheery

_____

10. supply

_____

11. sticky

_____

12. heavy

_____

13. magnify

_____

14. merry

_____

15. hasty

_____

16. obey

_____

17. friendly

_____

18. classify

_____

19. sleepy

_____

20. occupy

_____

Missing Words

Write a **list word** to complete each sentence.

1. Job seekers read the _____ ads in the newspaper.

2. This plant needs sun, so place it in the _____ spot.

3. The hungry dog gobbled the food _____.

4. A _____ glass will allow you to see small objects in more detail.

5. He was in a hurry and wrote the word so _____ that he made a spelling mistake.

6. Alex won the spelling bee by quickly _____ one correct answer after another.

7. Rather than trying to figure out a solution, I spent the day _____ about my problem.

8. Since the bags were _____ than I thought, I needed help carrying them up the stairs.

9. As a political candidate, her past experience as mayor was _____ by others.

10. Melted ice cream can make one of the _____ messes.

Word Building

Add and subtract letters to form **list words**. Write the **list words** on the line.

1. fries – es + end + l + funnier – funn _____

2. slam – am + keep – k + tie – t + best – be _____

3. no + ion – on + silly – l _____

4. mane – me + grace – ace + busily – bus _____

5. me + starry – stay + ill – l + y _____

6. rob – r + hey – h + staring – star _____

7. stare – are + tour – to + dice – ice + flier – fl _____

8. occupant – pant + spying – sing + hearing – hear _____

9. ache – a + ear – a + messily – mess _____

10. red – d + had – h + chill – chl + y _____

Spelling and Writing

Proofreading

Proofreading Marks

◯ spelling mistake

≡ capital letter

The following speech has nine mistakes. Use the proofreading marks to correct them. Then, write the misspelled **list words** correctly on the lines.

    I envyed my brother's baseball-card collection until I started my own stamp collection. My uncle, who lives in london and travels a lot, is always supplyng me with interesting stamps on the letters he sends. I have classyfied my stamps by country. I can usually peel a stamp off the envelope without tearing it. For the stickyest ones, though, i cut the envelope around the stamp. with a magnifing lens, I can see designs within the pictures on the stamps. I like to learn about each of the people or symbols on stamps. I find my collection occuping a lot of my free time, but it's lots of fun.

1. _____
2. _____
3. _____
4. _____
5. _____
6. _____

Writing a Speech

Think about something you enjoy collecting. Write a short speech to tell people about your collection. Use any **list words** that you can. Remember to proofread your speech and fix any mistakes.

_____
_____
_____
_____
_____
_____
_____
_____

BONUS WORDS

modified

levying

surveying

tardiest

displayed

Plurals of Words Ending in y

Spelling Words in Action

Why do people leave their homelands to live in America?

In Search of a Better Life

July 26, 1910
New York, New York

Dear Michael,

I'm writing to let you know that our younger sister, Rose, arrived safely here in New York after her Atlantic crossing. Doesn't it seem as if **centuries** have passed since we last saw her in Ireland?

I must say, our **journeys** to this country were easier than Rose's. She experienced such a fearful storm at sea that she lost her footing on a stairway, experiencing some minor **injuries**. Sleeping

quarters were cramped, and the passengers sorely missed fresh **groceries**. When she reached Ellis Island, the **authorities** said there might be a problem with Rose's **kidneys**, and they kept her for a full week. Finally they released her into my care.

Rose is enjoying many small **victories** as she begins to learn her way around New York. She has already visited some of the city's **libraries** and **bakeries**. She has also applied for a position as a cook with several **families** who seem quite kind. You will be glad to know that she embraces her new country's customs, just as we do.

Your loving brother,
John

Look back at the boldfaced words in the selection. How are the words alike? What do you notice about their spellings?

TIP

Follow these rules to write the plural form of words ending in **y**:

- If the letter before the **y** is a consonant, change the **y** to **i** and add **es**, as in <u>victories</u>.
- If the letter before the **y** is a vowel, just add **s**, as in <u>relays</u>.

Spelling Practice

LIST WORDS

1. centuries
2. groceries
3. countries
4. journeys
5. families
6. delays
7. kidneys
8. decoys
9. bakeries
10. libraries
11. cavities
12. cranberries
13. mysteries
14. activities
15. injuries
16. apologies
17. secretaries
18. authorities
19. victories
20. relays

Writing the Plural Form of Words

Write each **list word** below its singular form.

1. victory

2. injury

3. apology

4. journey

5. country

6. delay

7. grocery

8. authority

9. mystery

10. activity

11. relay

12. decoy

13. century

14. secretary

15. family

16. kidney

17. library

18. cranberry

19. cavity

20. bakery

Write the **list word** that belongs in each group.

1. years, decades, _____

2. cities, states, _____

3. wins, triumphs, _____

4. parents, children, _____

5. schools, museums, _____

6. hearts, lungs, _____

7. scrapes, cuts, _____

8. secrets, clues, _____

9. lures, traps, _____

10. pastries, breads, _____

11. clerks, typists, _____

12. regrets, sorrows, _____

13. trips, travels, _____

14. apples, grapes, _____

Write a **list word** to match each definition clue. Then, use the numbered letters to solve the riddle. Copy each numbered letter on the line with the same number.

1. long waits   —— —— —— —— —— ——
  7

2. decay in teeth   —— —— —— —— —— —— —— ——
           3

3. actions, movements   —— —— —— —— —— —— —— —— —— ——
                   4

4. groups of related people   —— —— —— —— —— —— —— ——
          6

5. Sorry! Sorry! Sorry!   —— —— —— —— —— —— —— —— ——
             5   10

6. those who enforce laws   —— —— —— —— —— —— —— —— —— ——
              9   11 2

7. kinds of races   —— —— —— —— —— ——
          1

8. food and supplies   —— —— —— —— —— —— —— —— ——
            8

Riddle: What do you need before you can own a dozen bakeries?

Answer: —— —— —— —— —— —— —— —— —— —— ——
    1   2   3   4   5   6   7   8   9 10 11

Spelling and Writing

Proofreading

The following article has eleven mistakes. Use the proofreading marks to correct them. Then, write the misspelled **list words** correctly on the lines.

Proofreading Marks

 spelling mistake

 capital letter

add something

Ellis Island opened as an immigration center on january 1 1892. On its first day, it welcomed over 2000 people after their difficult journys from faraway contries. A fifteen-year-old irish girl named Annie Moore was the first official immigrant. There were special activites to celebrate the opening of Ellis island. Annie was given a ten-dollar gold piece by the authorites of the center. Examinations for injurries and illnesses caused a few more delays. Finally, Annie and her brothers joined their parents.

1. _____ 2. _____ 3. _____

4. _____ 5. _____ 6. _____

Writing a Letter

Imagine you are traveling on a ship as an immigrant to America. Write a letter to a friend at home about your thoughts and hopes on the journey. Try to use as many **list words** as you can. Remember to proofread your letter and fix any mistakes.

_____

_____

_____

_____

_____

_____

BONUS WORDS

attorneys

missionaries

alloys

walkways

theories

Spelling Words in Action

How do animals adapt to a harsh climate?

Adaptable Animals

Around the world, animals can be found living in extreme climates. How do they adapt?

The gila monster is an animal that has adapted well to desert life. The gila monster can store fat in its tail and abdomen to use in times when food is scarce. The animal is one of only two **species** of lizards that are venomous.

The caribou is a good example of an Arctic survivor. Like **moose** and elks, it is a member of the deer family. The caribou has no **scarves** or mittens to protect it from the bitter cold, but it does have a long coat! Dense hairs trap air and help to keep the caribou warm. Because both humans and **wolves** hunt caribou, its newborn **calves** must be able to keep up with the herd. The calves can run soon after birth.

A tide pool is another extreme place for animals to live. The periwinkle protects itself from the waves with its hard, round shell. Mussels protect themselves by living very close to one another. A mussel's shell has two **halves**, like a clam's.

There is one threat that some animals cannot adapt to: humans. The use of river water for irrigation, for instance, has threatened some types of **salmon** and **trout**. However, people's **beliefs** can also help animals. In one part of Florida, for example, **sheriffs** patrol the waters to keep speedboats away from slow-moving manatees.

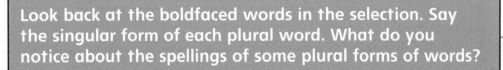

Look back at the boldfaced words in the selection. Say the singular form of each plural word. What do you notice about the spellings of some plural forms of words?

137

Spelling Practice

TIP

Some singular nouns, like <u>moose</u>, do not change when they become plurals. When singular nouns end in **f** or **fe**, usually change the **f** or **fe** to **v** and add **es**: <u>calf</u> → <u>calves</u>. Some words are exceptions to this rule, such as <u>chiefs</u>. Words that end in **ff** also form the plural by adding **s**: <u>cuff</u> → <u>cuffs</u>. When singular nouns end in **o**, add **s** to form the plural: <u>radio</u> → <u>radios</u>. Some nouns that end in **o** take **es** to form the plural: <u>potato</u> → <u>potatoes</u>.

LIST WORDS

1. moose
2. trout
3. salmon
4. wolves
5. calves
6. halves
7. scarves
8. broccoli
9. spaghetti
10. radios
11. tomatoes
12. sheriffs
13. cuffs
14. potatoes
15. beliefs
16. chiefs
17. volcanoes
18. species
19. igloos
20. tornadoes

Writing the Plural Form of Words

Write each **list word** below its singular form.

1. volcano

_____

2. cuff

_____

3. spaghetti

_____

4. trout

_____

5. tomato

_____

6. calf

_____

7. tornado

_____

8. chief

_____

9. broccoli

_____

10. radio

_____

11. sheriff

_____

12. igloo

_____

13. potato

_____

14. half

_____

15. salmon

_____

16. wolf

_____

17. belief

_____

18. species

_____

19. scarf

_____

20. moose

_____

Comparing Words

Study the relationship between the first two underlined words. Then, write a **list word** that has the same relationship with the third underlined word.

1. <u>Reading</u> is to <u>books</u> as <u>listening</u> is to _____.

2. <u>Farm animals</u> are to <u>chickens</u> as <u>pasta</u> is to _____.

3. <u>Meat</u> is to <u>beef</u> as <u>vegetable</u> is to _____.

4. <u>Snow</u> is to <u>blizzards</u> as <u>wind</u> is to _____.

5. <u>Badges</u> are to <u>police officers</u> as <u>stars</u> are to _____.

6. <u>Dimes</u> are to <u>nickels</u> as <u>wholes</u> are to _____.

7. <u>Water</u> is to <u>hoses</u> as <u>lava</u> is to _____.

8. <u>Necks</u> are to <u>collars</u> as <u>wrists</u> are to _____.

Puzzle

Read each clue. Write **list words** to complete the puzzle.

ACROSS

2. large fish with orange-pink meat when cooked
4. heads of tribal nations or groups
7. large animals related to deer
8. houses made of snow
9. a cow's young
10. food eaten baked or mashed
11. firmly held ideas

DOWN

1. fly fishermen often catch these
2. groups of similar plants or animals
3. wild animals of the dog family
5. clothing worn around the neck
6. ketchup is made from these

Spelling and Writing

Proofreading

Proofreading Marks

 spelling mistake

 capital letter

add something

The naturalist's journal entry below has eleven mistakes. Use the proofreading marks to correct them. Then, write the misspelled **list words** correctly on the lines.

ellesmere Island, may 19

   I watched a pack of wolfs attack a herd of musk oxen today. The adults formed a circle around the calfes. the pack killed aweak musk ox. The pack leaders, who are like the chieves of their group, ate first. People hold mistaken believes about wolves. They feel that they are a threat to the survival of the musk ox. Actually, they help this speeces by weeding out the sick animals. we put transmitter radioes on three musk oxen so that we can keep track of them.

1. _____   2. _____   3. _____

4. _____   5. _____   6. _____

Writing a Plan

You are lost deep in the woods in moose country. What will you eat? Whom will you contact for help, and how? Write how you would survive until you are rescued. Use any **list words** that you can. Remember to proofread your survival plan and fix any mistakes.

_____

_____

_____

_____

_____

_____

BONUS WORDS

loaves

torpedoes

thieves

piccolos

pliers

Spelling Words in Action

Why is the *Mona Lisa* the world's most famous portrait?

Lisa's Smile

In the 1500s, a woman named Lisa del Giocondo lived in Florence, Italy. Today, this woman's face is **familiar** the world over because of a portrait painted by the **famous** artist Leonardo da Vinci. He called his painting *La Gioconda*, a name that is often **misspelled**. We know it as the *Mona Lisa*.

The *Mona Lisa* is probably the best-known painting in the world. What makes it so special? Most people agree that it's Lisa's mysterious smile. Leonardo used a technique that shaded the corners of his subject's mouth and eyes. The woman seems to change before the viewer's eyes.

There are **weird** facts about this portrait. Until Leonardo did this work, no artist had **chosen** to portray a subject from the head down to the **stomach**. The **fashion** was to show only a subject's head. The painting was also stolen in 1911. Luckily, it was found again.

With the **wisdom** of modern technology, a scientist used a computer to put a self-portrait of Leonardo over Lisa's face. She found some **surprises**. The two **separate** portraits almost seem to merge into one face. This may be another clue to the puzzle of *La Gioconda*.

Look back at the boldfaced words in the selection. Say the words. Do you notice anything unusual about their spellings?

141

TIP

Some words don't follow the usual spelling rules. The best way to become familiar with these unexpected spellings is to practice using them as often as you can.

<u>yolk</u>   <u>stomach</u>   <u>forfeit</u>

Spelling Practice

LIST WORDS

1. yolk
2. familiar
3. separate
4. weird
5. February
6. column
7. surprises
8. islands
9. misspelled
10. ballet
11. fashion
12. stomach
13. recommend
14. famous
15. prairie
16. forfeit
17. wisdom
18. chosen
19. weather
20. punctuation

Words with Unexpected Spellings

Write each **list word** below the unexpected spelling it contains.

1. fei

_____

2. ose

_____

3. liar

_____

4. par

_____

5. rpr

_____

6. umn

_____

7. ach

_____

8. wis

_____

9. wea

_____

10. let

_____

11. wei

_____

12. rair

_____

13. punc

_____

14. isl

_____

15. lk

_____

16. hion

_____

17. mous

_____

18. mmen

_____

19. sspe

_____

20. bru

_____

Complete the Paragraph

Write the **list word** that best completes each sentence of the paragraph.

Megan loved to dance and had taken _____ lessons for four

years. She was willing to work hard at it, even to _____ time

with friends. Daily practice kept the muscles in her legs, arms, back,

and _____ strong and limber. Megan was _____

with all the famous ballets. Her favorite was "Coppélia," though she

_____ the title the first time she wrote it down. Her ballet

school had a performance scheduled for _____. Megan

hoped to be _____ for a lead role. She even hoped to

be a _____ ballerina some day. Megan would

_____ ballet lessons for any person who enjoyed

dance and was willing to work hard.

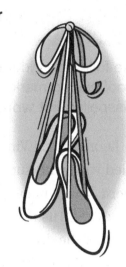

Word Search

Find these eleven **list words** in the puzzle below: <u>column</u>, <u>fashion</u>, <u>islands</u>, <u>prairie</u>, <u>punctuation</u>, <u>separate</u>, <u>surprises</u>, <u>weird</u>, <u>weather</u>, <u>wisdom</u>, <u>yolk</u>. The words can appear forward or backward, horizontally, vertically, or diagonally. Then, write the **list words** on the lines.

```
Z A D O S E P A R A T E
H Q N M U L O C L N F T
R M E I R S D U W O X J
L S A K P R A I R I E B
K N L C R M N S I T P I
M O D S I W C L B A S R
Y I X M S E R A J U B S
F H Q D E A D N N T O R
E S E L S T A D I C G L
G A P Q W H C S L N T U
L F M F X E E K I U O H
Z C W E I R D S V P J D
```

1. _____   2. _____

3. _____   4. _____

5. _____   6. _____

7. _____   8. _____

9. _____   10. _____

11. _____

Spelling and Writing

Proofreading

The following biography has ten mistakes. Use the proofreading marks to fix the mistakes. Then, write the misspelled **list words** correctly on the lines.

Proofreading Marks

- ⬭ spelling mistake
- ⊙ add period
- ℓ take out something

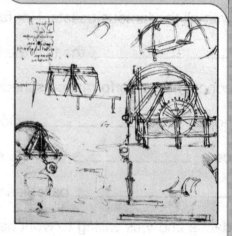

Leonardo da Vinci (1452–1519) created several notebooks filled with with suprizes At first glance, the writing looks wierd. That's because Leonardo had had chozen to write backward. His famus books can only be read with a mirror. Many of the drawings in the notebooks will look famillar to us today They include sketches of a parachute and a simple helicopter. Despite his great wizdum, his designs for flying machines are not workable. They all have flapping wings that require too much effort to be effective.

1. _____ 2. _____ 3. _____

4. _____ 5. _____ 6. _____

Writing a Dialogue

Write a dialogue that might have taken place between Lisa del Giocondo and Leonardo da Vinci. Did they know that someday they would both be <u>famous</u>? Use any **list words** that you can. Remember to proofread your dialogue and fix any mistakes.

_____

_____

_____

_____

_____

_____

eerie

seize

orchid

conscience

basically

Lessons 31–35 · Review

Lesson
36

In lessons 31 through 35, you learned how to add suffixes and endings to words that end with a single vowel and consonant, and words that end in **e** or **y**. You also learned how plurals are formed and how to spell words with unexpected spellings.

Check Your Spelling Notebook

Look at the words in your spelling notebook. Which words for lessons 31 through 35 did you have the most trouble with? Write them here.

_____

_____

_____

Practice writing your troublesome words with a partner. Underline the letters that change when adding a suffix or ending or when forming the plural of the word.

Lesson 31

 Before adding a suffix or ending to a word, sometimes you need to double the final consonant, as in <u>shredded</u>, or drop the final **e**, as in <u>amazing</u>.

List Words

planned
spinning
hoping
shredded
decided
strangest
usable
valuable
skidded
pleasing
imagination
amazing

Add a suffix or ending to each base word to form a **list word**. Write the word on the line. Not all the words will be used.

1. decide + ed _____

2. plan + ed _____

3. skid + ed _____

4. imagine + ation _____

5. please + ing _____

6. value + able _____

7. strange + est _____

8. hope + ing _____

9. use + able _____

10. spin + ing _____

145

Before adding a suffix or ending to a word that ends in **y**, sometimes you need to change the **y** to **i**, as in <u>stickiest</u>.

List Words

sturdier
cheerily
worrying
envied
stickiest
greedily
hastily
sleepiest
heavier
magnifying
sunniest
noisily

Write a **list word** that is an antonym for the word given. Not all the words will be used.

1. reducing _____

2. generously _____

3. weaker _____

4. sadly _____

5. slowly _____

6. lighter _____

7. quietly _____

8. most awake _____

9. relaxing _____

10. cloudiest _____

 Use the following rules to make words that end in **y** plural:
- If a consonant precedes the **y**, change the **y** to **i** and add **es**, as in <u>centuries</u>.
- If a vowel precedes the **y**, add **s**, as in <u>decoys</u>.

List Words

delays
cavities
injuries
victories
decoys
kidneys
cranberries
journeys
apologies
bakeries
mysteries
families

Write a **list word** that matches each clue. Not all the words will be used.

1. wounds; harm done to people _____

2. groups of related people _____

3. trips; excursions _____

4. the opposite of losses _____

5. areas of decay in teeth _____

6. places to buy baked goods _____

7. pair of major body organs _____

8. unexplained things; secrets _____

9. postponements _____

10. sour, red berries _____

Some words don't change in the plural form. For some words that end in **f** or **fe**, change **f** or **fe** to **v** and add **es**; for others, just add **s**. Some words that end in **o** take an **es**; others just take an **s**.

List Words

wolves
volcanoes
calves
broccoli
spaghetti
radios
tomatoes
sheriffs
beliefs
species
igloos
cuffs

Fill in **list words** to complete the sentences. Not all the words will be used.

1. _____ are assisted by deputies.

2. _____, _____, and _____ are things you eat.

3. _____ and _____ have four legs.

4. People listen to music and news on _____.

5. _____ are built out of blocks of snow.

6. What we believe in are our _____.

7. There are numerous _____ of animals.

 There are some words that you just need to practice using to become familiar with their spellings.

famous
yolk
column
stomach
surprises
separate
islands
misspelled
weather
February
ballet
punctuation

Write a **list word** to complete each sentence. Not all the words will be used.

1. A comma is a form of _____.

2. A word with letters missing is _____.

3. The yellow center of an egg is a _____.

4. The month after January is _____.

5. A dance performed on toes is _____.

6. Places surrounded by water are _____.

7. A vertical list of numbers is a _____.

8. Another word for unattached is _____.

9. Rain and snow are kinds of _____.

10. Food is digested in a person's _____.

Show What You Know

One word in misspelled in each set of **list words**. Fill in the circle next to the **list word** that is spelled incorrectly.

1. ○ sturdyer ○ kidneys ○ stomach ○ valuable ○ potatoes

2. ○ famous ○ spagheti ○ victories ○ magnifying ○ imagination

3. ○ stickiest ○ libraries ○ supplying ○ broccolli ○ wisdom

4. ○ familiar ○ surprizes ○ decoys ○ decided ○ sunniest

5. ○ centuries ○ pleged ○ moose ○ apologies ○ injuries

6. ○ weird ○ calves ○ scraping ○ families ○ volcanos

7. ○ introducing ○ balet ○ fashion ○ heavier ○ spinning

8. ○ column ○ tornadoes ○ wheather ○ classified ○ shipping

9. ○ separate ○ sheriffs ○ noisely ○ hoping ○ authorities

10. ○ Febuary ○ islands ○ countries ○ groceries ○ yolk

11. ○ shreaded ○ planned ○ envied ○ journeys ○ trout

12. ○ amazing ○ cheerily ○ relays ○ igloos ○ puntuation

13. ○ usable ○ hastily ○ backeries ○ radios ○ tomatoes

14. ○ chossen ○ forfeit ○ species ○ chiefs ○ secretaries

15. ○ unforgivable ○ disapproved ○ angrily ○ occupying ○ prairy

16. ○ cavitys ○ cranberries ○ strangest ○ worrying ○ friendlier

17. ○ obeying ○ delays ○ throbbing ○ misteries ○ recommend

18. ○ activities ○ salmon ○ wolfes ○ pleasing ○ skidded

19. ○ readily ○ greadily ○ sleepiest ○ merrily ○ halves

20. ○ scarves ○ cuffs ○ beliefs ○ mispelled ○ persuaded

Writing and Proofreading Guide

1. Choose a topic to write about.

2. Write your ideas. Don't worry about mistakes.

3. Now organize your writing so that it makes sense.

4. Proofread your work.

    Use these proofreading marks to make changes.

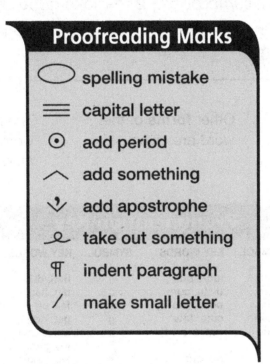

Proofreading Marks

- ⬭ spelling mistake
- ≡ capital letter
- ⊙ add period
- ⌃ add something
- ˯ add apostrophe
- ℓ take out something
- ¶ indent paragraph
- / make small letter

tomorrow well interview the auther of of our favorite Mystery story

5. Write your final copy.

    Tomorrow we'll interview the author of our favorite mystery story.

6. Share your writing.

Using Your Dictionary

The *Spelling Workout* Dictionary shows you many things about your spelling words.

The **entry word** listed in alphabetical order is the word you are looking up.

The **sound-spelling** or **respelling** tells how to pronounce the word.

The **part of speech** is given as an abbreviation.

im·prove (im proo͞v′) *v.* **1** to make or become better [Business has *improved*.] **2** to make good use of [She *improved* her spare time by reading.] —**im·proved**′, **im·prov′ing**

Sample sentences or **phrases** show how to use the word.

Other **forms** of the word are given.

The **definition** tells what the word means. There may be more than one definition.

Pronunciation Key

SYMBOL	KEY WORDS	SYMBOL	KEY WORDS	SYMBOL	KEY WORDS	SYMBOL	KEY WORDS
a	ask, fat	o͞o	look, pull	b	bed, dub	t	top, hat
ā	ape, date	yo͞o	unite, cure	d	did, had	v	vat, have
ä	car, lot	o͞o	ooze, tool	f	fall, off	w	will, always
		yo͞o	cute, few	g	get, dog	y	yet, yard
e	elf, ten	ou	out, crowd	h	he, ahead	z	zebra, haze
er	berry, care			j	joy, jump		
ē	even, meet	u	up, cut	k	kill, bake	ch	chin, arch
		u	fur, fern	l	let, ball	ŋ	ring, singer
i	is, hit			m	met, trim	sh	she, dash
ir	mirror, here	ə	a in ago	n	not, ton	th	thin, truth
ī	ice, fire		e in agent	p	put, tap	th	then, father
			e in father	r	red, dear	zh	s in pleasure
ō	open, go		i in unity	s	sell, pass		
ô	law, horn		o in collect				
oi	oil, point		u in focus				

An Americanism is a word or usage of a word that was born in this country. An open star (☆) before an entry word or definition means that the word or definition is an Americanism.

Aa

ab·sen·tee (ab sən tē′) *n.* a person who is absent, as from school, work, etc. ◆*adj.* living far away from land or a building that one owns [an *absentee* landord]

ab·sorb·ent (ab sôr′bənt *or* ab zôr′bənt) *adj.* able to absorb moisture, light, etc. [*absorbent* cotton]

a·bun·dant (ə bun′dənt) *adj.* **1** very plentiful; more than enough [The farmers had an *abundant* crop of grain last year.] **2** rich; well-supplied [a lake *abundant* in fish]

ac·cept·ance (ak sep′təns) *n.* **1** the act of accepting [the actor's *acceptance* of the award] **2** the condition of being accepted [his *acceptance* as a member of the club] **3** approval or belief [a theory that has the *acceptance* of most scientists]

ac·count·ant (ə kount′nt) *n.* a person whose work is keeping or examining accounts, or business records

ac·cu·mu·late (ə kyoom′yoo lāt′) *v.* to pile up, collect, or gather over a period of time [Junk has *accumulated* in the garage. Our school has *accumulated* a large library.] —**ac·cu′mu·lat·ed, ac·cu′mu·lat·ing**

ache (āk) *v.* **1** to have or give a dull, steady pain [My head *aches*.] **2** to want very much; long; *used only in everyday talk* [She is *aching* to take a trip.] —**ached, ach′ing**

a·chieve (ə chēv′) *v.* **1** to do; succeed in doing, accomplish [He *achieved* very little while he was mayor.] **2** to get or reach by trying hard; gain [She *achieved* her ambition to be a lawyer.] —**a·chieved′, a·chiev′ing**

a·cre (āk′ər) *n.* **1** a measure of land equal to 43,560 square feet **2 acres,** —*pl.* lands *or* fields [golden *acres* of grain]

ac·tiv·i·ty (ak tiv′ə tē) *n.* **1** the condition of being active; action; motion [There was not much *activity* in the shopping mall today.] ◆*v.* **1** normal power of mind or body; liveliness; alertness [His mental *activity* at age eighty was remarkable.] **2** something that one does besides one's regular work [We take part in many *activities* after school.] —*pl.* **ac·tiv′i·ties**

ad·here (ad hir′) *v.* **1** to stick and not come loose; stay attached [This stamp won't *adhere* to the envelope.] **2** to follow closely or faithfully [to *adhere* to a plan] —**ad·her′ing**

ad·min·is·tra·tion (əd min′i strā′shən) *n.* **1** an administering; management; direction **2** *often* Administration, the president and the other people who work in the executive branch of a government [The *Administration* was criticized for its foreign policy.] **3** their term of office [Johnson was vice-president during Kennedy's *administration*.] **4** the people who manage a company, school, or other organization —**ad·min′is·tra′tive** *adj.*

a·dopt (ə däpt′) *v.* **1** to take into one's family by a legal process [to *adopt* a child] **2** to take and use as one's own [He *adopted* her teaching methods for his own classroom.] **3** to choose or follow [to *adopt* a plan of action] —**a·dop′tion** *n.*

ad·vance (ad vans′) *v.* **1** to go or bring forward; move ahead [The trail became rougher as we *advanced*.] **2** to make or become higher; increase [Prices continue to *advance*.] —**ad·vanced′, ad·vanc′ing**

af·ter·ward (af′tər wərd) *or* **af·ter·wards** (af′ter werdz) *adv.* at a later time; later [We had dinner and went for a walk *afterward*.]

a·gree·a·ble (ə grē′ə bəl) *adj.* **1** pleasing or pleasant [an *agreeable* odor] **2** willing or ready to say "yes" [The principal was *agreeable* to our plan.] —**a·gree′a·bly** *adv.*

a·gree·ment (ə grē′mənt) *n.* **1** the fact of agreeing or being similar [The news report was not in *agreement* with the facts.] **2** a fixing of terms between two or more people, countries, etc., as in a treaty [The U.S. has trade *agreements* with many nations.]

aisle (īl) *n.* **1** an open way for passing between sections of seats, as in a theater **2** a part of a church along the inside wall, set off by a row of pews

a·lign (ə līn′) *v.* **1** to put into a straight line [*Align* the chairs along the wall.] —**a·ligned′, a·lign′ing**

al·low·ance (ə lou′əns) *n.* **1** an amount of money, food, etc. given regularly to a child or to anyone who depends on others for support **2** an amount added or taken off to make up for something [We give an *allowance* of $5 on your used tire when you buy a new one.]

al·loy (al′oi) *n.* a metal that is a mixture of two or more metals, or of a metal and something else [Bronze is an *alloy* of copper and tin.]

al·pha·bet·ize (al′fə bə tīz) *v.* to arrange in alphabetical order —**al′pha·bet·ized′, al′pha·bet·iz′ing**

a·maz·ing (ə māz′iŋ) *adj.* causing amazement; astonishing —**a·maz′ing·ly** *adv.*

A·mer·i·ca (ə mer′ə kə) **1** either North America or South America **2** North America and South America together ☆**3** the United States of America

a	ask, fat
ā	ape, date
ä	car, lot
e	elf, ten
ē	even, meet
i	is, hit
ī	ice, fire
ō	open, go
ô	law, horn
oi	oil, point
oo	look, pull
oo	ooze, tool
ou	out, crowd
u	up, cut
ʉ	fur, fern
ə	a in ago
	e in agent
	e in father
	i in unity
	o in collect
	u in focus
ch	chin, arch
ŋ	ring, singer
sh	she, dash
th	thin, truth
th	then, father
zh	s in pleasure

an·ces·tor (an′ses tər) *n.* **1** a person who comes before one in a family line, especially someone earlier than a grandparent; forefather [Their *ancestors* came from Poland.] **2** an early kind of animal from which later kinds have developed [The *ancestor* of the elephant was the mammoth.]

an·gri·ly (aŋ′grə lē) *adv.* in an angry manner

an·gry (aŋ′grē) *adj.* **1** feeling or showing anger [*angry* words; an *angry* crowd] **2** wild and stormy [an *angry* sea] —**an′gri·er, an′gri·est**

an·i·mal (an′ə məl) *n.* **1** any living being that can move about by itself, has sense organs, and does not make its own food as plants do from inorganic matter [Insects, snakes, fish, birds, cattle, and people are all *animals*.] **2** any such being other than a human being; especially, any four-footed creature; beast

an·i·mat·ed (an′ə māt′əd) *adj.* vigorous; lively [an *animated* conversation] —**an′i·mat′ed·ly** *adv.*

☆**animated cartoon** *n.* a motion picture made by filming a series of drawings, each changed slightly from the one before: the drawn figures seem to move when the drawings are shown on a screen, one quickly after the other

an·swer (an′sər) *n.* **1** something said, written, or done in return to a question, argument, letter, action, etc.; reply; response [The only *answers* required for the test were "true" or "false." His *answer* to the insult was to turn his back.] **2** a solution to a problem, as in arithmetic ➧*v.* to give an answer; reply or react, as to a question or action

a·pol·o·gy (ə päl′ə jē) *n.* a statement that one is sorry for doing something wrong or being at fault [Please accept my *apology* for sending you the wrong book.] —*pl.* **a·pol′o·gies**

ap·pli·cant (ap′li kənt) *n.* a person who applies or asks for something [*applicants* for a job]

ap·point·ee (ə poin tē′) *n.* a person who has been appointed to some position

a·pri·cot (ap′rə kät′ *or* ā′prə kät′) *n.* **1** a pale orange fruit that is a little like a peach, but smaller **2** the tree it grows on ➧*adj.* a pale orange color

ar·e·a (er′ē ə) *n.* **1** the amount or size of a surface, measured in square units [If a floor is 10 meters wide and 20 meters long, its *area* is 200 square meters.] **2** a part of the earth's surface; region [Our family lives mostly in rural *areas*.] **3** a space used for a special purpose [a picnic *area*]

ar·row (er′ō) *n.* **1** a slender rod that is shot from a bow: arrows usually have a point at the front end and feathers at the back end **2** anything that looks or is used like an arrow; especially, a sign (◄——) used to point out a direction or place

ar·ter·y (är′tər ē) *n.* **1** any of the tubes that carry blood from the heart to all parts of the body **2** a main road or channel [a railroad *artery*] —*pl.* **ar′ter·ies**

ar·tis·tic (är tis′tik) *adj.* **1** of art or artists **2** done with skill and a good sense of color, form, design, etc. [an *artistic* job of redecorating] **3** knowing and enjoying what is beautiful —**ar·tis′ti·cal·ly** *adv.*

as·sign (ə sīn′) *v.* **1** to set apart for a special purpose; designate [Let's *assign* a day for the trip.] **2** to place at some task or work [Two pupils were *assigned* to write the report.] **3** to give out as a task; allot [The teacher *assigned* some homework.]

as·sist·ant (ə sis′tənt) *n.* a person who assists or helps another; helper; aid [an *assistant* to the president] ➧*adj.* assisting or helping the person under whom one works [an *assistant* principal]

as·so·ci·ate (ə sō′shē āt′ *or* ə sō′sē āt′) *v.* **1** to connect in one's mind; think of together [We *associate* the taste of something with its smell.] **2** to bring or come together as friends or partners [Don't *associate* with people who gossip.] —**as·so′ci·at·ed, as·so′ci·at·ing** ➧*n.* (ə sō′shē āt *or* ə sō′sē āt) a person with whom one is joined in some way; friend, partner, or fellow worker

ath·let·ic (ath let′ik) *adj.* **1** of or for athletes or athletics **2** like an athlete; physically strong and active —**ath·let′i·cal·ly** *adv.*

at·mos·phere (at′məs fir) *n.* **1** all the air around the earth **2** the gases around any planet or star **3** the air in any particular place

at·tach·ment (ə tach′mənt) *n.* **1** the act of attaching something **2** anything used for attaching; fastening **3** strong liking or love; friendship; affection

at·tend·ance (ə ten′dəns) *n.* **1** the act of attending **2** people present [The *attendance* at the ball game was 36,000.]

at·ti·tude (at′ə tōōd *or* at′ə tyōōd) *n.* **1** the position of the body in doing a particular thing [We knelt in an *attitude* of prayer.] **2** a way of acting or behaving that shows what one is thinking or feeling [a friendly *attitude*]

at·tor·ney (ə tur′nē) *n.* a person whose profession is giving advice on law or acting for others in lawsuits —*pl.* **at·tor′neys**

auc·tion·eer (ôk shə nir′ *or* äk shə nir′) *n.* a person whose work is selling things at auctions

au·di·ence (ô′dē əns *or* ä′dē əns) *n.* a group of persons gathered together to hear and see a speaker, a play, or a concert [The *audience* cheered the singer.]

au·thor (ô′thər *or* ä′thər) *n.* **1** a person who writes something, as a book or story [The Brontë sisters were the *authors* of novels.] **2** a person who makes or begins something; creator [the author of a new plan for peace] ➧*v.* to be the author of

au·thor·i·ty (ə thôr′ə tē) *n.* **1** the right to give orders, make decisions, or take action [Do you have the *authority* to spend the money?] **2** a person or agency that has the right to govern or the power to enforce laws [The city *authorities* have approved the plan.] **3** a person, book, etc. that can be trusted to give the right information or advice [an *authority* on rare diseases] —*pl.* **au·thor′i·ties**

au·to·graph (ôt′ə graf *or* ät′ə graf) *n.* something written in a person's own handwriting, especially that person's name ◆*v.* to write one's name on [Please *autograph* this baseball.]

a·vi·a·tor (ā′ vē āt′ər) *n.* a person who flies airplanes; pilot

a·void (ə void′) *v.* **1** to keep away from; get out of the way of; shun [to *avoid* crowds] **2** to keep from happening [Try to *avoid* spilling the milk.] —**a·void′a·ble** *adj.* —**a·void′ance** *n.*

awe (ô *or* ä) *n.* deep respect mixed with fear and wonder [The starry sky filled them with *awe*.]

aw·ful·ly (ô′ fəl ē *or* ä′ fəl ē) *adv.* **1** in an awful way ☆**2** very; extremely; *used only in everyday talk* [I'm *awfully* glad you came.]

awk·ward (ôk′wərd *or* äk′wərd) *adj.* **1** not having grace or skill; clumsy; bungling [an *awkward* dancer; an *awkward* writing style] **2** hard to use or manage; not convenient [an *awkward* tool] **3** uncomfortable; cramped [sitting in an *awkward* position] **4** embarrassed or embarrassing [an *awkward* remark] —**awk′ward·ly** *adv.* —**awk′ward·ness** *n.*

Bb

back·ward (bak′wərd) *adv.* **1** toward the back; behind [to look *backward*] **2** with the back toward the front [If a man rides *backward*, he can see where he has been.] **3** in a way opposite to the usual way [Noel is Leon spelled *backward*.]

☆**bak·er·y** (bāk′ər ē) *n.* a place where bread, cakes, etc. are baked or sold —*pl.* **bak′er·ies**

bal·let (bal′ā *or* ba lā′) *n.* **1** a dance performed on a stage, usually by a group of dancers in costume: it often tells a story by means of its graceful, fixed movements **2** a group of such dancers

bas·i·cal·ly (bā′ sik lē) *adv.* in a basic way

beau·ti·ful (byo͞o′ti fəl) *adj.* very pleasant to look at or hear; giving delight to the mind [a *beautiful* face] —**beau′ti·ful·ly** *adv.*

be·hav·ior (bē hāv′yər) *n.* the way a person or thing behaves, or acts; conduct or action [His *behavior* at the dance was rude. The Curies studied the *behavior* of radium.]

be·lief (bē lēf′) *n.* **1** a believing or feeling that certain things are true or real; faith [You cannot destroy my *belief* in the honesty of most people.] **2** trust or confidence [I have *belief* in Pat's ability.] **3** anything believed or accepted as true; opinion [What are your religious *beliefs*?]

be·lieve (bē lēv′) *v.* **1** to accept as true or real [Can we *believe* that story?] **2** to have religious faith [to *believe* in life after death] **3** to have trust or confidence [I know you will win; I *believe* in you.] **4** to suppose; guess —**be·lieved′, be·liev′ing** —**be·liev′a·ble** *adj.* —**be·liev′er** *n.*

ben·e·fit (ben′ə fit) *n.* **1** help or advantage; also, anything that helps [Speak louder for the *benefit* of those in the rear.] **2** *often* **benefits**, *pl.* money paid by an insurance company, the government, etc. as during old age or sickness, or for death **3** any public event put on to raise money for a certain person, group, or cause [The show is a *benefit* for children.]

be·tray (bē trā′) *v.* to fail to keep a promise, secret, or agreement; be unfaithful [My cousin *betrayed* my trust by wasting my money.] —**be·trayed′, be·tray′ing**

bi·ceps (bī′saps) *n.* the large muscle in the front of the upper arm

bi·cy·cle (bī′si kəl) *n.* a vehicle to ride on that has two wheels, one behind the other: it is moved by foot pedals and steered by a handlebar ◆*v.* to ride a bicycle —**bi′cy·cled, bi′cy·cling** —**bi′cy·clist** (bī′si klist) *n.*

bi·fo·cals (bī′fō kəlz) *pl.n.* eyeglasses in which each lens has two parts, one for reading and seeing nearby objects and the other for seeing things far away

bi·og·ra·phy (bī äg′rə fē) *n.* the story of a person's life written by another person —*pl.* **bi·og′ra·phies** —**bi·o·graph·i·cal** (bī′ə graf′i kəl) *adj.*

bi·sect (bī sekt′ *or* bī′sekt) *v.* **1** to cut into two parts [Budapest is *bisected* by the Danube River.] **2** to divide into two equal parts [A circle is *bisected* by its diameter.]

blue (blo͞o) *adj.* having the color of the clear sky or the deep sea

blue-green (blo͞o′grēn) *adj.* having a combination of the colors blue and green

boast (bōst) *v.* **1** to talk about with too much pride and pleasure; praise too highly; brag [We're tired of hearing him *boast* of his bravery.] **2** to be proud of having [Our city *boasts* a fine new zoo.] —**boast′er** *n.*

a	ask, fat
ā	ape, date
ä	car, lot
e	elf, ten
ē	even, meet
i	is, hit
ī	ice, fire
ō	open, go
ô	law, horn
oi	oil, point
o͞o	look, pull
o͞o	ooze, tool
ou	out, crowd
u	up, cut
ᵿ	fur, fern
ə	a in ago
	e in agent
	e in father
	i in unity
	o in collect
	u in focus
ch	chin, arch
ŋ	ring, singer
sh	she, dash
th	thin, truth
th	then, father
zh	s in pleasure

bond (bänd) *n.* **1** anything that binds or ties [Handcuffs or shackles are called *bonds*.] **2** an agreement that binds one, as to pay certain sums or to do or not do certain things **3** a certificate sold by a government or business as a way of raising money: it promises to return the money to the buyer by a certain date, along with interest [The city issued *bonds* to build a subway.]

book·keep·er (book'kēp ər) *n.* a person whose work is to keep accounts for a business

bor·row (bär'ō *or* bôr'ō) *v.* **1** to get to use something for a while by agreeing to return it later [You can *borrow* that book from the library.] **2** to take another's word, idea, etc. and use it as one's own [The Romans *borrowed* many Greek myths.]

bot·a·ny (bät'n ē) *n.* the science that studies plants and how they grow —**bot'a·nist** *n.*

bound·a·ry (boun'drē *or* bou'dər ē) *n.* a line or thing that marks the outside edge or limit [The Delaware River forms the eastern *boundary* of Pennsylvania.] —*pl.* **bound'a·ries**

braid (brād) *v.* **1** to weave together three or more strands of hair, straw, ribbon, etc. **2** to make by weaving such strands [to *braid* a rug] ➤*n.* **1** a length of braided hair **2** a band of braided cloth, ribbon, etc. used for trimming or decoration

breathe (brēth) *v.* **1** to take air into the lungs and then let it out **2** to live [While I *breathe*, you are safe.] **3** to speak quietly; whisper [Don't *breathe* a word of it to anyone.] **4** to stop for breath; rest [to *breathe* a horse after a long run] —**breathed, breath'ing**

brief (brēf) *adj.* **1** not lasting very long; short in time [a *brief* visit] **2** using just a few words; concise [a *brief* news report]

broad·cast (brôd'kast) *v.* to send over the air by means of radio or television [to *broadcast* a program] —**broad'cast** *or* **broad'cast·ed, broad'cast·ing**

broc·co·li (bräk'ə lē) *n.* a vegetable whose tender shoots and loose heads of tiny green buds are cooked for eating

broil (broil) *v.* **1** to cook or be cooked close to a flame or other high heat [to *broil* steaks over charcoal] **2** to make or be very hot [a *broiling* summer day] ➤*n.* the act or state of broiling —**broiled**

broth·er·hood (bruth'ər hood) *n.* the tie between brothers or between people who feel they all belong to one big family.

bu·reau (byoor'ō) *n.* ☆**1** a chest of drawers for holding clothes: it usually has a mirror. **2** an office, as for a certain part of a business [an information *bureau*] ☆**3** a department of the government [The *Bureau* of Internal Revenue is in charge of collecting Federal taxes.] —*pl.* **bu'reaus** *or* **bu·reaux** (byoor'ōz)

bus·y (biz'ē) *adj.* **1** doing something; active; at work; not idle [The students are *busy* at their desks.] **2** full of activity; with much action or motion [a *busy* morning; a *busy* store] —**bus'i·er, bus'i·est** —**bus'ied, bus'y·ing** *v.* —**bus'y·ness** *n.*

cab·i·net (kab'i nət) *n.* **1** a case or cupboard with drawers or shelves for holding or storing things [a china *cabinet*; a medicine *cabinet*] ☆**2** *often* **Cabinet**, a group of officials who act as advisers to the head of a nation: our president's cabinet is made up of the heads of the departments of our government

calf (kaf) *n.* **1** a young cow or bull **2** a young elephant, whale, hippopotamus, seal, etc. —*pl.* **calves**

cam·paign (kam pān') *n.* **1** a series of battles or other military actions having a special goal [Napoleon's Russian *campaign* ended in his defeat.] **2** a series of planned actions for getting something done [a *campaign* to get someone elected] ➤*v.* to take part in a campaign —**cam·paign'er** *n.*

Can·a·da (kan'ə də) a country in the northern part of North America

can·cel (kan'səl) *v.* **1** to cross out with lines or mark in some other way [Postage stamps and checks are *canceled* to show that they have been used.] **2** to do away with; wipe out; say that it will no longer be [to *cancel* an order] **3** to balance something so that it has no effect [My gains and losses *cancel* each other.] —**can'celed** *or* **can'celled, can'cel·ing** *or* **can'cel·ling**

ca·pac·i·ty (kə pas'ə tē) *n.* **1** the amount of space that can be filled; room for holding [a jar with a *capacity* of 2 quarts; a stadium with a seating *capacity* of 80,000] **2** the ability to be, learn, become, etc.; skill or fitness [the *capacity* to be an actor] **3** position or office [He made the decision in his *capacity* as president.] —*pl.* **ca·pac'i·ties**

cap·il·lar·y (kap'i ler'ē) *n.* **1** a tube that is very narrow inside [The ordinary thermometer is a *capillary*.] **2** any of the tiny blood vessels joining the arteries and the veins —*pl.* **cap'il·lar'ies**

☆**cap·tion** (kap'shən) *n.* a title at the head of an article or below a picture, as in a newspaper

cap·tive (kap'tiv) *n.* a person caught and held prisoner, as in war ➤*adj.* **1** held as a prisoner ☆**2** forced to listen, whether wanting to or not [a *captive* audience]

carbon dioxide (kär′bən dī äks′īd) *n.* a gas made up of carbon and oxygen, that has no color and no smell and is heavier than air: it is breathed out of the lungs and is taken in by plants, which use it to make their food

ca·reer (kə rir′) *n.* **1** the way one earns one's living; profession or occupation [Have you thought of teaching as a *career*?] **2** one's progress through life or in one's work [a long and successful *career* in politics]

car·toon (kär tōōn′) *n.* **1** a drawing, as in a newspaper or magazine, that shows how the editor or artist feels about some person or thing in the news: it is often a caricature that criticizes or praises **2** a humorous drawing ☆**3** *same as* **comic strip** ☆**4** *same as* **animated cartoon** ☆◆*v.* to draw cartoons —**car·toon′ist** *n.*

cas·sette (kə set′) *n.* **1** a case with a roll of film in it, for loading a camera quickly and easily **2** a case with recording tape in it, for quick, easy use in a tape recorder

cas·u·al (kazh′ōō əl) *adj.* **1** happening by chance; not planned [a *casual* visit] **2** for wear at times when dressy clothes are not needed [*casual* sports clothes] —**cas′u·al·ly** *adv.* —**cas′u·al·ness** *n.*

cat·a·log or **cat·a·logue** (kat′ə lôg *or* kat′ə läg) *n.* ☆**1** a card file in alphabetical order giving a complete list of things in a collection, as of all the books in a library **2** a book or paper listing all the things for sale or on display ◆*v.* to make a list of or put into a list —**cat′a·loged** or **cat′a·logued, cat′a·log·ing** or **cat′a·logu·ing**

cau·li·flow·er (kôl′ə flou′ər *or* käl′ə flou′ər) *n.* a kind of cabbage with a head of white, fleshy flower clusters growing tightly together: it is eaten as a vegetable

cau·tion (kô′shən *or* kä′shən) *n.* **1** the act of being careful not to get into danger or make mistakes [Use *caution* in crossing streets.] **2** a warning [Let me give you a word of *caution*.] ◆*v.* to warn; tell of danger [The sign *cautioned* us to slow down.]

cav·i·ty (kav′i tē) *n.* **1** a hollow place, such as the one caused by decay in a tooth **2** a natural hollow space in the body [the chest *cavity*] —*pl.* **cav′i·ties**

cel·e·brate (sel′ə brāt) *v.* **1** to honor a victory, the memory of something, etc. in some special way [to *celebrate* a birthday with a party; to *celebrate* the Fourth of July with fireworks] **2** to honor or praise widely [Aesop's fables have been *celebrated* for centuries.] **3** to perform a ceremony in worshiping [to *celebrate* Mass] **4** to have a good time; used only in everyday talk [Let's *celebrate* when we finish painting the garage.] —**cel′e·brat·ed, cel′e·brat·ing** —**cel′e·bra′tion** *n.*

cen·tu·ry (sen′chər ē) *n.* **1** any of the 100-year periods counted forward or backward from the beginning of the Christian Era [From 500 to 401 B.C. was the fifth *century* B.C. From 1901 to 2000 is the twentieth *century* A.D.] **2** any period of 100 years [Mark Twain was born over a *century* ago.] —*pl.* **cen′tu·ries**

cer·e·mo·ny (ser′ə mō′ nē) *n.* **1** an act or set of acts done in a special way, with all the right details [a wedding *ceremony* in church; the *ceremony* of inaugurating the president.] **2** very polite behavior that follows strict rules; formality [The special dinner was served with great *ceremony*.] —*pl.* **cer′e·mo′nies**

cer·tain (surt′n) *adj.* **1** without any doubt or question; sure; positive [Are you *certain* of your facts?] **2** bound to happen; not failing or missing [to risk *certain* death; the soldier's *certain* aim] **3** not named or described, though perhaps known [It happened in a *certain* town out west.]

cer·tif·i·cate (sur tif′i kət) *n.* a written or printed statement that can be used as proof of something because it is official [A birth *certificate* proves where and when someone was born.]

chal·lenge (chal′ənj) *v.* **1** to question the right or rightness of; refuse to believe unless proof is given [to *challenge* a claim; to *challenge* something said or the person who says it] **2** to call to take part in a fight or contest; dare [He *challenged* her to a game of chess.] **3** to refuse to let pass unless a certain sign is given [The sentry waited for the password after *challenging* the soldier.] **4** to call for skill, effort, or imagination [That puzzle will really *challenge* you.] —**chal′lenged, chal′leng·ing**

cham·pi·on (cham′pē ən) *n.* **1** a person or thing that wins first place or is judged to be best, as in a contest or sport [a spelling *champion*; a tennis *champion*] **2** a person who fights for another or for a cause; defender [a *champion* of the poor]

cham·pi·on·ship (cham′pē ən ship′) *n.* **1** the position or title of a champion; first place **2** the act of championing, or defending

chan·nel (chan′əl) *n.* **1** the bed of a river or stream **2** the deeper part of a river, harbor, etc. **3** a body of water joining two larger bodies of water [The English *Channel* links the Atlantic Ocean to the North Sea.] **4** the band of frequencies on which a single radio or television station sends out its programs —**chan′neled** or **chan′nelled, chan′nel·ing** or **chan′nel·ling** *v.*

a	ask, fat
ā	ape, date
ä	car, lot
e	elf, ten
ē	even, meet
i	is, hit
ī	ice, fire
ō	open, go
ô	law, horn
oi	oil, point
ōō	look, pull
ōō	ooze, tool
ou	out, crowd
u	up, cut
ʉ	fur, fern
ə	a in ago
	e in agent
	e in father
	i in unity
	o in collect
	u in focus
ch	chin, arch
ŋ	ring, singer
sh	she, dash
th	thin, truth
th	then, father
zh	s in pleasure

char·ac·ter (kar'ək tər) *n.* **1** all the things that a person does, feels, and thinks by which that person is judged as being good or bad, strong or weak, etc. [That insulting remark showed her true *character*.] **2** all those things that make one person or thing different from others; special quality; nature [The fields and woods around the school gave it a rural *character*.] **3** any letter, figure, or symbol used in writing and printing **4** a person in a story or play

☆**check·book** (chək'book) *n.* a book that holds forms for writing checks

cheer·ful (chir'fəl) *adj.* **1** full of cheer; glad; joyful [a *cheerful* smile] **2** bright and gay [a *cheerful* room] **3** willing; glad to help [a *cheerful* worker] —**cheer'ful·ly** *adv.* —**cheer'ful·ness** *n.*

cheer·y (chir'ē) *adj.* cheerful; lively and happy [They gave us a *cheery* welcome.] —**cheer'i·er, cheer'i·est** —**cheer'i·ly** *adv.* —**cheer'i·ness** *n.*

chem·i·cal (kem'i kəl) *adj.* **1** of or in chemistry [a *chemical* process] **2** made by or used in chemistry [*chemical* compounds] —**chem'i·cal·ly** *adv.*

chief (chēf) *n.* the leader or head of some group [an Indian *chief*; the *chief* of a hospital staff] ◆*adj.* **1** having the highest position [the *chief* foreman] **2** main; most important [Jill's *chief* interest is golf.]

chim·pan·zee (chim'pan zē' *or* chim pan'zē) *n.* an ape of Africa that is smaller than a gorilla and is a very intelligent animal: *the word is often shortened to* **chimp** (chimp)

chin·chil·la (chin chil'ə) *n.* **1** a small, ratlike animal found in the Andes Mountains in South America **2** a soft, gray fur, which is very expensive **3** a heavy wool cloth with a rough surface, used for making coats

Chi·nese (chī nēz') *n.* **1** a member of a people whose native country is China —*pl.* **Chi·nese'** **2** the language of China ◆*adj.* of China, its people, language, or culture

choc·o·late (chôk'lət *or* chäk'lət *or* chôk'ə lət *or* chäk'ə lət) *n.* **1** a paste, powder, syrup, or bar made from cacao seeds that have been roasted and ground **2** a drink made of chocolate, sugar, and milk or water **3** a candy made of chocolate or covered with chocolate **4** reddish brown ◆*adj.* made of or flavored with chocolate

choir (kwīr) *n.* **1** a group of people trained to sing together, especially as part of a church service **2** the part of a church where the choir sits or stands

choose (chooz) *v.* **1** to pick out one or more from a number or group [*Choose* a subject from this list.] **2** to make up one's mind; decide or prefer [She *chose* to stay home.] —**chose, cho'sen, choos'ing**

cho·sen (chō'zen) *past participle of* **choose** ◆*adj.* picked out carefully, as for a special purpose [a *chosen* few soldiers formed the king's guard.]

cir·cus (sur'kəs) *n.* **1** a traveling show held in tents or in a hall, with clowns, trained animals, acrobats, etc. ☆**2** a very funny or entertaining person or thing: *used only in everyday talk* **3** a stadium or arena in ancient Rome, where games or races were held

cir·rus (sīr'əs) *n.* a kind of cloud that looks like thin strips of woolly curls —*pl.* **cir'rus**

cit·i·zen (sit'i zən) *n.* **1** a person who is a member of a country or state either because of being born there or having been made a member by law: citizens have certain duties to their country and are entitled to certain rights **2** a person who lives in a particular city or town [the *citizens* of Atlanta]

class (klas) *n.* **1** a number of people or things thought of as a group because they are alike in certain ways [Whales belong to the *class* of mammals. She is a member of the working *class*.] ☆**2** a group of students meeting together to be taught; also, a meeting of this kind [My English *class* is held at nine o'clock.] ☆**3** a group of students who are or will be graduating together [the *class* of 1981] **4** a division or grouping according to grade or quality [to travel first *class*]

clas·si·fy (klas'i fī') *v.* to arrange by putting into classes or groups according to some system [Plants and animals are *classified* into various orders, families, species, etc.] —**clas'si·fied, clas'si·fy·ing**

cli·ent (klī'ənt) *n.* **1** a person or company for whom a lawyer, accountant, etc. is acting **2** a customer

clos·et (kläz'ət *or* klôz'ət) *n.* a small room or cupboard for clothes, linens, supplies, etc. ◆*v.* to shut up in a room for a private talk [The president was *closeted* with his close advisers.]

☆**cloud·burst** (kloud'burst) *n.* a sudden, very heavy rain

coast (kōst) *n.* **1** land along the sea; seashore. ☆**2** a slide or ride downhill, as on a sled ◆*v.* **1** to sail along a coast ☆**2** to ride or slide downhill, as on a sled ☆**3** to keep on moving after the driving power is cut off [We ran out of gas, but the car *coasted* into the gas station.]

co·coa (kō'kō) *n.* **1** a powder made from roasted cacao seeds, used in making chocolate **2** a drink made from this powder by adding sugar and hot water or milk **3** a light, reddish brown

co·co·nut *or* **co·coa·nut** (kō'kə nut) *n.* the large, round fruit of a tall, tropical palm tree (called the **coconut palm** or **coco palm**): coconuts have a thick, hard, brown shell that has an inside layer of sweet white matter used as a food: the hollow center is filled with a sweet, milky liquid

col·lect (kə lekt′) *v.* **1** to gather in one place; assemble [*Collect* the rubbish and burn it. Water *collects* around the drain.] **2** to gather things as a hobby [She *collects* stamps.] **3** to call for and get money owed [The building manager *collects* the rent.]

col·lege (käl′ij) *n.* **1** a school that one can go to after high school for higher studies: colleges give degrees to students when they graduate; often a part of a university, which may have a number of special colleges, as of law or medicine **2** a school where one can get training in some special work [a business *college*]

co·logne (kə lōn′) *n.* a sweet-smelling liquid like perfume, but not so strong

co·lon (kō′lən) *n.* the main part of the large intestine, that leads to the rectum

col·umn (käl′əm) *n.* **1** a long, generally round, upright support; pillar: columns usually stand in groups to hold up a roof or other part of a building, but they are sometimes used just for decoration **2** any long, upright thing like a column [a *column* of water; the spinal *column*] **3** any of the long sections of print lying side by side on a page and separated by a line or blank space [Each page of this book has two *columns*.] **4** any of the articles by one writer or on a special subject, that appear regularly in a newspaper or magazine [a chess *column*]

com·fort·a·ble (kumf′tər bəl or kum′fər tə bəl) *adj.* **1** giving comfort or ease; not giving pain [a *comfortable* pair of shoes] **2** feeling comfort; not uneasy [Are you *comfortable* in that chair?] —**com′fort·a·bly** *adv.*

com·ic (käm′ik) *adj.* **1** having to do with comedy **2** funny or amusing; making one laugh ☆➛*n.* **comics**, *pl.* a section of comic strips, as in a newspaper

com·mand (kə mand′) *v.* **1** to give an order to; direct [I *command* you to halt!] **2** to be in control of [Captain Stone *commands* Company B.] **3** to deserve to have [Her courage *commands* our respect.] ➛*n.* **1** an order or direction [He obeyed the queen's *commands*.] **2** the power or ability to control or command; control [Who is in *command* here? He has no *command* of his temper.]

com·mence (kə mens′) *v.* to begin or start [The trial will *commence* at noon.] —**com·menced′, com·menc′ing**

com·mend (kə mend′) *v.* **1** to mention with approval; praise [a ballet company *commended* by all the dance critics] **2** to put in someone's care or keeping; commit —**com·men·da·tion** (käm′ən dā′shən) *n.*

com·mit·tee (kə mit′ē) *n.* a group of people chosen to study some matter or to do a certain thing [a *committee* to plan the party]

com·pan·ion (kəm pan′yən) *n.* **1** a person who goes along with another; especially, one who often shares or supports the other's activities; comrade; associate **2** either one of a pair of matched things [Where is the *companion* to this glove?]

com·pa·ny (kum′pə nē) *n.* **1** a group of people; especially, a group joined together in some work or activity [a *company* of actors; a business *company*] **2** a group of soldiers that is usually under the command of a captain **3** the state of being companions; companionship [We enjoy each other's *company*.] **4** friends or companions [One is judged by the *company* one keeps.] **5** a guest or guests [We've invited *company* for dinner.] —*pl.* **com′pa·nies**

com·pen·sa·tion (käm′pən sā′shən) *n.* **1** the act of compensating **2** something given or done to make up for something else [She was given an expensive gift as extra *compensation* for her services.]

com·pete (kəm pēt′) *v.* to take part in a contest; be a rival for something [Two hundred students *competed* for the scholarship.] —**com·pet′ed, com·pet′ing**

com·pe·tent (käm′pə tənt) *adj.* having enough ability to do what is needed; capable [a *competent* typist] —**com′pe·tent·ly** *adv.*

com·plain (kəm plān′) *v.* **1** to find fault with something or show pain or displeasure [Everyone *complained* about the poor food in the cafeteria.] **2** to make a report about something bad [We *complained* to the police about the noisy party next door.]

con·ceive (kən sēv′) *v.* **1** to form or develop in the mind; think of; imagine [I have *conceived* a plan for making a fortune.] **2** to understand [It is difficult to *conceive* how this motor works.] **3** to become pregnant —**con·ceived′, con·ceiv′ing**

con·cern (kən surn′) *v.* to have a relation to; be important to; involve [This matter *concerns* all of us.] —**con·cerned′, con·cern′ing** ➛*n.* worry or anxiety [He felt great *concern* over his wife's health.]

con·cert (kän′sərt) *n.* a musical program, especially one in which a number of musicians perform together

con·di·tion (kən dish′ən) *n.* **1** the particular way a person or thing is [What is the *condition* of the patient? Weather *conditions* won't allow us to go.] **2** the right or healthy way to be [The whole team is in *condition*.] **3** anything which must be or must happen before something else can take place [Her parents made it a *condition* that she had to do her homework before she could watch TV.]

a	ask, fat
ā	ape, date
ä	car, lot
e	elf, ten
ē	even, meet
i	is, hit
ī	ice, fire
ō	open, go
ô	law, horn
oi	oil, point
oo	look, pull
o͞o	ooze, tool
ou	out, crowd
u	up, cut
ʉ	fur, fern
ə	a in ago
	e in agent
	e in father
	i in unity
	o in collect
	u in focus
ch	chin, arch
ŋ	ring, singer
sh	she, dash
th	thin, truth
th	then, father
zh	s in pleasure

157

con·fi·dence (kän′ fi dəns) *n.* **1** strong belief or trust in someone or something; reliance [They have *confidence* in my skill.] **2** a belief in oneself; self-confidence [I began to play the piano with *confidence*.] **3** trust in another to keep one's secret [She told it to him in strict *confidence*.] **4** a secret [Don't burden me with your *confidences*.]

con·gress (kän′ grəs) *n.* **1** a coming together; meeting; convention ☆**2 Congress**, the group of elected officials that makes the laws: it consists of the Senate and the House of Representatives

con·gru·ent (kän′ grōō ənt) *adj.* in agreement or harmony; corresponding

con·nect (kə nekt′) *v.* **1** to join together; unite [Several bridges *connect* Ohio and Kentucky.] **2** to relate in some way; think of together [Do you *connect* his silence with her arrival?] —**con·nect′ ed, con·nect′ ing**

con·quer (käŋ′ kər) *v.* **1** to get or gain by using force, as by winning a war [The Spaniards *conquered* Mexico.] **2** to overcome by trying hard; get the better of; defeat [She *conquered* her bad habits.] —**con′ quer·or** *n.*

con·science (kän′ shəns) *n.* a sense of right and wrong; feeling that keeps one from doing bad things [My *conscience* bothers me after I tell a lie.]

con·serve (kən surv′) *v.* to keep from being hurt, lost, or wasted [to *conserve* one's energy] —**con·served′**

con·sid·er·ate (kən sid′ər ət) *adj.* thoughtful of other people's feelings; kind [It was *considerate* of you to invite her too.] —**con·sid′ er·ate·ly** *adv.*

con·sole (kən sōl′) *v.* to make less sad or troubled; comfort [A toy *consoled* the lost child.] —**con·soled′, con·sol′ ing**

con·sti·tu·tion (kän′sti tōō′shən *or* kän′sti tyōō′shən) *n.* **1** the act of setting up, forming, establishing, etc. **2** the way in which a person or thing is formed; makeup; structure [My strong *constitution* keeps me from catching cold.] **3** the system of basic laws or rules of a government, society, etc. **4** a document in which these laws and rules are written down [The *Constitution* of the U.S. is the supreme law here.]

con·trib·ute (kən trib′yōōt) *v.* **1** to give together with others [I *contribute* to my church.] **2** to write an article, poem, etc. as for a magazine or newspaper —**con·trib′ut·ed, con·trib′ut·ing**

con·vex (kän veks′ *or* kän′vəks) *adj.* curving outward like the outside of a ball [a *convex* lens] —**con·vex′i·ty** *n.* —**con·vex′ly** *adv.*

cook (kook) *v.* **1** to prepare food by heating; boil, roast, bake, etc. **2** to be cooked [The roast should *cook* longer.]

co·op·er·ate (kō äp′ər āt′) *v.* to work together to get something done [If we all *cooperate*, we can finish sooner.] —**co·op′er·at·ed, co·op′er·at·ing** —**co·op′er·a′ tion** *n.*

☆**corn·bread** (kôrn′bred) *n.* bread made with cornmeal

cor·rect (kə rekt′) *v.* **1** to make right; get rid of mistakes in [*Correct* your spelling before turning in your papers.] **2** to point out the mistakes of; sometimes, to punish or scold for such mistakes [to *correct* a child's behavior] ►*adj.* **1** without a mistake; right; true [a *correct* answer] **2** agreeing with what is thought to be proper [*correct* behavior] —**cor·rect′ ly** *adv.* —**cor·rect′ness** *n.*

cough (kôf *or* käf) *v.* to force air from the lungs with a sudden, loud noise —**coughed, cough′ ing** ►*n.* the act or sound of coughing [I have a bad *cough*.]

coun·se·lor *or* **coun·sel·lor** (koun′sə lər) *n.* **1** a person who advises; adviser **2** a lawyer **3** a person in charge of children at a camp

count (kount) *v.* **1** to name numbers in a regular order [I'll *count* to five.] **2** to add up so as to get a total [*Count* the people here.] **3** to take account of; include [There are ten here, *counting* you.] **4** to be taken into account; have importance, value, etc. [Every bit of help *counts*.] —**count′ ed**

☆**count·down** (kount′doun) *n.* the schedule of things that take place in planned order just before the firing of a rocket, the setting off of a nuclear explosion, etc.; also, the counting backward in units of time while these things take place

coun·try (kun′ trē) *n.* **1** an area of land; region [wooded *country*] **2** the whole land of a nation [The *country* of Japan is made up of islands.] **3** the people of a nation [The speech was broadcast to the whole *country*.] **4** the nation to which one belongs ["My *country*, 'tis of thee"] —*pl.* **coun′ tries**

cou·ple (kup′əl) *n.* **1** two things of the same kind that go together; pair [a *couple* of book ends] **2** a man and woman who are married, engaged, or partners, as in a dance ►*v.* to join together; unite; connect [to *couple* railroad cars] —**cou′ pled, cou′ pling**

cou·pon (kōō′ pän *or* kyōō′ pän) *n.* **1** a ticket or part of a ticket that gives the holder certain rights [The *coupon* on the cereal box is worth 10¢ toward buying another box.] **2** a part of a bond which is cut off at certain times and turned in for payment of interest **3** a part of a printed advertisement that can be used for ordering goods, samples, etc.

cou·ra·geous (kə rā′ jəs) *adj.* having or showing courage; brave

cour·te·ous (kur′tē əs) *adj.* polite and kind; thoughtful of others

cous·in (kuz′ən) *n.* **1** the son or daughter of one's uncle or aunt: *also called* **first cousin** [You are a second *cousin* to the children of your parents' first *cousins*, and you are a first *cousin* once removed to the children of your first cousins] **2** a distant relation

cov·er (kuv′ər) *v.* **1** to place one thing over another; spread over [*Cover* the bird cage at night. *Cover* the wall with white paint. Water *covered* the fields.] **2** to keep from being seen or known; hide [He tried to *cover* up the scandal.] **3** to protect, as from harm or loss [Are you *covered* by insurance?] **4** to provide for; take care of [Is this case *covered* by the rules?] **5** to have to do with; be about; include [This book *covers* the Civil War.]

cran·ber·ry (kran′ber′ē) *n.* **1** a hard, sour, red berry used in sauces and jellies **2** the marsh plant it grows on —*pl.* **cran′ber′ries**

crea·ture (krē′chər) *n.* a living being; any person or animal

cred·it (kred′it) *n.* **1** belief; trust [I give little *credit* to what he says.] **2** praise or approval [I give her *credit* for trying.] **3** official recognition in a record [You will receive *credit* for your work on this project.] **4** a person or thing that brings praise [She is a *credit* to the team.] **5** trust that a person will be able and willing to pay later [That store doesn't give *credit*, so you have to pay cash.]

crim·i·nal (krim′i nəl) *adj.* **1** being a crime; that is a crime [a *criminal* act] **2** having to do with crime [*criminal* law] ✦*n.* a person guilty of a crime —**crim′i·nal·ly** *adv.*

crowd (kroud) *n.* **1** a large group of people together [*crowds* of Christmas shoppers] **2** the common people; the masses ☆**3** a group of people having something in common; set: *used only in everyday talk* [My brother's *crowd* is too old for me.] ✦*v.* **1** to push or squeeze [Can we all *crowd* into one car?] **2** to come together in a large group [People *crowded* to see the show.] —**crowd′ed**

cu·cum·ber (kyoo′kum bər) *n.* **1** a long vegetable with green skin and firm, white flesh: it is used in salads and made into pickles **2** the vine that it grows on —**cool as a cucumber,** calm; not excited

cuff (kuf) *n.* **1** a band at the wrist of a sleeve, either fastened to the sleeve or separate **2** a fold turned up at the bottom of a trouser leg **3** a handcuff

cu·mu·lus (kyoom′yə ləs) *n.* a kind of cloud in which round masses are piled up on each other

cur·rant (kur′ənt) *n.* **1** a small, sweet, black raisin, used in cooking **2** a small, sour berry used in jams and jellies; also, the bush it grows on

cus·tom·er (kus′tə mər) *n.* **1** a person who buys, especially one who buys regularly [I have been a *customer* of that shop for many years.] **2** any person with whom one has dealings: *used only in everyday talk*

Dd

dan·ger·ous (dān′jər əs) *adj.* full of danger; likely to cause injury, pain, etc.; unsafe [This shaky old bridge is *dangerous*.] —**dan′ger·ous·ly** *adv.*

Dan·ube (dan′yoob) a river in southern Europe, flowing from southwestern Germany eastward into the Black Sea

dark (därk) *adj.* **1** having little or no light [a *dark* room; a *dark* night] **2** closer to black than to white; deep in shade; not light [*dark* green] **3** hidden; full of mystery [a *dark* secret] **4** gloomy or hopeless [Things look *dark* for Lou.] —**dark′ly** *adv.* —**dark′ness** *n.*

dark·en (där′kən) *v.* to make or become dark

daugh·ter (dôt′ər *or* dät′ər) *n.* **1** a girl or woman as she is related to a parent or to both parents **2** a girl or woman who is influenced by something in the way that a child is by a parent [a *daughter* of France]

de·cay (dē kā′) *v.* **1** to become rotten by the action of bacteria [The fallen apples *decayed* on the ground.] **2** to fall into ruins; become no longer sound, powerful, rich, beautiful, etc. [Spain's power *decayed* after its fleet was destroyed.] **3** to break down so that there are fewer radioactive atoms

de·ceit (dē sēt′) *n.* **1** a deceiving or lying **2** a lie or a dishonest act or acts

de·ceive (dē sēv′) *v.* to make someone believe what is not true; fool or trick; mislead [The queen *deceived* Snow White by pretending to be her friend.] —**de·ceived′, de·ceiv′ing** —**de·ceiv′er** *n.*

de·cid·ed (dē sīd′əd) *adj.* **1** clear and sharp; definite [a *decided* change in the weather] **2** sure or firm; without doubt [Clem has very *decided* ideas on the subject.] —**de·cid′ed·ly** *adv.*

de·code (dē kōd′) *v.* to figure out the meaning of something written in code —**de·cod′ed, de·cod′ing**

dec·o·ra·tive (dek′ə rə tiv *or* dek′ə rā′tiv) *adj.* that serves to decorate; ornamental

de·coy (dē′koi *or* dē koi′) *n.* **1** an artificial bird or animal used to attract wild birds or animals to a place where they can be shot or trapped; also, a live bird or animal used in the same way **2** a thing or person used to lure someone into a trap

a	ask, fat
ā	ape, date
ä	car, lot
e	elf, ten
ē	even, meet
i	is, hit
ī	ice, fire
ō	open, go
ô	law, horn
oi	oil, point
oo	look, pull
oo	ooze, tool
ou	out, crowd
u	up, cut
ʉ	fur, fern
ə	a in ago
	e in agent
	e in father
	i in unity
	o in collect
	u in focus
ch	chin, arch
ŋ	ring, singer
sh	she, dash
th	thin, truth
th	then, father
zh	s in pleasure

de·gree (dē grē′) *n.* **1** a step in a series; stage in the progress of something [He advanced by *degrees* from office clerk to president.] **2** a unit used in measuring temperature that is shown by the symbol °: the boiling point of water is 100° Celsius or 212° Fahrenheit **3** a unit used in measuring angles and arcs of circles [There are 360 *degrees* in the circumference of a circle.] **4** a rank given by a college to a student who has satisfactorily completed a course of study, or to an outstanding person as an honor [a B.A. *degree*]

de·lay (dē lā′) *v.* **1** to put off to a later time; postpone [The bride's illness will *delay* the wedding.] **2** to make late; hold back; keep from going on [We were *delayed* by the storm.]

de·light·ful (dē līt′fəl) *adj.* giving delight or pleasure; very pleasing [a *delightful* party] —**de·light′ful·ly** *adv.*

de·part·ment (dē pärt′mənt) *n.* a separate part or branch, as of a government or business [the police *department*; the shipping *department*; the *department* of mathematics in a college] —**de·part·men·tal** (dē′pärt ment′l) *adj.*

de·pend·a·ble (dē pen′də bəl) *adj.* that can be depended on; reliable [a *dependable* friend] —**de·pend′a·bil·i·ty** *n.*

de·pos·it (dē päz′it) *v.* **1** to place for safekeeping, as money in a bank **2** to give as part payment or as a pledge [They *deposited* $500 on a new car.] **3** to lay down [I *deposited* my books on the chair. The river *deposits* tons of mud at its mouth.] ◆*n.* **1** something placed for safekeeping, as money in a bank **2** money given as a pledge or part payment

de·scend·ant (dē sen′dənt) *n.* a person who is descended from a certain ancestor

de·sign (dē zīn′) *n.* **1** a drawing or plan to be followed in making something [the *designs* for a house] **2** the arrangement of parts, colors, etc.; pattern or decoration [the *design* in a rug] ◆*v.* **1** to think up and draw plans for [to *design* a new model of a car] **2** to arrange the parts, colors, etc. of [Who *designed* this book?] **3** to set apart for a certain use; intend [This chair was not *designed* for hard use.] —**de·signed′**

de·stroy (dē stroi′) *v.* to put an end to by breaking up, tearing down, ruining, or spoiling [The flood *destroyed* 300 homes.] —**de·stroyed′, de·stroy′ing**

de·tec·tor (dē tek′tər) *n.* a person or thing that detects; especially, a device used to show that something is present

di·am·e·ter (dī am′ət ər) *n.* **1** a straight line passing through the center of a circle or sphere, from one side to the other **2** the length of such a line [The *diameter* of the moon is about 2,160 miles.]

di·a·ry (dī′ə rē) *n.* **1** a record written day by day of some of the things done, seen, or thought by the writer **2** a book for keeping such a record —*pl.* **di′a·ries**

dic·tion·ar·y (dik′shə ner′ē) *n.* **1** a book in which some or most of the words of a language, or of some special field, are listed in alphabetical order with their meanings, pronunciations, etc. [a school *dictionary*; a medical *dictionary*] **2** a book like this in which words of one language are explained in words of another language [a Spanish-English *dictionary*] —*pl.* **dic′tion·ar′ies**

dig·it (dij′it) *n.* **1** any number from 0 through 9 **2** a finger or toe

di·plo·ma (di plō′mə) *n.* a certificate given to a student by a school or college to show that the student has completed a required course of study

di·rec·tion (də rek′shən) *n.* **1** a directing or managing; control [The choir is under the *direction* of Ms. Jones.] **2** an order or command **3** *usually* **directions**, *pl.* instructions on how to get to some place or how to do something [*directions* for driving to Omaha; *directions* for building a model boat] **4** the point toward which something faces or the line along which something moves or lies ["North," "up," "forward," and "left" are *directions*.] —**di·rec′tion·al** *adj.*

di·rec·tor (də rek′tər) *n.* **1** a person who directs or manages the work of others [the *director* of a play, a band, a government bureau] **2** a member of a group chosen to direct the affairs of a business —**di·rec′tor·ship** *n.*

dis·ap·pear (dis ə pir′) *v.* to stop being seen or to stop existing; vanish [The car *disappeared* around a curve. Dinosaurs *disappeared* millions of years ago.] —**dis·ap·pear′ance** *n.*

dis·ap·prove (dis ə prōōv′) *v.* to refuse to approve; have an opinion or feeling against; think to be wrong [The Puritans *disapproved* of dancing.] —**dis·ap·proved′, dis·ap·prov′ing** —**dis′ap·prov′ing·ly** *adv.*

dis·be·lief (dis bə lēf′) *n.* the state of not believing; lack of belief [The guide stared at me in *disbelief*.]

dis·con·tin·ue (dis′kən tin′yōō) *v.* to stop doing, using, etc; give up [to *discontinue* a subscription to a magazine] —**dis′con·tin′ued, dis′con·tin′u·ing**

dis·cov·er (di skuv′ər) *v.* **1** to be the first to find, see, or learn about [Marie and Pierre Curie *discovered* radium.] **2** to come upon, learn, or find out about [I *discovered* my name on the list.] **3** to be the first person who is not a native to come to or see a continent, river, etc. [De Soto *discovered* the Mississippi River.] —**dis·cov′ered**

dis·grace (dis grās′) *n.* **1** loss of favor, respect, or honor; dishonor; shame [She is in *disgrace* for cheating on the test.] **2** a person or thing bringing shame [Slums are a *disgrace* to a city ◆*v.* to bring shame or dishonor upon; hurt the reputation of [My cousin's crime has *disgraced* our family.] —**dis·graced′, dis·grac′ing**

dis·mal (diz′məl) *adj.* **1** causing gloom or misery; sad [a *dismal* story] **2** dark and gloomy [a *dismal* room] —**dis′mal·ly** *adv.*

dis·play (di splā′) *v.* to put or spread out so as to be seen; exhibit [to *display* a collection of stamps] —**dis·played′, dis·play′ing** ◆*n.* something that is displayed [a *display* of jewelry]

dis·tance (dis′təns) *n.* **1** the length of a line between two points [The *distance* between New York and Chicago is 713 miles.] **2** the condition of being far apart in space or time; remoteness ["*Distance* lends charm." There was quite a *distance* between their views.] **3** a place far away [viewing things from a *distance*] —**dis′tanced, dis′tanc·ing** ◆*v.*

dis·turb (dis tᴜrb′) *v.* **1** to break up the quiet or calm of [The roar of motorcycles *disturbed* the peace.] **2** to make worried or uneasy; upset [They are *disturbed* by their parents' divorce.] **3** to put into disorder; mix up [Someone *disturbed* the books on my shelf.]

di·vide (də vīd′) *v.* **1** to separate into parts; split up [a classroom *divided* by a movable wall] **2** to separate into equal parts by arithmetic [If you *divide* 12 by 3, you get 4.] **3** to put into separate groups; classify [Living things are *divided* into plants and animals.] **4** to make separate or keep apart [A stone wall *divides* their farms.]

dol·phin (dôl′fin) *n.* a water animal related to the whale but smaller: the common dolphin has a long snout and many teeth

dom·i·nant (däm′ə nənt) *adj.* most important or most powerful; ruling, controlling [a *dominant* world power]

dou·ble (dub′əl) *adj.* **1** having two parts that are alike [a *double* house; a *double* door; gun with a *double* barrel] **2** being of two kinds [Sometimes a word is used in a joke because it has a *double* meaning and can be understood in two different ways.] **3** twice as much, as many, as great, as fast, etc. [a *double* portion; *double* time] **4** made for two [a *double* bed; a *double* garage] ◆*adv.* two at one time; in a pair [to ride *double* on a bicycle] —**dou′bled, doub′ling** *v.*

doz·en (duz′ən) *n.* a group of twelve. —*pl.* **doz′ens** or, *especially after a number,* **doz′en.**

drain (drān) *v.* **1** to make flow away [*Drain* the water from the potatoes.] **2** to draw off water or other liquid from; make empty [to *drain* a swamp; to *drain* one's glass] **3** to flow off [Water won't *drain* from a flat roof.] **4** to become empty or dry [Our bathtub *drains* slowly.] **5** to flow into [The Ohio River *drains* into the Mississippi.]

dra·ma (drä′mə *or* dram′ə) *n.* **1** a story that is written to be acted out, as on a stage; play **2** the art of writing or performing plays **3** a series of interesting or exciting events [the *drama* of the American Revolution]

draw·er (drô′r *or* drôr) *n.* **1** a person or thing that draws **2** a box that slides in and out of a table, chest, desk, etc.

drear·y (drir′ē) *adj.* without happiness or cheer; gloomy, sad, or dull [a long, *dreary* tale] —**drear′i·er, drear′i·est** —**drear′i·ly** *adv.* —**drear′i·ness** *n.*

du·ra·ble (dōor′ə bəl *or* dᴜr′ə bəl) *adj.* lasting in spite of hard wear or much use —**du′ra·bil′i·ty** *n.* —**du′ra·bly** *adv.*

earth·quake (ᴜrth′kwäk) *n.* a shaking or trembling of the ground, caused by the shifting of underground rock or by the action of a volcano

ea·sel (ē′zəl) *n.* a standing frame for holding an artist's canvas or a picture

ee·rie or **ee·ry** (ir′ē) *adj.* giving a person a feeling of fear or mystery; weird [an *eerie* house that looked haunted]

ef·fort (ef′ərt) *n.* **1** the use of energy to get something done; a trying hard with the mind or body [It took great *effort* to climb the mountain.] **2** a try or attempt [They made no *effort* to be friendly.] **3** something done with effort [My early *efforts* at poetry were not published.]

eight·een (ā′tēn′) *n., adj.* the cardinal number between seventeen and nineteen; 18

eight·y (āt′ē) *n., adj.* eight times ten; the number 80 —*pl.* **eight′ies** —**the eighties,** the numbers or years from 80 through 89

ei·ther (ē′thər *or* ī′thər) *adj.* **1** one or the other of two [Use *either* exit.] **2** both one and the other; each [She had a tool in *either* hand.] ◆*pron.* one or the other of two [*Either* of the suits will fit you.]

e·lec·tion (ē lek′shən) *n.* the act of choosing or the fact of being chosen, especially by voting

e·lec·tric (ē lek′trik) *adj.* **1** of or having to do with electricity [*electric* current; *electric* wire] **2** making or made by electricity [an *electric* generator; *electric* lighting] **3** worked by electricity [an *electric* toothbrush]

e·lec·tron·ic (ē lek′trän·ik *or* el′ek trän′ik) *adj.* working or produced by the action of electrons [*electronic* equipment]

el·e·va·tion (el′ə vā′shən) *n.* **1** a raising up or being raised up [her *elevation* to the position of principal] **2** a higher place or position [The house is on a slight *elevation*.] **3** height above the surface of the earth or above sea level [The mountain has an *elevation* of 20,000 feet.]

em·per·or (em′pər ər) *n.* a man who rules an empire

a	ask, fat
ā	ape, date
ä	car, lot
e	elf, ten
ē	even, meet
i	is, hit
ī	ice, fire
ō	open, go
ô	law, horn
oi	oil, point
ᴏᴏ	look, pull
ᴏ̄ᴏ̄	ooze, tool
ou	out, crowd
u	up, cut
ᴜ	fur, fern
ə	a in ago
	e in agent
	e in father
	i in unity
	o in collect
	u in focus
ch	chin, arch
ŋ	ring, singer
sh	she, dash
th	thin, truth
th	then, father
zh	s in pleasure

em·pire (em′pīr) *n.* **1** a group of countries or territories under the control of one government or ruler [Much of Europe was once a part of the Roman *Empire*.] **2** any government whose ruler has the title of emperor or empress **3** a large business or group of businesses controlled by one person, family, or group

em·ploy·ee or **em·ploy·e** (em ploi′ē *or* em′ploi ē′) *n.* a person who works for another in return for pay

en·a·ble (en ā′bəl) *v.* to make able; give the means or power to [A loan *enabled* Lou to go to college.] —**en·a′bled, en·a′bling**

en·cour·age (en kʉr′ij) *v.* to give courage or hope to; make feel more confident [Praise *encouraged* the children to try harder.] —**en·cour′aged, en·cour′′ag·ing**

en·cy·clo·pe·di·a or **en·cy·clo·pae·di·a** (en sī′klə pē′ dē ə) *n.* a book or set of books that gives information on all branches of knowledge or, sometimes, on just one branch of knowledge: it is made up of articles usually in alphabetical order

en·dan·ger (en dān′jər) *v.* to put in danger or peril [to *endanger* one's life]

en·dan·gered species (en dān′jərd) *n.* a species of animal or plant in danger of becoming extinct, or dying off [The whooping crane is an *endangered* species.]

en·dure (en dŏŏr′ *or* en dyŏŏr′) *v.* **1** to hold up under pain, weariness, etc.; put up with; bear; stand [to *endure* torture; to *endure* insults] **2** to go on for a long time; last; remain [The Sphinx has *endured* for ages.] —**en·dured′, en·dur′ing** —**en·dur′a·ble** *adj.*

en·force (en fôrs′) *v.* **1** to force people to pay attention to; make people obey [to *enforce* traffic laws] **2** to bring about by using force or being strict [He is unable to *enforce* his views on others.] —**en·forced′, en·forc′ing** —**en·force′ment** *n.*

en·gage (en gāj′) *v.* **1** to promise to marry [Harry is *engaged* to Grace.] **2** to promise or undertake to do something [She *engaged* to tutor the child after school.] **3** to get the right to use something or the services of someone; hire [to *engage* a hotel room; to *engage* a lawyer] **4** to take part or be active [I have no time to *engage* in dramatics.] —**en·gaged′, en·gag′ing**

en·gi·neer (en′jə nir′) *n.* **1** a person who is trained in some branch of engineering **2** a person who runs an engine, as the driver of a railroad locomotive **3** a soldier whose special work is the building or wrecking of roads, bridges, etc.

en·joy·a·ble (en joi′ə bəl) *adj.* giving joy or pleasure; delightful [What an *enjoyable* concert!]

e·nough (ē nuf′) *adj.* as much or as many as needed or wanted; sufficient [There is *enough* food for all.] ◆*n.* the amount needed or wanted [I have heard *enough* of that music.] ◆*adv.* as much as needed; to the right amount [Is your steak cooked *enough*?]

en·rich (en rich′) *v.* to make richer in value or quality [Music *enriches* one's life.] —**en·riched′, en·rich′ing**

en·ter·prise (en′tər prīz) *n.* **1** any business or undertaking, especially one that takes daring and energy **2** willingness to undertake new or risky projects [They succeeded because of their *enterprise*.]

en·tire (en tīr′) *adj.* **1** including all the parts; whole; complete [I've read the *entire* book.] **2** not broken, not weakened, not lessened, etc. [We have his *entire* support.] —**en·tire′ly** *adv.*

en·vi·ron·ment (en vī′rən mənt) *n.* the things that surround anything; especially, all the conditions that surround a person, animal, or plant and affect growth, actions, character, etc. [Removing pollution from water and air will improve our *environment*.] —**en·vi′ron·men′tal** *adj.*

en·vy (en′vē) *n.* **1** jealousy and dislike felt toward another having some thing, quality, etc. that one would like to have [He glared at the winner with a look of *envy*.] **2** the person or thing one has such feelings about [Their new car is the *envy* of the neighborhood.] —*pl.* **en′vies** ◆*v.* to feel envy toward or because of [to *envy* a person for her wealth] —**en′vied, en′vy·ing**

e·qual (ē′kwəl) *adj.* **1** of the same amount, size, or value [The horses were of *equal* height.] **2** having the same rights, ability, or position [All persons are *equal* in a court of law in a just society.] ◆*v.* **1** to be equal to; match [His long jump *equaled* the school record. Six minus two *equals* four.] **2** to do or make something equal to [You can *equal* my score easily.] —**e′qualed** or **e′qualled, e′qual·ing** or **e′qual·ling** —**e′qual·ly** *adv.*

e·qual·i·ty (ē kôwl′ə tē) *n.* the condition of being equal, especially of having the same political, social, and economic rights and duties

e·quip·ment (ē kwip′mənt) *n.* **1** the special things needed for some purpose; outfit, supplies, etc. [fishing *equipment*] **2** the act of equipping

er·rand (er′ənd) *n.* a short trip to do a thing, often for someone else [I'm going downtown on an *errand* for my sister.]

e·soph·a·gus (e säf′ə gəs) *n.* the tube through which food passes from the throat to the stomach

e·vap·o·rate (e vap′ə rāt) **v. 1** to change into vapor [Heat *evaporates* water. The perfume in the bottle has *evaporated*.] **2** to disappear like vapor; vanish [Our courage *evaporated* when we saw the lion.] **3** to make thicker by heating so as to take some of the water from [to *evaporate* milk] —**e·vap′o·rat·ed, e·vap′o·rat·ing** —**e·vap′o·ra′tion** *n.*

ev·i·dence (ev′ə dəns) *n.* something that shows or proves, or that gives reason for believing; proof or indication [The footprint was *evidence* that someone had been there. Clear skin gives *evidence* of a good diet.] ➛*v.* to show clearly; make plain [His smile *evidenced* his joy.] —**ev′i·denced, ev′i·denc·ing**

ex·act·ly (eg zakt′lē) *adv.* **1** in an exact way; precisely [That's *exactly* the bike I want.] **2** quite true; I agree: *used as an answer to something said by another*

ex·ceed (ek sēd′) *v.* **1** to go beyond what is allowed [to *exceed* the speed limit] **2** to be more or better than [Her success *exceeded* her own wildest dreams.] —**ex·ceed′ed, ex·ceed′ing**

ex·cel·lent (ek′sə lənt) *adj.* better than others of its kind; very good [Their cakes are fairly good, but their pies are *excellent*.] —**ex′cel·lent·ly** *adv.*

ex·change (eks chānj′) *v.* **1** to give in return for something else; trade [She *exchanged* the bicycle for a larger one.] **2** to give each other similar things [The bride and groom *exchanged* rings during the ceremony.] —**ex·changed′, ex·chang′ing** ➛*n.* **1** a giving of one thing in return for another; trade [I'll give you my pen in *exchange* for that book.] **2** a giving to one another of similar things [Our club has a gift *exchange* at Christmas time.]

ex·cite·ment (ek sīt′mənt) *n.* **1** the condition of being excited [The hotel fire caused great *excitement* in the town.] **2** anything that excites

ex·claim (eks klām′) *v.* to speak out suddenly and with strong feeling, as in surprise, anger, etc. ["I won't go!" she *exclaimed*.]

ex·haust (eg zôst′ *or* eg zäst′) *v.* **1** to use up completely [Our drinking water was soon *exhausted*.] **2** to let out the contents of; make completely empty [The leak soon *exhausted* the gas tank.] **3** to use up the strength of; tire out; weaken [They are *exhausted* from playing tennis.] ➛*n.* **1** the used steam or gas that comes from the cylinders of an engine; especially, the fumes from the gasoline engine in an automobile

ex·ist (eg zist′) *v.* **1** to be; have actual being [The unicorn never really *existed*.] **2** to occur or be found [Tigers do not *exist* in Africa.] **3** to live [Fish cannot *exist* long out of water.]

ex·pe·di·tion (ek′ spə dish′ən) *n.* **1** a long journey or voyage by a group of people, as to explore a region or to take part in a battle **2** the people, ships, etc. making such a trip **3** speed or quickness with little effort or waste [We finished our task with *expedition*.] —**ex′pe·di′tion·ar′y** *adj.*

ex·pe·ri·ence (ek spir′ē əns) *n.* **1** the fact of living through a happening or happenings [*Experience* teaches us many things.] **2** something that one has done or lived through [This trip was an *experience* that I'll never forget.] **3** skill that one gets by training, practice, and work [a lawyer with much *experience*] —**ex·pe′ri·enced, ex·pe′ri·enc·ing** *v.*

ex·pert (eks′pərt *or* ek spurt′) *adj.* **1** having much special knowledge and experience; very skillful [an *expert* golfer] **2** of or from an expert [*expert* advice] ➛*n.* (ek′spərt) an expert person; authority [an *expert* in art]

ex·plain (ek splān′) *v.* **1** to make clear or plain; give details of [He *explained* how the engine works.] **2** to give the meaning of [The teacher *explained* the story.] **3** to give reasons for [Can you *explain* your absence?]

ex·port (ek spôrt′) *v.* to send goods from one country for sale in another [Japan *exports* many radios.] ➛*n.* (eks′pôrt) **1** the act of exporting [Brazil raises coffee for *export*.] **2** something exported [Oil is Venezuela's chief *export*.] —**ex·por·ta′tion, ex·port′er**

ex·pres·sion (ek spresh′ən) *n.* **1** an expressing, or putting into words [This note is an *expression* of my gratitude.] **2** a way of speaking, singing, or playing something that gives it real meaning or feeling [to read with *expression*] **3** the act of showing how one feels, what one means, etc. [Laughter is an *expression* of joy.]

ex·tend (ek stend′) *v.* **1** to make longer; stretch out [Careful cleaning *extends* the life of a rug.] **2** to lie or stretch [The fence *extends* along the meadow.] **3** to make larger or more complete; enlarge; increase [to *extend* one's power] **4** to offer or give [May I *extend* congratulations to the winner?] —**ex·tend′ed** *adj.*

ex·tinc·tion (ek stiŋk′shən) *n.* **1** the fact of becoming extinct, or dying out [The California condor faces *extinction*.] **2** a putting an end to or wiping out [the *extinction* of all debts] **3** an extinguishing, or putting out [the *extinction* of a fire]

a	ask, fat
ā	ape, date
ä	car, lot
e	elf, ten
ē	even, meet
i	is, hit
ī	ice, fire
ō	open, go
ô	law, horn
oi	oil, point
σσ	look, pull
ōσ	ooze, tool
ou	out, crowd
u	up, cut
ʉ	fur, fern
ə	a in ago
	e in agent
	e in father
	i in unity
	o in collect
	u in focus
ch	chin, arch
ŋ	ring, singer
sh	she, dash
th	thin, truth
th	then, father
zh	s in pleasure

faint (fānt) *adj.* **1** weak; not strong or clear; dim or feeble [a *faint* whisper; a *faint* odor; *faint* shadows] **2** weak and dizzy, as if about to swoon **3** not very certain; slight [a *faint* hope] ►*n.* a condition in which one becomes unconscious because not enough blood reaches the brain, as in sudden shock ►*v.* to fall into a faint; swoon —**faint′ed** —**faint′ly** *adv.*

false·hood (fôls′hood) *n.* a lie or the telling of lies

fa·mil·iar (fə mil′yər) *adj.* **1** friendly; intimate; well-acquainted [a *familiar* face in the crowd] **2** too friendly; intimate in a bold way [We were annoyed by the *familiar* manner of our new neighbor.] **3** knowing about; acquainted with [Are you *familiar* with this book?] **4** well-known; common; ordinary [Car accidents are a *familiar* sight.] ► *n.* a close friend

fam·i·ly (fam′ə lē) *n.* **1** a group made up of one or two parents and all of their children **2** the children alone [a widow who raised a large *family*] **3** a group of people who are related by marriage or a common ancestor; relatives; clan **4** a large group of related plants or animals [The robin is a member of the thrush *family*.] —*pl.* **fam′i·lies**

fa·mous (fā′məs) *adj.* much talked about as being outstanding; very well known

fan·cy (fan′sē) *adj.* having much design and decoration; not plain; elaborate [a *fancy* dress] —**fan′ci·er, fan′ci·est**

farm (färm) *n.* **1** a piece of land used to raise crops or animals; also, the house, barn, orchards, etc. on such land **2** any place where certain things are raised [An area of water for raising fish is a fish *farm*.]

farm·er (fär′mər) *n.* a person who owns or works on a farm

fash·ion (fash′ən) *n.* **1** the popular or up-to-date way of dressing, speaking, or behaving; style [It was once the *fashion* to wear powdered wigs.] **2** the way in which a thing is done, made, or formed [tea served in the Japanese *fashion*] ►*v.* to make, form, or shape [Bees *fashion* honeycombs out of wax.]

fau·cet (fô′sət *or* fä′sət) *n.* a device with a valve which can be turned on or off to control the flow of a liquid, as from a pipe; tap; cock

feath·er (feth′ər) *n.* **1** any of the parts that grow out of the skin of birds, covering the body and filling out the wings and tail: feathers are soft and light **2** anything like a feather in looks, lightness, etc. **3** the same class or kind [birds of a *feather*] —**feath′er·y** *adj.*

Feb·ru·ar·y (feb′roo er′ ē *or* feb′yoo er′ ē) *n.* the second month of the year: it usually has 28 days but in leap year it has 29 days; abbreviated **Feb.**

fed·er·al (fed′ər əl) *adj.* **1** of or describing a union of states having a central government **2** of such a central government [a *federal* constitution] ☆**3** *usually* **Federal,** of the central government of the U.S. [the *Federal* courts] —**fed′er·al·ist** *adj., n.*

fel·low·ship (fel′ō ship′) *n.* **1** friendship; companionship **2** a group of people having the same activities or interests **3** money given to a student at a university or college to help him or her study for a higher degree

fer·ry (fer′ē) *v.* to take or go across a river or bay in a boat or raft [They *ferried* our cars to the island.] —**fer′ried, fer′ry·ing**

fes·ti·val (fes′tə vəl) *n.* **1** a happy holiday [The Mardi Gras in New Orleans is a colorful *festival*.] **2** a time of special celebration or entertainment [Our town holds a garlic *festival* every spring.]

fierce (firs) *adj.* **1** wild or cruel; violent; raging [a *fierce* dog; a *fierce* wind] **2** very strong or eager [a *fierce* effort] —**fierc′er, fierc′est** —**fierce′ly** *adv.* —**fierce′ness** *n.*

fi·nal (fi′nəl) *adj.* **1** coming at the end; last; concluding [the *final* chapter in a book] **2** allowing no further change; deciding [The decision of the judes is *final*.] ►*n.* **1** anything final **2 finals,** *pl.* the last set in a series of games, tests, etc. —**fi′nal·ly** *adv.*

fi·nance (fi nans′ *or* fī′nans) *n.* **1 finances,** *pl.* all the money or income that a government, company, person, etc. has ready for use **2** the managing of money matters [Bankers are often experts in *finance*.] ►*v.* to give or get money for [loans to *finance* new business] —**fi·nanced′, fi·nanc′ing**

fin·ger·nail (fiŋ′gər nāl) *n.* the hard, tough cover at the top of each finger tip

fin·ger·print (fiŋ′ gər print) *n.* the mark made by pressing the tip of a finger against a flat surface: the fine lines and circles form a pattern that can be used to identify a person ►*v.* to take the fingerprints of someone by pressing the finger tips on an inked surface and then on paper

flaw (flô *or* flä) *n.* **1** a break, scratch, crack, etc. that spoils something; blemish [There is a *flaw* in this diamond.] **2** any fault or error [a *flaw* in one's reasoning] —**flaw′less** *adj.* —**flaw′less·ly** *adv.*

flur·ry (flur′ē) *n.* **1** a sudden, short rush of wind, or a sudden, light fall of rain or snow **2** a sudden, brief excitement or confusion —*pl.* **flur′ries** ►*v.* to confuse or excite [New drivers get *flurried* when they are in heavy traffic.] —**flur′ried, flur′ry·ing**

foam·y (fōm′ē) *adj.* foaming, full of foam, or like foam [the *foamy* water in the rapids] —**foam′i·er, foam′i·est** —**foam′i·ness** *n.*

for·bid (fər bid′) **v.** to order that something not be done; not allow; prohibit [The law *forbids* you to park your car there. Talking out loud is *forbidden* in the library.] —**for·bade**′or **for·bad**′, **for·bid**′**den**, **for·bid**′**ding**

fore·arm (fôr′ärm) **v.** to arm beforehand; get ready for trouble before it comes ☛**n.** The part of the arm between the elbow and the wrist

fore·cast (fôr′kast) **v.** to tell or try to tell how something will turn out; predict [Rain is *forecast* for tomorrow.] —**fore**′**cast** or **fore**′**cast·ed, fore**′**cast·ing** ☛**n.** a telling of what will happen; prediction [a weather *forecast*] —**fore**′**cast· er n.**

for·eign (fôr′in *or* fär′in) **adj.** **1** that is outside one's own country, region, etc. [a *foreign* land] **2** of, from, or dealing with other countries [*foreign* trade; *foreign* languages; *foreign* policy] **3** not belonging; not a natural or usual part [conduct *foreign* to one's nature; *foreign* matter in the eye]

fore·see (fôr sē′) **v.** to see or know beforehand [to *foresee* the future] —**fore·saw**′, **fore· seen**′, **fore·see**′**ing**

fore·sight (fôr′sīt) **n.** the ability to look ahead and plan for the future [Amy had the *foresight* to bring a snack on our hike.]

fore·warn (fôr wôrn′) **v.** to warn ahead of time [We were *forewarned* we wouldn't get tickets later.]

for·feit (fôr′fit) **v.** to give up or lose something because of what one has done or has failed to do [Because our team was late in arriving, we had to *forfeit* the game.] ☛**n.** the thing that is forfeited; penalty

for·giv·a·ble (fər giv′ə bəl) **adj.** deserving to be forgiven; excusable [*forgivable* anger]

for·give (fər giv′) **v.** to give up feeling angry or wanting to punish; show mercy to; excuse or pardon [She *forgave* him for his unkindness to her.] —**for· gave**′, **for·giv**′ **en**, **for·giv**′**ing** —**for· giv·a·ble adj.**

for·ty-six (fôrt′ē siks) **n.** the cardinal number equal to four times ten plus six; 46

for·ward (fôr′wərd) **adj.** **1** at, toward, or of the front **2** ahead of others in ideas, growth, progress, etc.; advanced **3** ready or eager; prompt [She was *forward* in helping.] **4** too bold or free in manners; rude or impudent —**for**′**ward·ness n.**

fos·sil (fäs′əl) **n.** **1** any hardened remains or prints, as in rocks or bogs, of plants or animals that lived many years ago **2** a person who is very set or old-fashioned in his or her ideas or ways ☛**adj.** **1** of or like a fossil **2** taken from the earth [Coal and oil are *fossil* fuels.]

freight (frāt) **n.** **1** a load of goods shipped by train, truck, ship, airplane, etc. **2** the cost of shipping such goods **3** the shipping of goods in this way [Send it by *freight*.]

friend·ly (frend′lē) **adj.** **1** of, like, to, or from a friend; kindly [some *friendly* advice] **2** showing good and peaceful feelings; ready to be a friend [a *friendly* nation] —**friend**′**li·er, friend**′**li·est** ☛**adv.** in a friendly way [to act *friendly*] —**friend**′**li·ness n.**

fright·en (frīt′n) **v.** **1** to make or become suddenly afraid; scare **2** to force to do something by making afraid [He was *frightened* into confessing.] —**fright**′**ened**

frol·ic (fräl′ik) **n.** a lively game or party; merry play ☛**v.** to play or romp about in a happy and carefree way —**frol**′**icked, frol**′**ick·ing**

fu·el (fyo͞o′əl) **n.** **1** anything that is burned to give heat or power [Coal, gas, oil, and wood are *fuels*.] **2** anything that makes a strong feeling even stronger [Their teasing only added *fuel* to her anger.] ☛**v.** **1** to supply with fuel **2** to get fuel —**fu**′**eled** or **fu**′**elled, fu**′**el·ing** or **fu**′**el·ling**

fund (fund) **n.** **1** an amount of money to be used for a particular purpose [a scholarship *fund*] **2 funds**, *pl.* money on hand, ready for use **3** a supply; stock [a *fund* of good will]

fu·ture (fyo͞o′chər) **adj.** **1** in the time to come; after the present time [a *future* date; my *future* happiness] **2** showing time to come ["Shall" and "will" are used with a verb to express *future* tense.] ☛**n.** **1** the time that is to come [We'll buy a new car sometime in the *future*.] **2** what is going to be [We all have some control over the *future*.] **3** chance to succeed [She has a great *future* as a lawyer.] —**fu**′**tur·is′tic adj.**

Gg

gadg·et (gaj′ ət) **n.** **1** a small, mechanical thing having some special use [a *gadget* for opening cans] **2** any interesting but not very useful device

gain (gān) **n.** **1** a thing or amount added; increase or addition [a *gain* in weight] **2** *often* **gains**, *pl.* profit or winnings [the *gains* from our business] **3** the act of getting something, especially money [A love of *gain* can make a person greedy.] ☛**v.** **1** to get as an increase or advantage [He *gained* ten pounds in two months.] **2** to become better; improve [She *gained* in health.] —**gained, gaining**

gall·blad·der (gôl′blad ər) **n.** a small sac attached to the liver; the gall, or bile, is stored in it

ga·rage (gər äzh′*or* gər äj′) **n.** **1** a closed place where automobiles are sheltered **2** a place where automobiles are repaired

a	ask, fat
ā	ape, date
ä	car, lot
e	elf, ten
ē	even, meet
i	is, hit
ī	ice, fire
ō	open, go
ô	law, horn
oi	oil, point
o͞o	look, pull
o͞o	ooze, tool
ou	out, crowd
u	up, cut
ʉ	fur, fern
ə	a in ago
	e in agent
	e in father
	i in unity
	o in collect
	u in focus
ch	chin, arch
ŋ	ring, singer
sh	she, dash
th	thin, truth
th	then, father
zh	s in pleasure

gen·er·al (jen′ər əl) *adj.* **1** of, for or from the whole or all, not just a part or some [to promote the *general* welfare] **2** widespread or common [The *general* opinion of him is unfavorable.] **3** having to do with the main parts but not with details [the *general* features of a plan] **4** not special or specialized [*general* science; a *general* store] **5** highest in rank; most important [the attorney *general*]

gen·er·a·tion (jen′ ər ā′shən) *n.* **1** a single stage in the history of a family [Grandmother, mother, and son are three *generations*.] **2** all the people born at about the same time [Most of his *generation* of men spent time in the army.] **3** the average time between the birth of one generation and the birth of the next, about 30 years

gen·er·ous (jen′ər əs) *adj.* **1** willing to give or share; not selfish or stingy; openhanded **2** large; great in amount [*generous* helpings of dessert] **3** not mean; noble and forgiving [To forgive your enemy is a *generous* act.] —**gen′er·ous·ly** *adv.* —**gen′er·ous·ness** *n.*

ge·og·ra·phy (jē ôg′rə fē *or* jē ä′grə fē) *n.* **1** the study of the surface of the earth and how it is divided into continents, countries, seas, etc.: geography also deals with the climates, plants, animals, minerals, etc. of the earth **2** the natural features of a certain part of the earth [the *geography* of Ohio] —**ge·og′ra·pher**

ge·ol·o·gy (jē ä′lə jē) *n.* the study of the earth's crust and of the way in which its layers were formed: it includes the study of rocks and fossils —**ge·ol′o·gist**

ge·om·e·try (jē äm′ə trē) *n.* the branch of mathematics that deals with lines, angles, surfaces, and solids, and with their measurement

Geor·gia (jôr′jə) **1** a state in the southeastern part of the U.S.: abbreviated **Ga., GA 2** a republic southwest of Russia —**Geor′gian** *adj., n.*

ges·ture (jes′ cher) *n.* **1** a motion made with some part of the body, especially the hands or arms, to show some idea or feeling **2** anything said or done to show one's feelings; sometimes, something done just for effect, and not really meant [Our neighbor's gift was a *gesture* of friendship.] ◆*v.* to make a gesture or gestures —**ges′tured, ges′tur·ing**

gi·gan·tic (jī gan′tik) *adj.* like a giant in size; very big; huge; enormous [a gigantic building]

gnaw (nô *or* nä) *v.* **1** to bite and wear away bit by bit with the teeth [The rat *gnawed* the rope in two. The dog *gnawed* on the bone.] **2** to make by gnawing [to *gnaw* a hole] **3** to keep on troubling for a long time [Jealousy *gnawed* at her heart.] —**gnawed, gnaw′ing, gnaws**

goose (go͞os) *n.* a swimming bird that is like a duck but has a larger body and a longer neck; especially, the female of this bird: the male is called a *gander* —*pl.* **geese**

gorge (gôrj) *n.* a narrow pass or valley between steep cliffs or walls ◆*v.* to stuff with food in a greedy way [to *gorge* oneself with cake] —**gorged, gorg′ing**

☆**go·ril·la** (gə ril′ə) *n.* **1** the largest and strongest of the apes, found in African jungles

gov·er·nor (guv′ər nər) *n.* ☆**1** the person elected to be head of a state of the United States **2** a person appointed to govern a province, territory, etc. **3** any of the people who direct some organization [the board of *governors* of a hospital] **4** a device in an engine, etc. that automatically controls its speed —**gov′er·nor·ship′**

grad·u·ate (gra′jo͞o ət) *n.* a person who has finished a course of study at a school or college and has been given a diploma or degree —**grad′u·a′tion** *n.* ◆*adj.* **1** that is a graduate [*Graduate* students work for degrees above the bachelor's.] ☆**2** of or for graduates [*graduate* courses] ◆*v.* (gra′jo͞o āt′) **1** to make or become a graduate of a school or college **2** to mark off with small lines for measuring [A thermometer is a tube *graduated* in degrees.] —**grad′u·at·ed, grad′u·at·ing**

grand·par·ent (grand′per ənt) *n.* a grandfather or grandmother

gran·ite (gran′it) *n.* a very hard rock used for buildings and monuments

grape·fruit (grāp′fro͞ot) *n.* a large, round citrus fruit with a yellow rind and a juicy, somewhat sour pulp

grate·ful (grāt′fəl) *adj.* **1** feeling thankful or showing thanks; appreciative **2** pleasing or welcome [a *grateful* blessing] —**grate′ful·ly** *adv.* —**grate′ful·ness** *n.*

great (grāt) *adj.* **1** much above the average in size, degree, power, etc.; big or very big; much or very much [the *Great* Lakes; a *great* distance; *great* pain] **2** very much of a [a *great* reader] **3** very important; noted; remarkable [a *great* composer; a great discovery] **4** older or younger by a generation: *used in words formed with a hyphen* [my *great*-aunt; my *great*-niece] —**great′er, great′est** —**great′ly** *adv.* —**great′ness** *n.*

greed·y (grēd′ē) *adj.* wanting or taking all that one can get with no thought of what others need [The *greedy* girl ate all the cookies.] —**greed′i·er, greed′i·est** —**greed′i·ly** *adv.* —**greed′i·ness** *n.*

green (grēn) *adj.* having the color of grass [*green* peas]

grief (grēf) *n.* **1** deep and painful sorrow, as that caused by someone's death **2** something that causes such sorrow

grieve (grēv) *v.* to feel grief; be sad [She is *grieving* over a lost cat.] —**grieved, griev′ing**

gro·cer·y (grō′sər ē) *n.* ☆**1** a store selling food and household supplies **2 groceries,** *pl.* the goods sold by a grocer

guest (gest) *n.* **1** a person who is visiting another's home, or who is being treated to a meal, etc. by another **2** any paying customer of a hotel or restaurant **3** any person invited to appear on a program

guilt·y (gil′tē) *adj.* **1** having done something wrong; being to blame for something [She is often *guilty* of telling lies.] **2** judged in court to be a wrongdoer [The jury found him *guilty* of robbery.] —**guilt′i·er, guilt′i·est** —**guilt′i·ly** *adv.* —**guilt′i·ness** *n.*

gust (gust) *n.* **1** a strong and sudden rush of air or of something carried by the air [a *gust* of wind; *gusts* of smoke] **2** a sudden outburst of laughter, rage, etc. ◆*v.* to blow in gusts —**gust′y** *adj.*

hab·i·tat (hab′i tat′) *n.* the place where an animal or plant is normally found [Woodland streams are the *habitat* of beavers.]

hair·cut (her′kut) *n.* the act or a style of cutting the hair of the head

half (haf) *n.* **1** either of the two equal parts of something [Five is *half* of ten.] **2** a half hour [It is *half* past two.] **3** either of the two parts of an inning in baseball, or of the two main time periods of a game of football, basketball, etc. —*pl.* **halves**

☆**hall·way** (hôl′wā) *n.* a passageway, as between rooms; corridor

ham·burg·er (ham′bʉrg ər) *n.* **1** ground beef **2** a small patty of ground beef, fried or broiled

ham·mock (ham′ək) *n.* a long piece of netting or canvas that is hung with ropes at each end and is used as a bed or couch

harsh (härsh) *adj.* **1** not pleasing to the senses [*harsh* music] **2** cruel or severe [*harsh* punishment] —**harsh′er, harsh′est**

har·vest (här′vəst) *n.* **1** the act of gathering a crop of grain, fruit, etc. when it becomes ripe **2** the time of the year when a crop is gathered **3** all the grain, fruit, etc. gathered in one season; crop [a large *harvest*] **4** the results of doing something [She reaped a *harvest* of love for all her good works.]

hast·y (hās′tē) *adj.* **1** done or made with haste; hurried [a *hasty* lunch] **2** done or made too quickly, without enough thought; rash [a *hasty* decision] —**hast′i·er, hast′i·est** —**hast′i·ly** *adv.* —**hast′i·ness** *n.*

haul (hôl) *v.* **1** to move by pulling; drag or tug [We *hauled* the boat up on the beach.] **2** to carry by wagon, truck, etc. [He *hauls* steel for a large company.] **3** to change the course of a ship by setting the sails —**hauled**

hawk (hôk *or* häk) *n.* a large bird with a strong, hooked beak and claws, and keen sight: it captures and eats smaller birds and animals ◆*v.* to hunt small game with the help of trained hawks

heal (hēl) *v.* to make or become well, sound, or healthy; cure or be cured [The wound *healed* slowly.] —**healed, heal′ing**

health·y (hel′thē) *adj.* **1** having good health; well [a *healthy* child] **2** showing good health [a *healthy* appetite] **3** good for one's health; healthful [a *healthy* climate] —**health′i·er, health′i·est** —**health′i·ness** *n.*

heav·y (hev′ē) *adj.* **1** hard to lift or move because of its weight; weighing very much [a *heavy* load] **2** weighing more than is usual for its kind [Lead is a *heavy* metal.] **3** larger, deeper, greater, etc. than usual [a *heavy* vote; a *heavy* sleep; a *heavy* blow] **4** full of sorrow; sad [a *heavy* heart] **5** hard to do, bear, etc.; difficult [*heavy* work; *heavy* sorrow] —**heav′i·er, heav′i·est** —**heav′i·ly** *adv.* —**heav′i·ness** *n.*

He·brew (hē′bro͞o) *n.* **1** a member of the ancient people of the Bible who settled in Canaan; Israelite: the Hebrews were the ancestors of the Jews **2** the ancient language of the Israelites or the modern form of this language, used in Israel today: it is written in a different alphabet from English ◆*adj.* of the Hebrews or of the Hebrew language

hel·met (hel′mət) *n.* a hard covering to protect the head, worn by soldiers, certain athletes, motorcycle riders, etc.

hem·i·sphere (hem′i sfir′) *n.* **1** half of a sphere or globe [The dome of the church was in the shape of a *hemisphere*.] **2** any of the halves into which the earth's surface is divided in geography

his·to·ry (his′tər ē) *n.* **1** what has happened in the life of a people, country, science, art, etc.; also, an account of this [the *history* of medicine; a *history* of England] **2** the record of everything that has happened in the past [Nero was one of the worst tyrants in *history*.] **3** the science or study that keeps a record of past events [How will *history* treat our times?] **4** a story or tale [This hat has a strange *history*.] —*pl.* **his′to·ries**

hoax (hōks) *n.* something that is meant to trick or fool others, especially a practical joke ◆*v.* to play a trick on; fool —**hoax′er** *n.*

hope (hōp) *n.* **1** a feeling that what one wants will happen [We gave up *hope* of being rescued.] **2** the thing that one wants [It is my *hope* to go to college.] **3** a person or thing on which one may base some hope [The 1500-meter run is our last *hope* for a victory.] ◆*v.* **1** to have hope; want and expect [I *hope* to see you soon.] **2** to want to believe [I *hope* I didn't overlook anybody.] —**hoped, hop′ing**

a	ask, fat
ā	ape, date
ä	car, lot
e	elf, ten
ē	even, meet
i	is, hit
ī	ice, fire
ō	open, go
ô	law, horn
oi	oil, point
o͝o	look, pull
o͞o	ooze, tool
ou	out, crowd
u	up, cut
ʉ	fur, fern
ə	a in ago
	e in agent
	e in father
	i in unity
	o in collect
	u in focus
ch	chin, arch
ŋ	ring, singer
sh	she, dash
th	thin, truth
th	then, father
zh	s in pleasure

hor·ri·ble (hôr′ə bəl) *adj.* **1** causing a feeling of horror; terrible; dreadful [a *horrible* accident] **2** very bad, ugly, unpleasant, etc.: *used only in everyday talk* [What a *horrible* color!] —**hor′ri·bly** *adv.*

hu·man·i·ty (hyoo man′ə tē) *n.* **1** all human beings; the human race [Could *humanity* survive an atomic war?] **2** kindness or sympathy [She showed her *humanity* by caring for the sick.] **3** the special qualities of all human beings; human nature [It is our common *humanity* to be selfish at one time and unselfish at another.] —*pl.* **hu·man′i·ties** —**the humanities,** studies that deal with human relations and human thought, as literature, philosophy, the fine arts, etc., but not the sciences

hu·mid·i·ty (hyoo mid′ə tē) *n.* dampness; especially, the amount of moisture in the air

hu·mor·ous (hyoo′mər əs) *adj.* funny or amusing; comical —**hu′mor·ous·ly** *adv.*

Hun·ga·ry (huŋ′gər ē) a country in central Europe —**Hun·gar′i·an** (huŋ ger′ē ən) *adj., n.*

hun·gry (huŋ′grē) *adj.* **1** wanting or needing food [Cold weather makes me *hungry*.] **2** having a strong desire; eager [*hungry* for praise] —**hun′gri·er, hun′gri·est** —**hun′gri·ly** *adv.* —**hun′gri·ness** *n.*

hy·phen (hī′fən) *n.* the mark (-) used between the parts of a compound word (as *court-martial*), or between the parts of a word divided at the end of a line ◆ *v.* to hyphenate

ice·berg (īs′bʉrg) *n.* a mass of ice broken off from a glacier and floating in the sea: the larger part of an iceberg is under water

i·ci·cle (ī′sik əl) *n.* a hanging stick of ice formed by water freezing as it drips down

i·den·ti·fi·ca·tion (ī den′tə fi kā′shən) *n.* **1** anything that identifies a person or thing [Fingerprints are used as *identification*.] **2** an identifying or being identified

ig·loo (ig′loo) *n.* a hut built by Eskimos using blocks of packed snow —*pl.* **ig′loos**

il·lus·trate (il′ə strāt *or* i lus′trāt) *v.* **1** to make clear or explain by giving examples, making comparisons, etc. [Census figures *illustrate* how the city has grown.] **2** to put drawings or pictures in that explain or decorate [an *illustrated* book] —**il′lus·trat·ed, il′lus·trat·ing**

i·mag·i·na·tion (i maj′ i nā′shən) *n.* **1** the act or power of making up pictures or ideas in the mind of what is not present or of how things might be [The flying saucer you thought you saw is just in your *imagination*. It takes great *imagination* to write a play.] **2** the ability to understand and appreciate what others imagine, especially in art and literature [She hasn't enough *imagination* to know what that short story is about.]

im·i·ta·tion (im′ i tā′shən) *n.* **1** the act of imitating or copying [The children danced in *imitation* of swaying trees.] **2** a copy or likeness [These jewels are clever *imitations* of precious gems.] ◆ *adj.* made to look like something better; not real [a belt of *imitation* leather]

im·mense (im mens′) *adj.* very large; huge; vast [an *immense* territory] —**im·mense′ly** *adv.*

im·merse (im mʉrs′) *v.* **1** to plunge or dip into a liquid **2** to baptize a person by dipping under water **3** to get or be deeply in; absorb [*immersed* in study; *immersed* in sadness] —**im·mersed′, im·mers′ing** —**im·mer·sion** (im mʉr′shən) *n.*

im·mo·bile (im mō′bəl) *adj.* not moving or changing; without motion [The frightened deer stood *immobile*.] —**im′mo·bil′i·ty** *n.*

im·po·lite (im pə līt′) *adj.* not polite; rude —**im·po·lite′ly** *adv.* —**im·po·lite′ness** *n.*

im·por·tance (im pôrt′ns) *n.* the fact of being important [news of little *importance*]

im·por·tant (im pôrt′nt) *adj.* **1** having much meaning or value [Our wedding anniversary is an *important* date in our lives.] **2** having power of authority, or acting as if one had power [an *important* official] —**im·por′tant·ly** *adv.*

im·pose (im pōz′) *v.* to put on as a duty, burden, or penalty [to *impose* a tax on furs] —**im·posed′, im·pos′ing**

im·pos·si·ble (im päs′ə bəl) *adj.* **1** that cannot be, be done, or happen; not possible [He found it *impossible* to lift the crate.] **2** very unpleasant or hard to put up with [You're always asking *impossible* questions!] —**im·pos·si·bil′i·ty** *n.* —**im·pos′si·bly** *adv.*

im·pres·sion (im presh′ən) *n.* **1** the act of impressing **2** a mark or imprint made by pressing [The police took an *impression* of his fingerprints.] **3** an effect produced on the mind [The play made a great *impression* on us.] **4** the effect produced by some action [Cleaning made no *impression* on the stain.] **5** a vague feeling [I have the *impression* that someone was here.]

im·prop·er (im präp′ər) *adj.* **1** not proper or suitable, unfit [Sandals are *improper* shoes for tennis.] **2** not true; wrong; incorrect [an *improper* street address] **3** not decent; in bad taste [*improper* jokes] —**im·prop′er·ly** *adv.*

im·prove (im proov′) **v. 1** to make or become better [Business has *improved*.] **2** to make good use of [She *improved* her spare time by reading.] —**im·proved′, im·prov′ing**

im·pure (im pyoor′) **adj. 1** not clean; dirty [Smoke made the air *impure*.] **2** mixed with things that do not belong [*impure* gold] **3** not decent or proper [*impure* thoughts]

in·clude (in klood′) **v.** to have or take in as part of a whole; contain [Prices *include* taxes.] —**in·clud′ed, in·clud′ing**

in·come (in′kum) **n.** the money that one gets as wages, salary, rent, interest, profit, etc.

in·com·plete (in kəm plēt′) **adj.** not complete; without all its parts; not whole or finished —**in·com·plete′ly adv.**

in·crease (in krēs′) **v.** to make or become greater, larger, etc.; add to or grow [When she *increased* her wealth, her power *increased*.] —**in·creased′, in·creas′ing** ◆**n.** (in′krēs) **1** an increasing; addition; growth [an *increase* in population] **2** the amount by which something increases [a population *increase* of 10 percent]

in·de·pend·ence (in′ dē pen′dəns) **n.** the state of being independent; freedom from the control of another or others

in·ex·pen·sive (in′ ek spen′siv) **adj.** not expensive; low-priced —**in′ex·pen′sive·ly adv.**

in·fant (in′fənt) **n.** a very young child; baby ◆**adj. 1** of or for infants [a book on *infant* care] **2** in a very early stage [an *infant* nation]

☆**in·field** (in′fēld) **n. 1** the part of a baseball field enclosed by the four base lines **2** all the infielders

in·for·ma·tion (in′ fər mā′shən) **n. 1** an informing or being informed [This is for your *information* only.] **2** something told or facts learned; news or knowledge; data [An encyclopedia gives *information* about many things.] **3** a person or service that answers certain questions [Ask *information* for the location of the shoe department.]

in·hale (in hāl′) **v.** to breathe in; draw into the lungs, as air or tobacco smoke —**in·haled′, in·hal′ing** —**in·ha·la·tion** (in′ hə lā′shən), **in·hal′er n.**

in·ju·ry (in′jər ē) **n.** harm or damage done to a person or thing [*injuries* received in a fall; *injury* to one's good name] —*pl.* **in′ju·ries**

in·quire (in kwīr′) **v.** to ask a question; ask about in order to learn [The students *inquired* about their grades. We *inquired* the way home.] —**in·quired′, in·quir′ing** —**in·quir′er n.**

in·se·cure (in′ si kyoor′) **adj. 1** not secure or safe; dangerous; not dependable [an *insecure* mountain ledge; an *insecure* partnership] **2** not feeling safe or confident [A person can feel *insecure* in a new job.] —**in′ se·cure′ly adv.** —**in·se·cu·ri·ty** (in′si kyoor′ ə tē) **n.**

in·spec·tor (in spek′ tər) **n. 1** a person who inspects, as in a factory **2** a police officer who ranks next below a superintendent

in·spire (in spīr′) **v. 1** to cause, urge, or influence to do something [The sunset *inspired* her to write a poem.] **2** to cause to have a certain feeling or thought [Praise *inspires* us with confidence.] **3** to arouse or bring about [Your kindness *inspired* his love.] **4** to do or make as if guided by some higher power [That was an *inspired* speech.] —**in·spired′, in·spir′ing**

in·stant (in′stənt) **n. 1** a very short time; moment [Wait just an *instant*.] **2** a particular moment [At that *instant* I fell.] ◆**adj. 1** with no delay; immediate [an *instant* response] **2** that can be prepared quickly; as by adding water [*instant* coffee]

in·sti·tu·tion (in′ stə too′shən *or* in′ stə tyoo′shən) **n. 1** an instituting or being instituted **2** an established law, custom, practice, etc. [the *institution* of marriage] **3** a school, church, prison, or other organization with a special purpose —**in′sti·tu′tion·al adj.**

in·ter·pret·er (in tur′prə tər) **n.** a person who interprets, especially one whose work is translating things said in one language into another language

in·ter·view (in′tər vyoo) **n. 1** a meeting of one person with another to talk about something [an *interview* with an employer about a job] ☆**2** a meeting in which a person is asked about his or her opinions, activities, etc., as by a reporter —**in′ter·view·er**

in·tes·tine (in tes′tin) **n.** *usually* **intestines,** *pl.* the tube through which food passes from the stomach: the long, narrow part with many coils is called the **small intestine,** and the shorter and thicker part is called the **large intestine** [Food is digested in the *intestines* as well as in the stomach.]

in·tro·duce (in trə doos′ *or* in trə dyoos′) **v. 1** to make known; make acquainted; present [Please *introduce* me to them.] **2** to bring into use; make popular or common [Science has *introduced* many new words.] **3** to make familiar with something [They *introduced* me to the music of Bach.] **4** to bring to the attention of others in a formal way [to *introduce* a bill into Congress] —**in·tro·duced′, in·tro·duc′ing**

in·ven·to·ry (in′vən tôr′ ē) **n. 1** a complete list of goods or property [The store makes an *inventory* of its stock every year.] **2** the stock of goods on hand [Because of fewer sales this year, dealers have large *inventories*.] —*pl.* **in′ ven·to′ries** ◆**v.** to make an inventory or list of [to *inventory* our books] —**in′ven·to·ried, in′ven·to′ry·ing**

in·ves·ti·gate (in ves′tə gāt′) **v.** to search into so as to learn the facts, examine in detail [to *investigate* an accident] —**in·ves′ti·gat′ed, in·ves′ti·gat′ing** —**in·ves′ti·ga′tion, in·ves′ti·ga′tor n.**

a	ask, fat
ā	ape, date
ä	car, lot
e	elf, ten
ē	even, meet
i	is, hit
ī	ice, fire
ō	open, go
ô	law, horn
oi	oil, point
oo	look, pull
oo	ooze, tool
ou	out, crowd
u	up, cut
ʉ	fur, fern
ə	a in ago
	e in agent
	e in father
	i in unity
	o in collect
	u in focus
ch	chin, arch
ŋ	ring, singer
sh	she, dash
th	thin, truth
th	then, father
zh	s in pleasure

in·vis·i·ble (in viz′ə bəl) *adj.* not able to be seen [The moon was *invisible* behind the clouds.] —**in·vis′i·bly** *adv.*

i·ron (ī′ərn) *n.* **1** a strong metal that is a chemical element: it can be molded or stretched into various shapes after being heated, and is much used in the form of steel **2** a device made of iron or other metal and having a flat, smooth bottom: it is heated and used for pressing clothes, etc. **3 irons,** *pl.* iron shackles or chains

is·land (ī′lənd) *n.* **1** a piece of land smaller than a continent and surrounded by water **2** any place set apart from what surrounds it [The oasis was an *island* of green in the desert.]

I·tal·ian (i tal′yən) *adj.* of Italy, its people, etc. ◆*n.* **1** a person born or living in Italy **2** the language of Italy

jack·et (jak′ət) *n.* **1** a short coat **2** an outer covering, as the skin of a potato, or the paper wrapper for a book ☆**3** a cardboard holder for a phonograph record

Ja·pan (jə pan′) a country east of Korea, made up of many islands

Jap·a·nese (jap ə nēz′) *n.* **1** a member of a people whose native country is Japan —*pl.* **Jap·a·nese′ 2** the language of Japan ◆*adj.* of Japan, its people, language, or culture

Jef·fer·son (jef′er sən), **Thomas** (täm′əs) 1743–1826; the third president of the United States, from 1801–1809

jel·ly·fish (jel′ē fish′) *n.* a sea animal with a body that feels like jelly

jin·gle (jiŋ′ gəl) *v.* **1** to make ringing, tinkling sounds, as bits of metal striking together [The pennies *jingled* in my pocket.] **2** to make jingle [She *jingled* her keys.] **3** to have simple rhymes and a regular rhythm, as some poetry and music —**jin′ gled, jin′gling** *n.* a ringing, tinkling sound

join (join) *v.* **1** to bring together; connect; fasten [We *joined* hands and stood in a circle.] **2** to come together; meet [Where do the Ohio and Mississippi rivers *join*?] **3** to become a part or a member of [Paula has *joined* our club.] **4** to go along with; accompany [*Join* us in a walk.] **5** to take part along with others [*Join* in the game.] —**joined**

joint (joint) *n.* **1** a place where two things or parts are joined [Water leaked from the *joint* in the pipe.] **2** a place or part where two bones are joined, usually so that they can move [the elbow *joint*] **3** a large cut of meat with the bone still in it ◆*v.* **1** to connect by a joint or joints [Bamboo is *jointed*.] **2** to cut at the joints [The butcher *jointed* the chicken.]

jour·ney (jur′nē) *n.* a traveling from one place to another; trip —*pl.* **jour′ neys** ◆*v.* to go on a trip; travel —**jour′neyed, jour′ ney·ing**

jun·gle (juŋ′gəl) *n.* land thickly covered with trees, vines, etc., as in the tropics: jungles are usually filled with animals that prey on one another

ju·ry (joor′ē *or* jur′ē) *n.* **1** a group of people chosen to listen to the evidence in a law trial, and then to reach a decision, or verdict **2** a group of people chosen to decide the winners in a contest —*pl.* **ju′ries**

jus·tice (jus′tis) *n.* **1** the condition of being just or fair [There is *justice* in their demand.] **2** reward or punishment as deserved [The prisoner asked only for *justice*.] **3** the upholding of what is just or lawful [a court of *justice*] **4** a judge [a *justice* of the Supreme Court]

Kan·sas (kan′zəs) a state in the central part of the U.S.: abbreviated **Kans., KS** —**Kan′ san** *adj., n.*

kar·at (ker′ət) *n.* one 24th part of pure gold [14 *karat* gold is 14 parts pure gold and 10 parts other metal.]

keep·ing (kēp′iŋ) *n.* **1** care or protection [He left his money in her *keeping*.] **2** the observing of a rule, holiday, etc.

kid·ney (kid′nē) *n.* **1** either of a pair of organs in the central part of the body that take water and waste products out of the blood and pass them through the bladder as urine **2** the kidney of an animal, used as food —*pl.* **kid′neys**

kind·ness (kīnd′nəs) *n.* the condition or habit of being kind

knead (nēd) *v.* **1** to keep pressing and squeezing dough, clay, etc. to make it ready for use **2** to rub or press with the hands; massage [to *knead* a muscle]

knee·cap (nē′kap) *n.* the flat, movable bone that forms the front of a person's knee

kneel (nēl) *v.* to rest on a knee or knees [Some people *kneel* when they pray.] —**knelt** or **kneeled, kneel′ ing**

knob (näb) *n.* a handle that is more or less round on a door or drawer

knock (näk) *v.* **1** to hit as with the fist; especially, to rap on a door [Who is *knocking*?] **2** to hit and cause to fall [The dog *knocked* down the papergirl.] **3** to make by hitting [to *knock* a hole in the wall] **4** to make a pounding or tapping noise [An engine *knocks* when the combustion is faulty.] —**knocked**

knot (nät) *n.* **1** a lump, as in a string or ribbon, formed by a loop or a tangle drawn tight **2** a fastening made by tying together parts or pieces of string, rope, etc. [Sailors make a variety of *knots.*] **3** a small group [a *knot* of people] **4** something that joins closely, as the bond of marriage **5** a unit of speed of one nautical mile (1,852 meters, or 6,076.12 feet) an hour [The ship averaged 20 *knots.*] —**knot´ted, knot´ting** *v.*

knot·hole (nät´hōl) *n.* a hole in a board or tree trunk where a knot has fallen out

know (nō) *v.* **1** to be sure of or have the facts about [Do you *know* why grass is green? She *knows* the law.] **2** to be aware of; realize [He suddenly *knew* he would be late.] **3** to have in one's mind or memory [The actress *knows* her lines.] **4** to be acquainted with [I *know* your brother well.] **5** to recognize [I'd *know* that face anywhere.] **6** to be able to tell the difference in [It's not always easy to *know* right from wrong.] —**knew, known, know´ing**

knowl·edge (nä´lij) *n.* **1** the fact or condition of knowing [*Knowledge* of the crime spread through the town.] **2** what is known or learned through study, experience, etc. [a great *knowledge* of history]

known (nōn) *past participle of* **know**

knuck·le (nuk´əl) *n.* **1** a joint of the finger; especially, a joint connecting a finger to the rest of the hand **2** the knee or hock joint of a pig, calf, etc., used as food —**knuck´led, knuck´ling** *v.*

la·bor (lā´bər) *n.* **1** work; toil **2** a piece of work; task [We rested from our *labors.*] **3** workers as a group [an agreement between *labor* and management on wages] **4** the act of giving birth to a child

lab·o·ra·to·ry (lab´rə tôr´ē) *n.* a room or building where scientific work or tests are carried on, or where chemicals, drugs, etc. are prepared —*pl.* **lab´o·ra·to´ries**

la·dies (lā´dēs) *n.* a polite form of address for women in a group ["*Ladies* and gentlemen," the speaker began.]

laugh (laf) *v.* **1** to make a series of quick sounds with the voice that show one is amused or happy or, sometimes, that show scorn: one usually smiles or grins when laughing **2** to bring about, get rid of, etc. by means of laughter [*Laugh* your fears away.] ◆*n.* the act or sound of laughing

laugh·ter (laf´tər) *n.* the act or sound of laughing [He shook with *laughter.*]

law·yer (lô´yər *or* lä´yər) *n.* a person whose profession is giving advice on law or acting for others in lawsuits

lead·er (lēd´ər) *n.* a person or thing that leads, or guides —**lead´er·ship**

leath·er (le*th*´ər) *n.* a material made from the skin of cows, horses, goats, etc. by cleaning and tanning it ◆*adj.* made of leather

leg·i·ble (lej´ə bəl) *adj.* clear enough to be read easily [*legible* handwriting]

lei·sure (lē´zhər *or* lezh´ər) *n.* free time not taken up with work or duty, that a person may use for rest or recreation ◆*adj.* free and not busy; spare [*leisure* time]

lep·re·chaun (lep´rə kôn *or* lep´rə kän) *n.* an elf in Irish folklore who can show a buried crock of gold to anyone who catches him

lev·y (lev´ē) *v.* **1** to order the payment of [to *levy* a tax] **2** to wage; carry on [to *levy* war] —**lev´ied, lev´y·ing**

li·brar·y (lī´brer´ē) *n.* **1** a place where a collection of books is kept for reading or borrowing **2** a collection of books —*pl.* **li´brar´ies**

li·cense (lī´səns) *n.* **1** a paper, card, etc. showing that one is permitted by law to do something [a marriage *license;* driver's *license*] **2** freedom to ignore the usual rules [To take poetic *license* is to ignore, as in a poem, the usual rules of style, logic, etc. in order to gain a special effect.] **3** freedom of action or speech that goes beyond what is right or proper [Booing in a courtroom isn't free speech—it's *license.*] ◆*v.* to give a license to; permit by law [Are they *licensed* to fish?] —**li´censed, li´cens·ing**

like·li·hood (līk´lē hood´) *n.* the fact of being likely to happen; probability [There is a strong *likelihood* he will win.]

Lin·coln (liŋ´kən), **Abraham** (ā´brə ham) 1809–1865; 16th president of the United States, from 1861–1865: he was assassinated

lit·er·a·ture (lit´ər ə chər) *n.* **1** all the writings of a certain time, country, etc.; especially, those that have lasting value because of their beauty, imagination, etc., as fine novels, plays, and poems **2** the work or profession of writing such things; also, the study of such writings **3** all the writings on some subject [medical *literature*]

liv·er (liv´ər) *n.* **1** a large organ of the body, near the stomach: it makes bile and helps break down food into substances that the body can absorb **2** the liver of some animals, used as food

loaf (lōf) *n.* a portion of bread baked in one piece, usually oblong in shape —*pl.* **loaves**

loud (loud) *adj.* **1** strong in sound; not soft or quiet [a *loud* noise; a *loud* bell] **2** noisy [a *loud* party] **3** so strong as to force attention; forceful [*loud* demands] ◆*adv.* in a loud way —**loud´er, loud´est** —**loud´ly** *adv.* —**loud´ness** *n.*

a	ask, fat
ā	ape, date
ä	car, lot
e	elf, ten
ē	even, meet
i	is, hit
ī	ice, fire
ō	open, go
ô	law, horn
oi	oil, point
oo	look, pull
oo	ooze, tool
ou	out, crowd
u	up, cut
u	fur, fern
ə	a in ago
	e in agent
	e in father
	i in unity
	o in collect
	u in focus
ch	chin, arch
ŋ	ring, singer
sh	she, dash
th	thin, truth
th	then, father
zh	s in pleasure

loy·al (loi′əl) *adj.* **1** faithful to one's country [a *loyal* citizen] **2** faithful to one's family, duty, beliefs, etc. [a *loyal* friend; a *loyal* member] —**loy′al·ly** *adv.*

loy·al·ty (loi′əl tē) *n.* the condition of being loyal; faithfulness —*pl.* **loy′al·ties**

lyr·ic (lir′ik) *adj.* **1** of or having to do with poetry that describes the poet's feelings and thoughts [Sonnets and odes are *lyric* poems.] **2** like a song or suitable for singing **3** of or having a high voice that moves lightly and easily from note to note [a *lyric* soprano] ►*n.* **1** a lyric poem **2** *usually* **lyrics**, *pl.* the words of a song

mag·a·zine (mag ə zēn′ *or* mag′ ə zēn) *n.* **1** a publication that comes out regularly, as weekly or monthly, and contains articles, stories, pictures, etc. **2** a place for storing things, as military supplies **3** a space, as in a warship, for storing explosives

mag·ni·fy (mag′nə fī) *v.* to make look or seem larger or greater than is really so [This lens *magnifies* an object to ten times its size. He *magnified* the seriousness of his illness.] —**mag′ni·fied, mag′ni·fy·ing**

ma·jor (mā′ jər) *adj.* **1** greater in size, importance, amount, etc. [the *major* part of his wealth; a *major* poet] **2** in music, that is separated from the next tone by a full step instead of a half step [a *major* interval] ►*n.* **1** a military officer ranking just above a captain ☆**2** the main subject that a student is studying [History is my *major*.]

mam·mal (mam′əl) *n.* any animal with glands in the female that produce milk for feeding its young —**mam·ma·li·an** (me mā′ lē ən) *adj., n.*

mam·moth (mam′əth) *n.* a large, extinct elephant with hairy skin and long tusks that curved upward ►*adj.* very big; huge [a *mammoth* arena]

man·ag·er (man′ij ər) *n.* a person who manages a business

man·ner (man′ər) *n.* **1** a way in which something happens or is done; style [the *manner* in which an artist sketches a scene] **2** a way of acting; behavior [an angry *manner*] **3** **manners**, *pl.* ways of behaving or living, especially polite ways of behaving [It is good *manners* to say "Thank you."] **4** kind; sort [What *manner* of man is he?]

man·tle (man′təl) *n.* a loose cloak without sleeves; cape

mas·sive (mas′iv) *adj.* large, solid, heavy, etc. [a *massive* statue] —**mas′sive·ly** *adv.* —**mas′sive·ness** *n.*

may·or (mā′ ər) *n.* the head of the government of a city or town

mead·ow (med′ō) *n.* **1** a piece of land where grass is grown for hay **2** low, level grassland near a stream or lake

meas·ure (mezh′ər) *v.* to find out the size, amount, or extent of something, often by comparing with something else [*Measure* the child's height with a yardstick.] —**meas′ured, meas′ur·ing** ►*n.* the size, amount, or extent of something, found out by measuring [The *measure* of the bucket is 15 liters.]

me·chan·ic (mə kan′ik) *n.* a worker skilled in using tools or in making, repairing, and using machinery

me·di·a (mē′ de ə) *n.* a plural of medium

med·i·cal (med′i kəl) *adj.* having to do with the practice or study of medicine [*medical* care]

me·di·um (mē′ dē əm) any way by which something is done; especially, a way of communicating with the general public, as TV or newspapers: *in this meaning the plural* **media** *is sometimes used as a singular noun* [The *media* is covering the president's inauguration.]

mem·ber·ship (mem′bər ship) *n.* **1** the condition of being a member **2** all the members of a group **3** the number of members

☆**mem·o·rize** (mem′ə rīz) *v.* to fix in one's memory exactly or word for word; learn by heart —**mem′o·rized, mem′o·riz·ing** —**mem′o·ri·za′tion** *n.*

men·tal (ment′l) *adj.* **1** of, for, by, or in the mind [*mental* ability; *mental* arithmetic] **2** sick in mind [a *mental* patient] **3** for the sick in mind [a *mental* hospital]

mer·ry (mer′ē) *adj.* filled with fun and laughter; lively and cheerful [a *merry* party] —**mer′ri·er, mer′ri·est** —**make merry,** to have fun —**mer′ri·ly** *adv.* —**mer′ri·ness** *n.*

Mex·i·co (mek′sī kō) a country in North America, south of the U.S.

mid·air (mid er′) *n.* any point in space, not touching the ground or other surface

mid·day (mid′dā) *n., adj. another word for* **noon**

mid·dle (mid′əl) *n.* the point or part that is halfway between the ends or that is in the center [the *middle* of the morning; an island in the *middle* of the lake] ►*adj.* being in the middle or center [the *middle* toe]

mid·night (mid′nīt) *n.* twelve o'clock at night; the middle of the night ►*adj.* **1** of or at midnight [a *midnight* ride] **2** like midnight; very dark [*midnight* blue]

mid·stream (mid′strēm) *n.* the middle of a stream

mid·way (mid′wā *or* mid wā′) *adj., adv.* in the middle; halfway ►*n.* (mid′wā) the part of a fair, circus, or amusement park where sideshows or rides are located

mid·win·ter (mid′win′tər) *n.* **1** the middle of the winter **2** the period around December 22

min·i·mize (min′ə mīz) *v.* to make as small as possible; reduce to a minimum [Safe storage of gas will *minimize* the danger of fire.] —**min′i·mized, min′i·miz·ing**

mir·ror (mir′ər) *n.* **1** a smooth surface that reflects light; especially, a piece of glass coated with silver on the back; looking glass **2** anything that gives a true description [A good novel is a *mirror* of life.] ◆*v.* to reflect as in a mirror [The moon was *mirrored* in the lake.]

mis·be·have (mis′bē hāv′) *v.* to behave in a bad way; do what one is not supposed to do —**mis′be·haved′, mis′be·hav′ing** —**mis·be·hav·ior** (mis′bi hāv′yər) *n.*

mis·for·tune (mis fôr′chən) *n.* bad luck; trouble

mis·judge (mis juj′) *v.* to judge unfairly or wrongly —**mis·judged′, mis·judg′ing**

mis·lead (mis lēd′) *v.* **1** to lead in a wrong direction [That old road map will *mislead* you.] **2** to cause to believe what is not true; deceive [She *misled* us into thinking she would help.] —**mis·led′, mis·lead′ing**

mis·place (mis plās′) *v.* **1** to put in a wrong place [He *misplaced* the book of poems in the art section.] **2** to give trust, love, etc. to one who does not deserve it [I *misplaced* my confidence in you.] —**mis·placed′, mis·plac′ing**

mis·pro·nounce (mis prə nouns′) *v.* to pronounce in a wrong way [Some people *mispronounce* "cavalry" as "calvary."] —**mis·pro·nounced′, mis·pro·nounc′ing** —**mis·pro·nun·ci·a·tion** (mis′prə nun′sē ā′ shən) *n.*

mis·sion (mish′ən) *n.* **1** the special duty or errand that a person or group is sent out to do, as by a church, government, air force, etc. [a *mission* to gain converts; a *mission* to increase trade; a *mission* to bomb a factory] **2** a group of missionaries, or the place where they live, work, etc. [the foreign *missions* of a church] **3** a group of persons sent to a foreign government to carry on dealings, as for trade, a treaty, etc.

mis·sion·ar·y (mish′ən er′ ē) *n.* a person sent out by a church to spread its religion in a foreign country —*pl.* **mis′sion·ar′ies**

mis·spell (mis spel′) *v.* to spell incorrectly —**mis·spelled′or mis·spelt′, mis·spell′ing**

mis·take (mi stāk′) *n.* an idea, answer, act, etc. that is wrong; error or blunder ◆*v.* **1** to get a wrong idea of; misunderstand [You *mistake* his real purpose.] **2** to think that someone or something is some other person or thing [to *mistake* one twin for the other.] —**mis·took′, mis·tak′en, mis·tak′ing**

mis·trust (mis trust′) *n.* a lack of trust or confidence; suspicion; doubt [He felt *mistrust* of the stranger.] ◆*v.* to have no trust or confidence in; doubt —**mis·trust′ful adj.**

mis·un·der·stand (mis′ un dər stand′) *v.* to understand in a way that is wrong; give a wrong meaning to —**mis·un·der·stood** (mis′ un dər stood′), —**mis′un·der·stand′ing**

mod·ern (mäd′ərn) *adj.* **1** of or having to do with the present time or the period we live in [a *modern* poet] **2** of the period after about 1450 [the *modern* history of Europe] **3** of or having to do with the latest styles, methods, or ideas; up-to-date [He travels the *modern* way, by jet airplane.] ◆*n.* a person who lives in modern times or has up-to-date ideas

mod·i·fy (mäd′ə fī) *v.* **1** to make a small or partial change in [Exploration has *modified* our maps of Antarctica.] **2** in grammar, to limit the meaning of; describe or qualify [In the phrase "old man" the adjective "old" *modifies* the noun "man."] —**mod′i·fied, mod′i·fy·ing**

mois·ture (mois′chər) *n.* liquid causing a dampness, such as fine drops of water in the air

mois·tur·ize (mois′chər īz) *v.* to add, supply, or restore moisture to the skin, the air, etc. —**mois′tur·ized, mois′tur·iz·ing** —**mois′tur·iz·er n.**

Mont·re·al (män′trē ôl′) a city in southern Quebec, Canada, on an island in the St. Lawrence River

mon·u·ment (män′yoo mənt) *n.* **1** something put up in memory of a person or happening, as a statue, building, etc. **2** something great or famous, especially from long ago [Shakespeare's plays are *monuments* of English culture.]

☆**moose** (moos) *n.* a large animal related to the deer, of the northern U.S. and Canada: the male has broad antlers with many points —*pl.* **moose**

mort·gage (môr′gij) *n.* **1** an agreement in which a person borrowing money gives the lender a claim to property as a pledge that the debt will be paid [The bank holds a *mortgage* of $15,000 on our house.] **2** the legal paper by which such a claim is given ◆*v.* to pledge by a mortgage in order to borrow money [to *mortgage* a home] —**mort′gaged, mort′gag·ing**

moth·er (muth′ər) *n.* **1** a woman as she is related to her child or children; a female parent **2** the origin, source, or cause of something [Virginia is the state known as the *mother* of presidents.] **3** a nun who is the head of a convent, school, etc.: *the full name is* **mother superior** ◆*adj.* of, like, or as if from a mother [*mother* love; one's *mother* tongue] ◆*v.* to care for as a mother does —**moth′er·hood n.** —**moth′er·less adj.**

mo·ti·vate (mōt′ə vāt) *v.* to give a motive to or be a motive for [Love *motivated* my actions.] —**mo′ti·vat·ed, mo′ti·vat·ing** —**mo′ti·va′tion n.**

a	ask, fat
ā	ape, date
ä	car, lot
e	elf, ten
ē	even, meet
i	is, hit
ī	ice, fire
ō	open, go
ô	law, horn
oi	oil, point
oo	look, pull
oo	ooze, tool
ou	out, crowd
u	up, cut
u	fur, fern
ə	a in ago
	e in agent
	e in father
	i in unity
	o in collect
	u in focus
ch	chin, arch
ŋ	ring, singer
sh	she, dash
th	thin, truth
th	then, father
zh	s in pleasure

173

moun·tain·eer (mount'n ir') *n.* **1** a person who lives in a region of mountains **2** a person who climbs mountains ◆*v.* to climb mountains, as for sport

moun·tain·ous (mount'n əs) *adj.* **1** full of mountains **2** very large [a *mountainous* debt]

move·ment (mo͞ov'mənt) *n.* **1** the act of moving or a way of moving [a *movement* of the branches; the regular *movement* of the stars] **2** a working together to bring about some result [the *movement* for world peace]

mus·cle (mus'əl) *n.* the tissue in the body that is made up of bundles of long cells or fibers that can be stretched or squeezed together to move parts of the body [Eating protein helps build *muscle*.]

mys·ter·y (mis'tər ē *or* mis'trē) *n.* **1** something that is not known or explained, or that is kept secret [the *mystery* of life] **2** anything that remains unexplained or is so secret that it makes people curious [That murder is still a *mystery*.] **3** a story or play about such a happening —*pl.* **mys'ter·ies**

nar·row (ner'ō) *adj.* **1** small in width; less wide than usual [a *narrow* road] **2** small or limited in size, amount, or degree [I was the winner by a *narrow* majority.] **3** with barely enough space, time, means, etc.; close [a *narrow* escape] —**nar'row·ly** *adv.* —**nar'row·ness** *n.*

nat·u·ral (nach'ər əl) *adj.* **1** produced by nature; not made by man [*natural* resources; *natural* curls] **2** of or dealing with nature [Biology and chemistry are *natural* sciences.] **3** that is part of one from birth; native [He has a *natural* ability in music.] **4** free and easy; not forced or artificial [a *natural* laugh] —**nat'u·ral·ness** *n.*

naugh·ty (nôt'ē *or* nät'ē) *adj.* **1** not behaving; bad, disobedient, mischievous, etc. [*naughty* children] **2** not nice or proper [*naughty* words] —**naugh'ti·er, naught'ti·est** —**naugh'ti·ly** *adv.* —**naugh'ti·ness** *n.*

nec·tar (nek'tər) *n.* **1** the sweet liquid in many flowers, made into honey by bees **2** the drink of the gods in Greek myths

nec·tar·ine (nek tə rēn') *n.* a kind of peach that has a smooth skin

nee·dle (nēd'əl) *n.* **1** a small, slender piece of steel with a sharp point and a hole for thread, used for sewing **2** a slender rod of steel, bone, plastic, etc., used in knitting or crocheting **3** a short, slender piece of metal, often tipped with diamond, that moves in the grooves of a phonograph record to pick up the vibrations **4** the pointer of a compass, gauge, meter, etc. —**nee'dled, nee'dling** *v.*

neg·a·tive (neg'ə tiv) *adj.* **1** saying that something is not so or refusing; answering "no" [a *negative* reply] **2** that does not help, improve, etc. [*negative* criticism] **3** opposite to or lacking something that is positive [He always takes a *negative* attitude and expects the worst.] **4** showing that a certain disease, condition, etc is not present [The reaction to her allergy test was *negative*.] —**neg'a·tive·ly** *adv.*

neigh·bor·hood (nā'bər ho͝od) *n.* **1** a small part or district of a city, town, etc. [an old *neighborhood*] **2** the people in such a district [The whole *neighborhood* helped.]

nei·ther (nē'thər *or* nī'thər) *adj., pron.* not one or the other of two; not either (*Neither* boy went. *Neither* of them was invited.] ◆*conj.* not either; nor yet

news·pa·per (no͞oz'pā pər *or* nyo͞oz'pā pər) *n.* a daily or weekly publication printed on large, folded sheets of paper and containing news, opinions, advertisements, etc.

niece (nēs) *n.* **1** the daughter of one's brother or sister **2** the daughter of one's brother-in-law or sister-in-law

no·ble (nō'bəl) *adj.* **1** having or showing a very good character or high morals; lofty [*noble* ideals] **2** of or having a high rank or title; aristocratic [a *noble* family]

nois·y (noi'zē) *adj.* **1** making noise [a *noisy* bell] **2** full of noise [a *noisy* theater] —**nois'i·er, nois'i·est** —**nois'i·ly** *adv.* —**nois'i·ness** *n.*

noon (no͞on) *n.* twelve o'clock in the daytime: also **noon'day, noon'tide, noon'time**

nor·mal (nôr'məl) *adj.* **1** agreeing with a standard or norm; natural; usual; regular; average [It is *normal* to make a mistake sometimes.] **2** in good health; not ill or diseased

north·east (nôrth ēst' *or* nôr ēst') *n.* **1** the direction halfway between north and east **2** a place or region in or toward this direction

nov·el (näv'əl) *adj.* new and unusual [In the year 1920, flying was still a *novel* way of travel.] ◆*n.* a long story, usually a complete book about imaginary people and happenings

nov·el·ist (näv'əl ist) *n.* a person who writes novels

☆**ny·lon** (nī'län) *n.* **1** a very strong, elastic material made from chemicals and used for thread, bristles, etc. **2** **nylons**, *pl.* stockings made of nylon yarn

Oo

o·bey (ō bā′) **v. 1** to carry out the orders of [Soldiers must *obey* their officers.] **2** to do as one is told [My dog always *obeys*.] —**o·beyed′, o·bey′ing, o·beys′** —**o·bey′ er** **n.**

ob·jec·tion (äb jek′shən) **n. 1** a feeling of dislike or disapproval; protest [I have no *objection* to that plan.] **2** a reason for disliking or disapproving [My main *objection* to this climate is its dampness.]

ob·ser·va·tion (äb zər vā′shən) **n.** the act or power of seeing or noticing [It's a good night for *observation* of the stars.] ◆**adj.** for observing [an *observation* tower]

oc·cu·pant (äk′yoō pənt) **n.** a person who occupies land, a house, or a position [a former *occupant* of the White House]

oc·cu·py (äk′yoō pī′) **v. 1** to take possession of a place by capturing it or settling in it [The Germans *occupied* much of France during World War II. Pioneers *occupied* the wilderness.] **2** to have or hold [She *occupies* an important post in the government.] **3** to live in [to *occupy* a house] **4** to keep busy; employ [Many activities *occupy* his time.] —**oc′cu·pied′, oc′cu·py′ing**

o·pin·ion (ə pin′yən) **n. 1** a belief that is not based on what is certain, but on what one thinks to be true or likely [In my *opinion*, it will rain before dark.] **2** what one thinks about how good or valuable something is [What is your *opinion* of that painting?] **3** a judgment made by an expert [It would be better to get several medical *opinions*.]

op·por·tu·ni·ty (äp′ ər toō′nə tē *or* äp′ ər tyoō′nə tē) **n.** a time or occasion that is right for doing something; good chance [You will have an *opportunity* to ask questions after the talk.] —*pl.* **op′por·tu′ ni·ties**

op·po·site (äp′ə zit) **adj. 1** different in every way; exactly reverse or in contrast [Up is *opposite* to down.] **2** at the other end or side; directly facing or back to back [the *opposite* end of a table; the *opposite* side of a coin] ◆**n.** anything opposite or opposed [Love is the *opposite* of hate.] ◆**prep.** across from; facing [We sat *opposite* each other.] —**op′po·site·ly adv.**

op·ti·cal (äp′ti kəl) **adj. 1** of the sense of sight; visual [an *optical* illusion] **2** made to give help in seeing [Lenses are *optical* instruments.] —**op′ti·cal·ly adv.**

o·rang·u·tan (ô raŋ′ə tan′) **n.** a large ape with very long arms and shaggy, reddish hair, found in Borneo and Sumatra: *also* **o·rang·ou·tang** (o raŋ′ə taŋ′)

or·ches·tra (ôr′kəs trə) **n. 1** a group of musicians playing together, especially with some stringed instruments **2** the instruments of such a group —**or·ches·tral** (ôr kəs′trəl) **adj.**

or·chid (ôr′kid) **n.** a plant with flowers having three petals: the middle petal is larger than the others and has the shape of a lip

Or·e·gon (ôr′ə gən *or* ôr′ə gän) a state in the northwestern part of the U.S.: abbreviated **Oreg., OR**

o·rig·i·nal (ə rij′ə nəl) **adj. 1** having to do with an origin; first or earliest [the *original* settlers of North America] **2** that has never been before; not copied; fresh; new [an *original* idea; *original* music] **3** able to think of new things; inventive [Edison had an *original* mind.] **4** being the one of which there are copies [the *original* letter and three carbon copies] —**o·rig·i·nal·i·ty** (ə rij′ə nal′ ə tē) **n.**

out·ra·geous (σut rā′jəs) **adj.** doing great injury or wrong [*outrageous* crimes] —**out·ra′geous·ly adv.**

o·val (ō′vəl) **adj.** shaped like an egg or like an ellipse ◆**n.** anything with such a shape

o·ver·board (ō′vər bôrd) **adv.** from a ship into the water [He fell *overboard*.]

o·ver·come (ō vər kum′) **v. 1** to get the better of; defeat; master [to *overcome* an enemy; to *overcome* a problem] **2** to make weak or helpless [We were *overcome* by laughter.] **3** to be victorious; win —**o·ver·came′, o·ver·come′, o·ver·com′ing**

o·ver·due (ō vər doō′ *or* ō vər dyoō′) **adj. 1** not paid by the time set for payment [an *overdue* bill] **2** delayed past the arrival time; late [Her bus was long *overdue*.]

o·ver·look (ō vər look′) **v. 1** to give a view of from above; look down on [Your room *overlooks* the sea.] **2** to fail to notice [I *overlooked* no detail.] **3** to pay no attention to; excuse [I can *overlook* her rudeness.] —**o·ver·looked′**

o·ver·re·act (ō′ vər rē akt′) **v.** to respond to something with greater feeling or force than seems necessary

own·er·ship (ōn′ər ship) **n.** the condition of being an owner; possession

ox·y·gen (äks′i jən) **n.** a gas that has no color, taste, or odor and is a chemical element: it makes up almost one fifth of the air and combines with nearly all other elements: all living things need oxygen

oys·ter (σis′tər) **n.** a shellfish with a soft body enclosed in two rough shells hinged together: some are used as food, and pearls are formed inside others

o·zone (ō′zōn) **n.** a pale-blue gas that is a form of oxygen with a sharp smell: it is formed by an electrical discharge in the air and is used as a bleach, water purifier, etc.

a	ask, fat
ā	ape, date
ä	car, lot
e	elf, ten
ē	even, meet
i	is, hit
ī	ice, fire
ō	open, go
ô	law, horn
σi	oil, point
oo	look, pull
o͞o	ooze, tool
ou	out, crowd
u	up, cut
ʉ	fur, fern
ə	a in ago
	e in agent
	e in father
	i in unity
	o in collect
	u in focus
ch	chin, arch
ŋ	ring, singer
sh	she, dash
th	thin, truth
th	then, father
zh	s in pleasure

pack·age (pak′ ij) *n.* **1** a thing or things wrapped or tied up, as in a box or in wrapping paper; parcel ☆**2** a number of things offered together as one [a retirement *package*] ◆☆*v.* to put into a package —**pack′aged, pack′ag·ing**

pain (pān) *n.* **1** a feeling of hurting in some part of the body [a sharp *pain* in a tooth] **2** suffering of the mind; sorrow [The memory of that loss brought us *pain*.] ◆*v.* to give pain to; cause to suffer; hurt [The wound *pains* me. Their insults *pained* us.]

pain·ful (pān′ fəl) *adj.* causing pain; hurting; unpleasant [a *painful* wound; *painful* embarrassment] —**pain′ful·ly** *adv.* —**pain′ful·ness** *n.*

pan·cake (pan′ kāk) *n.* a thin, flat cake made by pouring batter onto a griddle or into a pan and frying it; flapjack

pan·cre·as (pan′ krē əs) *n.* a large gland behind the stomach that sends a juice into the small intestine to help digestion —**pan·cre·at·ic** (pən′ krē at′ik) *adj.*

pan·el (pan′ əl) *n.* **1** a flat section or part of a wall, door, etc., either raised above or sunk below the surfaces around it **2** a board or section containing dials, controls, etc. as for an airplane or a system of electric wiring **3** a picture or painting that is long and narrow **4** a strip of different material sewn lengthwise into a skirt or dress —**pan′eled** or **pan′elled, pan′el·ing** or **pan′el·ling** *v.*

pa·pa·ya (pə pī′ə) *n.* **1** a tree of tropical America, a little like the palm, with a yellowish-orange fruit like a small melon **2** this fruit, used as food

pa·per·back (pā′ pər bak) *n.* a book bound in paper, instead of cloth, leather, etc.

par·a·graph (per′ ə graf) *n.* **1** a separate section of a piece of writing, that deals with a particular point and is made up of one or more sentences: each paragraph begins on a new line that is usually moved in from the margin **2** a short note or item in a newspaper or magazine

par·al·lel (per′ə lel) *adj.* **1** moving out in the same direction and always the same distance apart so as to never meet, as the tracks of a sled in the snow **2** similar or alike [Their lives followed *parallel* courses.] ◆*n.* **1** a parallel line, plane, etc. **2** something similar to or like something else [Your experience is a *parallel* to mine.] —**par′al·leled** or **par′al·lelled, par′al·lel·ing** or **par′al·lel·ling** *v.*

par·ent (per′ənt) *n.* **1** a father or mother **2** any animal or plant as it is related to its offspring **3** anything from which other things come; source; origin [Latin is the *parent* of various languages.] —**par′ent·hood**

par·tic·i·pant (pär tis′ə pənt) *n.* a person who takes part in something

part·ner (pärt′nər) *n.* **1** a person who takes part in something with another or others; especially, one of the owners of a business who shares in its profits and risks **2** either of two players on the same side or team [my tennis *partner*] **3** either of two persons dancing together **4** a husband or wife

part·ner·ship (pärt′nər ship) *n.* **1** the condition or relationship of being a partner **2** a business firm made up of two or more partners

pas·sage (pas′ij) *n.* the act of passing [the *passage* of a bill into law]

pat·tern (pat′ərn) *n.* **1** a plan or model used as a guide for making things [a dress *pattern*] **2** a person or thing taken as a model or example [Sir Galahad was the *pattern* of the pure knight.] **3** the arrangement of parts; design [wallpaper *patterns*] **4** a habit or way of acting that does not change [the migration *pattern* of the swallow]

pause (pôz *or* päz) *n.* **1** a short stop, as in speaking or working **2** a musical sign (⌢) placed above a note or rest that is to be held longer ◆*v.* to make a pause; stop for a short time [He *paused* to catch his breath.] —**paused, paus′ing**

pay·ee (pā ē′) *n.* the person to whom a check, money, etc. is to be paid

pay·ment (pā′ mənt) *n.* **1** a paying or being paid [the *payment* of taxes] **2** something paid [a monthly rent *payment* of $168]

peace·ful (pēs′fəl) *adj.* **1** free from noise or disorder; quiet; calm [the *peaceful* countryside] **2** fond of peace; not fighting [a *peaceful* people] **3** of or fit for a time of peace [*peaceful* trade between nations] —**peace′ful·ly** *adv.* —**peace′ful·ness** *n.*

peas·ant (pez′ənt) *n.* mainly in Europe and Asia, a member of the class of farm workers and farmers with small farms

peck (pēk) *n.* **1** a measure of volume for grain, fruit, vegetables, etc.: it is equal to 1/4 bushel or eight quarts **2** a basket, etc. that holds a peck

pent·a·gon (pen′tə gän) *n.* **1** a flat figure having five sides and five angles ☆**2 Pentagon**, the five-sided office building of the Defense Department, near Washington, D.C. —**pen·tag·o·nal** (pen tag′ə n′l) *adj.*

per·form (pər fôrm′) *v.* **1** to do or carry out [to *perform* a task; to *perform* a promise] **2** to do something to entertain an audience; act, play, music, sing, etc. —**per·form′er** *n.*

pe·ri·od·i·cal (pir′ ē äd′i kəl) *n.* a magazine published every week, month, etc. ◆*adj.* **1** published every week, month, etc. **2** of periodicals [a *periodical* index] —**pe′ri·od′i·cal·ly** *adv.*

per·sist·ent (pər sis′tənt) *adj.* refusing to give up; steady and determined [a *persistent* job seeker] —**per·sist′ent·ly** *adv.*

per·son·al·ly (pʉr′sə nəl ē) **adv.** **1** by oneself, without the help of others [I'll ask them *personally*.] **2** as a person [I dislike the artist *personally*, but I admire her paintings.] **3** speaking for oneself [*Personally*, I think you're right.] **4** as though aimed at oneself [You should not take my remarks *personally*.]

per·suade (pər swād′) **v.** to get someone to do or believe something, as by making it seem like a good idea; convince —**per·suad′ed, per·suad′ing**

pes·ti·cide (pes′tə sīd) **n.** any poison used to kill insects, weeds, etc.

pet·al (pet′l) **n.** any of the brightly colored leaves that make up the flower of a plant

pho·no·graph (fō′nə graf) **n.** an instrument for playing records with a spiral groove on them in which sounds of music or speech have been recorded

pho·tog·ra·phy (fə täg′rə fē) **n.** the art or method of making pictures by means of a camera

phys·i·cal (fiz′i kəl) **adj.** **1** of nature or matter; material; natural [the *physical* universe] **2** of the body rather than the mind [Swimming is good *physical* exercise.] **3** of or having to do with the natural sciences or the laws of nature [the *physical* force that makes an object move] ◆**n.** ☆a medical examination of the whole body

pic·co·lo (pik′ə lō) **n.** a small flute that sounds notes an octave higher than an ordinary flute does —*pl.* **pic′co·los**

pick·le (pik′el) **n.** **1** a cucumber or other vegetable preserved in salt water, vinegar, or spicy liquid **2** a liquid of this kind used to preserve food ◆**v.** to preserve in a pickle liquid [*pickled* beets] —**pick′led, pick′ling**

piece (pēs) **n.** **1** a part broken or separated from a whole thing [The glass shattered and I swept up the *pieces*.] **2** a part or section of a whole, thought of as complete by itself [a *piece* of meat; a *piece* of land] **3** any one of a set or group of things [a dinner set of 52 *pieces*; a chess *piece*] **4** a work of music, writing, or art [a *piece* for the piano] —**pieced, piec′ing v.**

pis·til (pis′təl) **n.** the part of a flower in which the seeds grow: a single pistil is made up of a stigma, style, and ovary

plan (plan) **n.** **1** a method or way of doing something, that has been thought out ahead of time [vacation *plans*] **2** a drawing that shows how the parts of a building or piece of ground are arranged [floor *plans* of a house; a *plan* of the battlefield] ◆**v.** **1** to think out a way of making or doing something [They *planned* their escape carefully.] **2** to make a drawing or diagram of beforehand [An architect is *planning* our new school.] —**planned, plan′ning**

plas·tic (plas′tik) **adj.** **1** that can be shaped or molded [Clay is a *plastic* material.] **2** that gives form or shape to matter [Sculpture is a *plastic* art.] **3** made of plastic [a *plastic* comb] ◆**n.** a substance, made from various chemicals, that can be molded and hardened into many useful products —**plas·tic·i·ty** (plas tis′ə tē) **n.**

Platte (plat) a river in central Nebraska

pleas·ant (plez′ənt) **adj.** **1** giving pleasure; bringing happiness; enjoyable [a *pleasant* day in the park] **2** having a look or manner that gives pleasure; likable [a *pleasant* person]

pleas·ing (plēz′iŋ) **adj.** giving pleasure; enjoyable [a *pleasing* smile]

pleas·ure (plezh′ər) **n.** **1** a feeling of delight or satisfaction; enjoyment [I get *pleasure* from taking long walks.] **2** a thing that gives pleasure [Her voice is a *pleasure* to hear.] **3** one's wish or choice [For dessert, what is your *pleasure*?]

pledge (plej) **n.** **1** a promise or agreement [the *pledge* of allegiance to the flag] **2** something promised, especially money to be given as to a charity **3** a thing given as a guarantee or token of something [They gave each other rings as a *pledge* of their love.] ◆**v.** to promise to give [to *pledge* $100 to a building fund] —**pledged, pledg′ing**

plen·ti·ful (plen′ti fəl) **adj.** great in amount or number; more than enough [a *plentiful* food supply] —**plen′ti·ful·ly adv.**

pli·ers (plī′ərz) **pl.n.** a tool like small pincers, used for gripping small objects or bending wire

plu·ral (ploor′əl) **adj.** showing that more than one is meant [The *plural* form of "box" is "boxes."] ◆**n.** the form of a word which shows that more than one is meant

poach (pōch) **v.** to cook an egg without its shell, in boiling water or in a small cup put over boiling water

poise (poiz) **n.** **1** balance, as in the way one carries oneself [the perfect *poise* of a tiger that is ready to spring] **2** calmness and easiness of manner; self-control [I lost my *poise* when they laughed at me.] ◆**v.** to balance or be held balanced [The stork *poised* itself on one leg. The earth is *poised* in space.] —**poised, pois′ing**

poi·son·ous (poi′zə nəs) **adj.** that is a poison; harming or killing by poison [a *poisonous* berry]

po·lar (pō′lər) **adj.** **1** of or near the North or South Pole **2** of a pole or poles

Pol·ish (pōl′ish) **adj.** of Poland, its people, language, etc. ◆**n.** the language of Poland

po·lite (pə līt′) **adj.** **1** having or showing good manners; thoughtful of others; courteous [a *polite* note of thanks] **2** behaving in a way that is considered refined or elegant [Such things aren't done in *polite* society.] —**po·lite′ly adv.** —**po·lite′ness n.**

a	ask, fat
ā	ape, date
ä	car, lot
e	elf, ten
ē	even, meet
i	is, hit
ī	ice, fire
ō	open, go
ô	law, horn
oi	oil, point
ၾၾ	look, pull
ᴏ̄ᴏ̄	ooze, tool
ou	out, crowd
u	up, cut
ʉ	fur, fern
ə	a in ago
	e in agent
	e in father
	i in unity
	o in collect
	u in focus
ch	chin, arch
ŋ	ring, singer
sh	she, dash
th	thin, truth
th	then, father
zh	s in pleasure

pol·li·nate (päl′ə nāt) **v.** to place pollen on the pistil of a flower; fertilize —**pol′li·nat′ed, pol′li·nat′ing** —**pol′li·na′tion** n.

pol·y·es·ter (päl′ē es′ tər) **n.** an artificial resin used in making plastics, fibers for fabrics, etc.

pop·u·lar (päp′yoo lər) **adj. 1** having many friends; very well liked **2** liked by many people **3** of, for, or by all the people or most people —**pop·u·lar·i·ty** (päp′yə lar′ə tē) **n.** —**pop′u·lar·ly adv.**

pop·u·la·tion (päp′yoo lā′shən) **n. 1** the people living in a country, city, etc.; especially, the total number of these **2** the act of populating or the fact of being populated

pos·si·ble (päs′ə bəl) **adj. 1** that can be [The highest *possible* score in bowling is 300.] **2** that may or may not happen [colder tomorrow, with *possible* showers] **3** that can be done, known, got, used, etc. [two *possible* routes to Denver]

post·game (pōst′gām′) **adj.** having to do with activities after a game

post·pone (pōst pōn′) **v.** to put off until later; delay [I *postponed* my trip because of illness.] —**post·poned′, post·pon′ing** —**post·pone′ment** n.

pos·ture (päs′chər) **n. 1** the way one holds the body in sitting or standing; carriage [good *posture* with the back held straight] **2** a special way of holding the body or of acting, as in posing [Doubling up a fist is a *posture* of defiance.] ◆**v.** to take on a posture; pose —**pos′tured, pos′tur·ing**

post·war (pōst′wôr′) **adj.** after the war

po·ta·to (pə tāt′ō) **n. 1** a plant whose tuber, or thick, starchy underground stem, is used as a vegetable **2** this tuber —*pl.* **po·ta′toes**

pow·der (pou′dər) **n.** a dry substance in the form of fine particles like dust, made by crushing or grinding [talcum *powder*; baking *powder*; gun*powder*] ◆**v.** to sprinkle, dust, or cover as with powder [Snow *powdered* the rooftops.]

pow·er·ful (pou′ər fəl) **adj.** having much power; strong or influential [a *powerful* leader] —**pow′er·ful·ly adv.**

☆**prai·rie** (prer′ē) **n.** a large area of level or rolling grassy land without many trees

preach·er (prēch′ər) **n.** a person who preaches; especially, a clergyman

pre·pare (prē per′) **v. 1** to make or get ready [to *prepare* for a test; to *prepare* ground for planting] **2** to furnish with what is needed; equip [to *prepare* an expedition] **3** to make or put together out of parts or materials [to *prepare* a medicine] —**pre·pared′, pre·par′ing**

pre·serv·a·tive (prē zurv′ə tiv) **n.** anything that preserves; especially, a substance added to food to keep it from spoiling

pre·serve (prē zurv′) **v. 1** to protect from harm or damage; save [to *preserve* our national forests] **2** to keep from spoiling or rotting **3** to prepare food for later use by canning, pickling, or salting it —**pre·served′, pre·serv′ing** ◆**n.** *usually* **preserves**, *pl.* fruit preserved by cooking it with sugar and canning it

pres·i·dent (prez′i dənt) **n.** ☆**1** the highest officer of a company, club, college, etc. **2** *often* **President**, the head of government in a republic

pres·sure (presh′ ər) **n. 1** a pressing or being pressed; force of pushing or of weight [the *pressure* of the foot on the brake] **2** a condition of trouble, strain, etc. that is hard to bear [She never gave in to the *pressure* of her grief.] **3** influence or force to make someone do something [His friends put *pressure* on him to resign as president.] **4** urgent demands; urgency [She neglected her homework and now has to work under *pressure* of time.] —**pres′ sured, pres′ sur·ing v.**

pre·tend (prē tənd′) **v. 1** to make believe, as in play [Let's *pretend* we're cowboys.] **2** to claim or act in a false way [She *pretended* to be angry, but she wasn't.] —**pre·tend′ ed adj.**

pre·vail (prē vāl′) **v. 1** to be successful or win out [to *prevail* over an enemy] **2** to be or become more common or widespread, as a custom or practice

pre·vent (prē vent′) **v. 1** to stop or hinder [A storm *prevented* us from going.] **2** to keep from happening [Careful driving *prevents* accidents.] —**pre·vent′ ed, pre·vent′ ing**

pris·on·er (priz′ən ər *or* priz′nər) **n.** a person who is kept shut up, as in a prison, or held as a captive, as in war

prob·lem (präb′ləm) **n. 1** a condition, person, etc. that is difficult to deal with or hard to understand [Getting the table through that narrow door will be a *problem*.] **2** a question to be solved or worked out [an arithmetic *problem*; the problem of reckless drivers]

pro·ceed (prō sēd′) **v.** to go on, especially after stopping for a while [After eating, we *proceeded* to the next town.] —**pro·ceed′ ed, pro·ceed′ ing**

pro·ces·sion (prə sesh′ən) **n. 1** a number of persons or things moving forward in an orderly way **2** the act of moving in this way

pro·duce (prə doos′ *or* prə dyoos′) **v. 1** to bring forth; bear; yield [trees *producing* apples; a well that *produces* oil] **2** to make or manufacture [a company that *produces* bicycles] **3** to bring out into view; show [*Produce* your fishing license.] **4** to get ready and bring to the public, as a play, movie, etc. —**pro·duced′, pro·duc′ing** ◆**n.** (prō′ doos) —**pro·duc′ er**

pro·fes·sion·al (prə fesh′ən əl) *adj.* **1** of or in a profession [the *professional* ethics of a lawyer] **2** earning one's living from a sport or other activity not usually thought of as an occupation [a *professional* golfer] **3** engaged in by professional players [*professional* football] —**pro·fes′sion·al·ism** *n.* —**pro·fes′sion·al·ly** *adv.*

prof·it·a·ble (präf′it ə bəl) *adj.* that brings profit or benefit [a *profitable* sale; a *profitable* idea] —**prof′it·a·bly** *adv.*

pro·mote (prə mōt′) *v.* **1** to raise to a higher rank, grade, or position [She was *promoted* to manager.] **2** to help to grow, succeed, etc. [New laws were passed to *promote* the general welfare.] ☆**3** to make more popular, increase the sales of, etc. by advertising or giving publicity [to *promote* a product] ☆**4** to move a student forward a grade in school —**pro·mot′ed, pro·mot′ing** —**pro·mot′er, pro·mo′tion** *n.*

pro·pose (prə pōz′) *v.* **1** to suggest for others to think about, approve, etc. [We *propose* that the city build a zoo. I *propose* Robin for treasurer.] **2** to plan or intend [Do you *propose* to leave us?] **3** to make an offer of marriage —**pro·posed′, pro·pos′ing**

pro·tec·tion (prō tek′shən) *n.* **1** a protecting or being protected [The guard carried a club for *protection*.] **2** a person or thing that protects [Being careful is your best *protection* against accidents.]

pro·test (prō test′ *or* prō′ test) *v.* **1** to speak out against; object [They joined the march to *protest* against injustice.] **2** to say in a positive way; insist [Bill *protested* that he would be glad to help.] ➧*n.* (prō′ test) the act of protesting; objection [They ignored my *protest* and continued hammering.] —**pro·test′er** or **pro·tes′tor**

pro·trac·tor (prō trak′ tər *or* prō′ trak tər) *n.* an instrument used for drawing and measuring angles: it is in the form of a half circle marked with degrees

pro·vide (prō vīd′) *v.* **1** to give what is needed; supply; furnish [The school *provides* free books.] **2** to furnish the means of support [How large a family do you *provide* for?] **3** to get ready ahead of time; prepare [You'd better *provide* for rain by taking umbrellas.] **4** to set forth as a condition, as in a contract [Our lease *provides* that rent will be paid monthly.] —**pro·vid′ed, pro·vid′ing**

prune (prōōn) *v.* **1** to cut off or trim branches, twigs, etc. from [to *prune* hedges] **2** to make shorter by cutting out parts [to *prune* a novel] —**pruned, prun′ing**

psy·chol·o·gy (sī käl′ ə jē) *n.* **1** the science that studies the mind and the reasons for the ways that people think and act **2** the ways of thinking and acting of a person or group [the *psychology* of the child; mob *psychology*] —*pl.* **psy·chol′o·gies** —**psy·chol′o·gist** *n.*

pub·lic (pub′ lik) *adj.* **1** of or having to do with the people as a whole [*public* affairs; *public* opinion] **2** for the use or the good of everyone [a *public* park] **3** acting for the people as a whole [a *public* official] **4** known by all or most people; open [a *public* figure; a *public* scandal]

pump·kin (pum′ kin *or* pump′ kin) *n.* a large, round, orange fruit that grows on a vine and has many seeds: the pulp is much used as a filling for pies

punc·tu·a·tion (puŋk′ chōō ā′ shən) *n.* **1** the use of commas, periods, etc. in writing [rules of *punctuation*] **2** punctuation marks [What *punctuation* is used to end sentences?]

pup·pet·eer (pup ə tir′) *n.* a person who works the strings that make puppets move or one who puts on puppet shows

pyr·a·mid (pir′ ə mid) *n.* **1** a solid figure whose sloping sides are triangles that come together in a point at the top **2** anything having this shape; especially, any of the huge structures with a square base and four sides in which ancient Egyptian rulers were buried ➧*v.* to build up or heap up in the form of a pyramid

Qq

qual·i·fi·ca·tion (kwôl′ ə fi kā′ shən *or* kwä′ lə fi kā′ shən) *n.* **1** a qualifying or being qualified **2** a thing that changes, limits, or holds back [I can recommend the book without any *qualification*.] **3** any skill, experience, special training, etc. that fits a person for some work, office, etc.

qual·i·fy (kwôl′ ə fī *or* kwä′ lə fī) *v.* to make or be fit or suitable for a particular role, job, or activity [Your training and education *qualify* you for the job.] —**qual′i·fied, qual′i·fy·ing**

quar·rel (kwôr′ əl) *n.* **1** an argument or disagreement, especially an angry one; dispute **2** a reason for arguing [I have no *quarrel* with the way things are being done.] ➧*v.* **1** to argue or disagree in an angry way **2** to find fault; complain [She *quarrels* with his methods, not with his results.] —**quar′reled** or **quar′relled, quar′rel·ing** or **quar′rel·ling**

quar·ter (kwôrt′ər) *n.* **1** any of the four equal parts of something; fourth [a *quarter* of a mile; the third *quarter* of a football game] **2** one-fourth of a year; three months **3** the point fifteen minutes before or after any given hour [It's a *quarter* after five.] **4** a coin of the U.S. or Canada, worth 25 cents; one-fourth of a dollar

a	ask, fat
ā	ape, date
ä	car, lot
e	elf, ten
ē	even, meet
i	is, hit
ī	ice, fire
ō	open, go
ô	law, horn
oi	oil, point
ōō	look, pull
o͞o	ooze, tool
ou	out, crowd
u	up, cut
₉	fur, fern
ə	**a** in ago
	e in agent
	e in father
	i in unity
	o in collect
	u in focus
ch	chin, arch
ŋ	ring, singer
sh	she, dash
th	thin, truth
th	then, father
zh	s in pleasure

ques·tion (kwes′chən) *n.* **1** something that is asked in order to learn or know [The athlete refused to answer the reporter's *questions*.] **2** doubt [There is no *question* about his honesty.] **3** a matter to be considered; problem [It's not a *question* of money.] ◆*v.* to ask questions of [The lawyer started to *question* the witness.] —**ques′tion·er** *n.*

quick (kwik) *adj.* **1** done with speed; rapid; swift [We took a *quick* trip.] **2** done or happening at once; prompt [I was grateful for her *quick* reply.] **3** able to learn or understand easily [You have a *quick* mind.] **4** easily stirred up; touchy [Lynn has a *quick* temper.] —**quick′ly** *adv.* —**quick′ness** *n.*

qui·et (kwī′ət) *adj.* **1** not noisy; hushed [a *quiet* motor] **2** not talking; silent [She was *quiet* during dinner.] **3** not moving; still; calm [a *quiet* pond] **4** peaceful and relaxing [We spent a *quiet* evening at home.] —**qui′et·ly** *adv.* —**qui′et·ness** *n.*

ra·dar (rā′där) *n.* a device or system that sends out radio waves and picks them up after they strike some object and bounce back

☆**ra·di·o** (rā′dē ō′) *n.* **1** a way of sending sounds through space by changing them into electric waves which are sent and picked up, without wires, by a receiver that changes them back to sounds **2** the act or business of broadcasting news, music, talks, etc. by radio —*pl.* **ra′di·os′** —**ra′di·oed′, ra′di·o′ing** *v.*

ra·di·us (rā′dē əs) *n.* **1** any straight line that goes from the center to the outside of a circle or sphere **2** a round area as measured by its radius [no houses within a *radius* of five miles] **3** the thicker of the two bones in the forearm —*pl.* **ra·di·i** (rā′dē ī′) or **ra′di·us·es**

rail·way (rāl′wā) *n.* a track made up of parallel steel rails along which trains run

rain·bow (rān′bō) *n.* a curved band across the sky with all the colors of the spectrum in it: it is seen when the sun's rays pass through falling rain or mist

rai·sin (rā′zən) *n.* a sweet grape dried for eating

rasp·ber·ry (raz′ber′ē) *n.* **1** a small, juicy, red or black fruit with many tiny seeds **2** the shrub it grows on —*pl.* **rasp′ber′ries**

☆**ray·on** (rā′än) *n.* a fiber made from cellulose, or a fabric woven from such fibers

read·i·ly (red′əl ē) *adv.* **1** without hesitation; willingly **2** without difficulty; easily

re·al·ist (rē′ə list) *n.* a person who sees things as they really are; practical person

re·ap·pear (rē ə pir′) *v.* to appear again —**re′ap·pear′ance** *n.*

re·ar·range (rē ə rānj′) *v.* to arrange again or in a different way —**re·ar·ranged′, re·ar·rang′ing** —**re′ar·range′ment** *n.*

re·ceive (rē sēv′) *v.* **1** to take or get what has been given or sent to one [to *receive* a letter] **2** to meet with; be given; undergo [to *receive* punishment; to receive applause] **3** to find out about; learn [He *received* the news calmly.] **4** to greet guests and let them come in [Our hostess *received* us at the door.] —**re·ceived′, re·ceiv′ing**

re·cent (rē′sənt) *adj.* of a time just before now; made or happening a short time ago [*recent* news; a *recent* storm] —**re′cent·ly** *adv.*

rec·og·nize (rek′əg nīz) *v.* **1** to be aware of as something or someone seen, heard, etc. before; know again [to *recognize* a street; to *recognize* a tune] **2** to know by a certain feature; identify [to *recognize* a giraffe by its long neck] **3** to take notice of; show approval of [a ceremony to *recognize* those employees with ten years or more of service] **4** to admit as true; accept [to *recognize* defeat] —**rec′og·nized, rec′og·niz·ing**

rec·om·mend (rek ə mend′) *v.* **1** to speak of as being good for a certain use, job, etc.; praise [to *recommend* a good plumber; to *recommend* a book] **2** to make pleasing or worth having [That summer camp has much to *recommend* it.] **3** to give advice; advise [I *recommend* that you study harder.]

rec·re·a·tion (rek′ rē ā′shən) *n.* **1** the act of refreshing one's body or mind, as after work [He plays chess for *recreation*.] **2** any sport, exercise, hobby, amusement, etc. by which one does this —**rec′re·a′tion·al** *adj.*

rec·tan·gle (rek′ taŋ′gəl) *n.* any flat figure with four right angles and four sides

re·cy·cle (rē sī′kəl) *v.* to use again and again, as a single supply of water in a fountain or for cooling, metal to be melted down and recast, or paper processed for use again —**re·cy′cled, re·cy′cling**

re·duce (rē dōōs′ *or* rē dyōōs′) *v.* **1** to make smaller, less, fewer, etc.; decrease [to *reduce* speed; to *reduce* taxes] **2** to lose weight, as by dieting **3** to make lower, as in rank or condition; bring down [to *reduce* a major to the rank of captain; a family *reduced* to poverty] **4** to change into a different form or condition [to *reduce* peanuts to a paste by grinding] —**re·duced′, re·duc′ing** —**re·duc′er** *n.* —**re·duc′i·ble** *adj.*

ref·er·ence (ref'ər əns *or* ref'rəns)
n. **1** the act or fact of referring; mention
[They made no *reference* to the accident.]
2 the fact of having to do with; relation;
connection [I am writing in *reference* to
your letter.] **3** a mention, as in a book, of
some other work where information can be
found; also, the work so mentioned [Most of
the author's *references* are useful.]
4 something that gives information [Look in
the encyclopedia and other *references*.]
re·flect (rē flekt') *v.* **1** to throw back or be
thrown back, as light, heat, or sound
[A polished metal surface *reflects* both light
and heat.] **2** to give back an image of
[The calm lake *reflected* the trees on the
shore.] **3** to bring as a result [Your success
reflects credit on your teachers.] **4** to bring
blame, doubt, etc.
reg·u·lar (reg'yə lər) *adj.* **1** formed or
arranged in an orderly way; balanced
[a *regular* pattern; a face with *regular*
features] **2** according to some rule or habit;
usual; customary [Sit in your *regular* place.]
3 steady and even; not changing [a *regular*
rhythm] **4** in grammar, changing form in
the usual way in showing tense, number,
etc. ["Walk" is a *regular* verb, but "swim" is
not.] —**reg·u·lar·i·ty** (reg'yə lar'ə tē) *n.*
—**reg'u·lar·ly** *adv.*
rel·a·tive (rel'ə tiv) *n.* a person of the same
family by blood or by marriage
re·lax (rē laks') *v.* **1** to make or become less
firm, tense, or strict; loosen up [The body
relaxes in sleep. The parents never *relaxed*
their watch over their child.] **2** to rest from
work or effort [He *relaxes* by going fishing.]
—**re'lax·a'tion** *n.*
re·lay (rē'lā) *n.* **1** a fresh group that takes
over some work from another group; shift
[The carpenters worked in *relays* to finish
the project on time.] **2** a race in which each
member of a team runs only a certain part
of the whole distance: the full name is **relay
race** ◆*v.* to get and pass on [to *relay* a
message] —**re'layed, re'lay·ing**
re·li·ant (rē lī'ənt) *adj.* having or showing
trust or confidence; depending [The needy
are *reliant* on our help.]
re·lieve (rē lēv') *v.* **1** to reduce or ease pain
or worry [Cold water *relieves* a swelling.]
2 to free from pain or worry [We were
relieved of our fear when the danger
passed.] —**re·lieved', re·liev'ing**
re·li·gion (rē lij'ən) *n.* **1** belief in, or the
worship of, God or a group of gods
2 a particular system of belief or worship
built around God, moral ideas, a philosophy
of life, etc.
re·mem·ber (rē mem'bər) *v.* **1** to think of
again [I suddenly *remembered* I was
supposed to mow the lawn.] **2** to bring back
to mind by trying; recall [I just can't
remember your name.] **3** to be careful not
to forget [*Remember* to look both ways
before crossing.] **4** to mention as sending
greetings [*Remember* me to your family.]

re·mote (rē mōt') *adj.* **1** far off or far
away in space or time; distant **2** not closely
related **3** slight or faint —**re·mot'er,
re·mot'est** —**re·mote'ly** *adv.*
—**re·mote'ness** *n.*
re·pel·lent (rē pel'ənt) *adj.* that repels in
any of various ways [a *repellent* smell; a
water-*repellent* jacket] ◆*n.* something that
repels, as a spray that keeps insects away
re·print (rē print') *v.* to print again [The
book was *reprinted*.] —**re·print'ed,
re·print'ing**
re·quire (rē kwīr') *v.* **1** to be in need of
[Most plants *require* sunlight.] **2** to order,
command, or insist upon [He *required* us to
leave.] —**re·quired', re·quir'ing**
res·cue (res'kyoo) *v.* to free or save from
danger, evil, etc. [*rescue* people from a
burning building] ◆*n.* the act of rescuing
—**res'cued, res'cu·ing** —**res'cu·er** *n.*
res·i·dent (rez'i dənt) *n.* a person who
lives in a place, not just a visitor ◆*adj.*
living or staying in a place, as while
working
re·sign (rē zīn') *v.* to give up one's office,
position, membership, etc. [We *resigned*
from the club.]
re·source·ful (rē sôrs'fəl) *adj.* skillful
at solving problems or getting out of
trouble —**re·source'ful·ly** *adv.*
—**re·source'ful·ness** *n.*
re·spon·si·ble (rē spän'sə bəl) *adj.*
1 supposed or expected to take care of
something or do something [Harry is
responsible for mowing the lawn.] **2** that
must get the credit or blame [All of us are
responsible for our own actions.] **3** having
to do with important duties [a *responsible*
job] **4** that can be trusted or depended
upon; reliable [a *responsible* person]
re·turn (rē turn') *v.* **1** to go or come back
[When did you *return* from your trip?]
2 to bring, send, carry, or put back [Our
neighbor *returned* the ladder.] **3** to pay
back by doing the same [to *return* a visit; to
return a favor] **4** to throw, hit, or run back a
ball —**re·turned', re·turn'ing, re·turns'**
re·view (rē vyoo') *v.* **1** to go over or study
again [to *review* a subject for a test]
2 to think back on [She *reviewed* the events
that led to their quarrel.] **3** to inspect or
examine in an official way [to *review*
troops] **4** to tell what a book, play, etc. is
about and give one's opinion of it
rev·o·lu·tion (rev'ə loo'shən) *n.*
1 overthrow of a government or a social
system, with another taking its place
[the American *Revolution*; the Industrial
Revolution] **2** a complete change of any
kind [The telephone caused a *revolution* in
communication.] **3** the act of revolving;
movement in an orbit [the *revolution* of
the moon around the earth] **4** a turning
motion of a wheel, etc. around a center
or axis; rotation

a	ask, fat
ā	ape, date
ä	car, lot
e	elf, ten
ē	even, meet
i	is, hit
ī	ice, fire
ō	open, go
ô	law, horn
oi	oil, point
oo	look, pull
oo	ooze, tool
ou	out, crowd
u	up, cut
u	fur, fern
ə	a in ago
	e in agent
	e in father
	i in unity
	o in collect
	u in focus
ch	chin, arch
ŋ	ring, singer
sh	she, dash
th	thin, truth
th	then, father
zh	s in pleasure

re·ward (rē wôrd′) *n.* **1** something given in return, especially for good work or a good deed [a *reward* for bravery] **2** money offered, as for returning something lost

ridge (rij) *n.* **1** a top or high part that is long and narrow; crest [the *ridge* of a roof] **2** a range of hills or mountains **3** any narrow, raised strip [Waves made tiny *ridges* in the sand.]

roast (rōst) *v.* **1** to cook with little or no liquid, as in an oven or over an open fire [to *roast* a chicken or a whole ox] **2** to dry or brown with great heat [to *roast* coffee] **3** to make or become very hot —**roast′ed, roast′ing**

rot (rät) *v.* to fall apart or spoil by the action of bacteria or dampness; to decay [A dead tree will *rot*.] —**rot′ted, rot′ting**

rub·ble (rub′əl) *n.* **1** rough, broken pieces of stone, brick, etc. **2** masonry made up of such pieces **3** broken pieces from buildings, etc. damaged or destroyed by an earthquake, bombing, etc.

Rus·sian (rush′ən) *n.* **1** a person born or living in Russia **2** the chief language of Russia ⬥*adj.* of Russia, its people, their language, etc.

sa·li·va (sə lī′və) *n.* the watery liquid produced in the mouth by certain glands; spit: it helps to digest food

salm·on (sam′ən) *n.* a large food fish with silver scales and flesh that is orange-pink when cooked: salmon live in the ocean but swim up rivers to lay their eggs —*pl.* **salm′on** or **salm′ons**

sat·in (sat′n) *n.* a cloth of silk, nylon or rayon having a smooth finish, glossy on the front side and dull on the back

sat·u·rate (sach′ər āt) *v.* **1** to soak through and through [The baby's bib was *saturated* with milk.] **2** to fill so completely or dissolve so much of something that no more can be taken up [to *saturate* water with salt] —**sat′u·rat·ed, sat′u·rat·ing** —**sat′u·ra′tion** *n.*

sau·cer (sô′sər *or* sä′sər) *n.* **1** a small, shallow dish, especially one for a cup to rest on **2** anything round and shallow like this dish

sau·sage (sô′sij *or* sä′sij) *n.* pork or other meat, chopped up and seasoned and, usually, stuffed into a tube made of thin skin

scan (skan) *v.* **1** to look at very carefully; examine [Columbus *scanned* the horizon for land.] ☆**2** to glance at or look over quickly [I *scanned* the list of names to find yours.] **3** to show the pattern of rhythm in the lines of a poem [We can *scan* a line this way: Má rў Má rў quíte cŏn trár ў.] —**scanned, scan′ning** —**scan′ner** *n.*

scare·crow (sker′krō) *n.* a figure of a man made with sticks, old clothes, etc. and set up in a field to scare birds away from crops

scarf (skärf) *n.* **1** a long or broad piece of cloth worn about the head, neck, or shoulders for warmth or decoration **2** a long, narrow piece of cloth used as a covering on top of a table, bureau, etc. —*pl.* **scarves** or **scarfs** (skärvz)

scar·y (sker′ē) *adj.* causing fear; frightening —**scar′i·er, scar′i·est** —**scar′i·ness** *n.*

schol·ar·ship (skä′lər ship) *n.* **1** the knowledge of a learned person; great learning **2** the kind of knowledge that a student shows [Her paper shows good *scholarship*.]

sci·ence (sī′əns) *n.* knowledge made up of an orderly system of facts that have been learned from study, observation, and experiments [*Science* helps us to understand how things happen.]

sci·en·tist (sī′ən tist) *n.* an expert in science, such as a chemist, biologist, etc.

scram·ble (skram′bəl) *v.* **1** to climb or crawl in a quick, rough way [The children *scrambled* up the steep hill.] **2** to struggle or scuffle for something [The puppies *scrambled* for the meat.] ☆**3** to cook eggs while stirring the mixed whites and yolks **4** to mix up electronic signals, as those containing a secret message, so that the message cannot be understood without special equipment —**scram′bled, scram′bling**

scrape (skrāp) *v.* **1** to make smooth or clean by rubbing with a tool or with something rough [to *scrape* the bottom of a ship] **2** to remove in this way [*Scrape* off the old paint.] **3** to scratch or rub the skin from [He fell and *scraped* his knee.] **4** to rub with a harsh or grating sound [The shovel *scraped* across the sidewalk.] —**scraped, scrap′ing**

☆**screen·play** (skrēn′plā) *n.* the written script from which a movie is made

sec·re·tar·y (sek′rə ter′ē) *n.* **1** a person whose work is keeping records, writing letters, etc. for a person, organization, etc. **2** the head of a department of government [the *Secretary* of State] **3** a writing desk, especially one with a bookcase built at the top —*pl.* **sec′re·tar′ies** —**sec·re·tar·i·al** (sek′rə ter′ē əl) *adj.*

seek (sēk) *v.* to try to find; search for [to *seek* gold] —**sought, seek′ing**

seize (sēz) *v.* to take hold of in a sudden, strong, or eager way; grasp [to *seize* a weapon and fight] —**seized, seiz′ing**

se·lec·tive (sə lek′tiv) *adj.* **1** of or set apart by selection **2** tending to select **3** having the power to select [A *selective* radio set brings in each station clearly.] —**se·lec′tive·ly** *adv.* —**se·lec·tiv·i·ty** (se lek′ tiv′ə tē) *n.*

self-con·trol (self′kən trōl′) *n.* control of oneself or of one's feelings and actions

self-pres·er·va·tion (self′prez ər vā′shən) *n.* the act or instinct of keeping oneself safe and alive

sen·ate (sen′ət) *n.* **1** an assembly or council **2 Senate**, the upper and smaller branch of Congress or of a state legislature

sen·a·tor (sen′ə tər) *n.* a member of a senate —**sen·a·to·ri·al** (sen′ə tôr′ē əl) *adj.*

sen·si·ble (sen′sə bəl) *adj.* **1** having or showing good sense; reasonable; wise [*sensible* advice] **2** having understanding; aware [She was *sensible* of his unhappiness.] **3** that can be felt or noticed by the senses [a *sensible* change in temperature] **4** that can receive sensation [The eye is *sensible* to light rays.] —**sen′si·ble·ness** *n.* —**sen′si·bly** *adv.*

se·pal (sē′pəl) *n.* any of the leaves that form the calyx at the base of a flower

sep·a·rate (sep′ər āt) *v.* **1** to set apart; divide into parts or groups [*Separate* the good apples from the bad ones.] **2** to keep apart or divide by being or putting between [A hedge *separates* his yard from ours.] **3** to go apart; stop being together or joined [The friends *separated* at the crossroads.] —**sep′a·rat·ed, sep′a·rat·ing** *adj.* (sep′ər ət *or* sep′ rət) single or individual [the body's *separate* parts] —**sep′a·rate·ly** *adv.* —**sep′a·ra·tion** *n.*

se·quence (sē′kwens) *n.* **1** the following of one thing after another; succession [The *sequence* of events in their lives led to marriage.] **2** the order in which things follow one another [Line them up in *sequence* from shortest to tallest.] **3** a series of things that are related [a *sequence* of misfortunes]

se·ri·ous (sir′ē əs) *adj.* **1** having or showing deep thought; not frivolous; solemn; earnest [a *serious* student] **2** not joking or fooling; sincere [Is she *serious* about wanting to help?] **3** needing careful thought; important [a *serious* problem] **4** that can cause worry; dangerous [a *serious* illness] —**se′ri·ous·ly** *adv.* —**se′ri·ous·ness** *n.*

set·tle·ment (set′l mənt) *n.* a place where people have gone to settle; colony [early English *settlements* in Virginia]

shake (shāk) *v.* **1** to move quickly up and down, back and forth, or from side to side [to *shake* one's head in approval] **2** to clasp another's hand, as in greeting **3** to bring, force, throw, stir up, etc. by short, quick movements [I'll *shake* salt on the popcorn. *Shake* the medicine well before taking it.] **4** to tremble or make tremble [His voice *shook* with fear. Chills *shook* his body.] —**shook, shak·en** (shak′n), **shak′ing**

shal·low (shal′ō) *adj.* **1** not deep [a *shallow* lake] **2** not serious in thinking or strong in feeling [a *shallow* mind] ◆*n.* a shallow place, as in a river

shame·ful (shām′fəl) *adj.* **1** bringing shame or disgrace **2** not moral or decent —**shame′ful·ly** *adv.*

sharp·en (shärp′ən) *v.* to make or become sharp or sharper —**sharp′en·er** *n.*

she'll (shēl) *contraction* **1** she will **2** she shall

sher·bet (shur′bət) *n.* a frozen dessert of fruit juice, sugar, and water or milk

☆**sher·iff** (sher′if) *n.* the chief officer of the law in a county

shield (shēld) *n.* **1** a piece of armor carried on the arm to ward off blows in battle **2** something that guards or protects, as a safety guard over machinery **3** anything shaped like a shield, as a coat of arms ◆*v.* to guard or protect [Trees *shield* our house from the sun.]

ship (ship) *n.* **1** any vessel, larger than a boat, for traveling on deep water **2** the crew of a ship **3** an aircraft or spaceship ◆*v.* to put, take, go, or send in a ship or boat [The cargo was *shipped* from New York.] —**shipped, ship′ping**

ship·wreck (ship′rek) *n.* **1** the remains of a wrecked ship **2** the loss or ruin of a ship, as in a storm or crash ◆*v.* to wreck or destroy a ship

shoe·lace (shoo′lās) *n.* a lace of cord, leather, etc. used for fastening a shoe

shore·ward (shôr′wərd) *adj., adv.* toward the shore [Two boats were headed *shoreward.*]

☆**short·age** (shôrt′ij) *n.* a lack in the amount that is needed or expected [a *shortage* of help]

shred (shred) *n.* **1** a long, narrow strip or piece cut or torn off [My shirt was torn to *shreds.*] **2** a tiny piece or amount; fragment [a story without a *shred* of truth] ◆*v.* to cut or tear into shreds [*shredded* coconut] —**shred′ded** or **shred, shred′ding**

shy (shī) *adj.* **1** easily frightened; timid [a shy animal] **2** not at ease with other people; bashful [a *shy* child] —**shi′er** or **shy′er, shi′est** or **shy′est** —**shied, shy′ing** *v.* —**shy′ly** *adv.* —**shy′ness** *n.*

a	ask, fat
ā	ape, date
ä	car, lot
e	elf, ten
ē	even, meet
i	is, hit
ī	ice, fire
ō	open, go
ô	law, horn
oi	oil, point
oo	look, pull
o͞o	ooze, tool
ou	out, crowd
u	up, cut
ʉ	fur, fern
ə	a in ago
	e in agent
	e in father
	i in unity
	o in collect
	u in focus
ch	chin, arch
ŋ	ring, singer
sh	she, dash
th	thin, truth
th	then, father
zh	s in pleasure

sig·nal (sig′nəl) *n.* **1** something that tells when some action is to start or end, or is used as a warning or direction [A loud bell is the *signal* for a fire drill. The traffic *signal* is green, telling us to go.] **2** the electrical waves sent out or received as sounds or pictures in radio and television —**sig′naled** or **sig′nalled, sig′nal·ing** or **sig′nal·ling** *v.*

si·lence (sī′ləns) *n.* **1** a keeping still and not speaking, making noise, etc. [His *silence* meant he agreed.] **2** absence of any sound or noise; stillness [There was complete *silence* in the deep forest.] —**si′lenc·er** —**si′lenced, si′lenc·ing** *v.*

sin·cere (sin sir′) *adj.* not pretending or fooling; honest; truthful [Are you *sincere* in wanting to help?] —**sin·cer′er, sin·cer′est**

sin·cer·i·ty (sin ser′ə tē) *n.* the condition of being sincere; honesty; good faith

six (siks) *n., adj.* one more than five; the number 6

six·ty-four (siks′tē fôr) *n., adj.* the cardinal number that is equal to six times ten plus four; 64

skid (skid) *n.* ☆**1** a plank, log, etc. used as a support or as a track on which to slide something heavy **2** a sliding wedge used as a brake on a wheel ➤*v.* to slide without turning, as a wheel does on ice when it is held by a brake —**skid′ded, skid′ding**

slaugh·ter (slôt′ər *or* slät′ər) *n.* the act of killing people or animals in a cruel way or in large numbers ➤*v.* to kill for food; butcher [to *slaughter* a hog] —**slaugh′tered, slaugh′ter·ing**

sleep·y (slē′pē) *adj.* **1** ready or likely to fall asleep; drowsy **2** not very active; dull; quiet [a *sleepy* little town] —**sleep′i·er, sleep′i·est** —**sleep′i·ly** *adv.* —**sleep′i·ness** *n.*

slight (slīt) *adj.* **1** small in amount or degree; not great, strong, important, etc. [a *slight* change in temperature; a *slight* advantage; a *slight* bruise] **2** light in build; slender [Most jockeys are short and *slight.*] ➤*v.* to pay little or no attention to; neglect, snub, etc. [to *slight* one's homework; to *slight* a neighbor] —**slight′ly** *adv.* —**slight′er, slight′est** *adj.*

snout (snout) *n.* the part, including the nose and jaws, that sticks out from the face of pigs, dogs, and certain other animals

snow·drift (snō′ drift) *n.* a bank or pile of snow heaped up by the wind

soil (soil) *n.* the act of soiling or a soiled spot; stain ➤*v.* **1** to make or become dirty; stain; spot **2** to disgrace [to *soil* one's honor] —**soiled**

sor·row (sär′ō) *n.* a sad or troubled feeling; sadness; grief

spa·ghet·ti (spə get′ē) *n.* long, thin strings of dried flour paste, cooked by boiling or steaming and served with a sauce

Span·ish (span′ish) *adj.* of Spain, its people, etc. ➤*n.* the language of Spain and Spanish America —**the Spanish,** the people of Spain

spark·le (spär′kəl) *v.* **1** to give off sparks or flashes of light; glitter; glisten [A lake *sparkles* in sunlight.] **2** to be lively and witty [There was much *sparkling* talk at the party.] **3** to bubble as ginger ale does —**spar′kled, spar′kling**

spar·row (sper′ō) *n.* a small, often brown or gray songbird with a short beak

speak·er (spē′kər) *n.* **1** a person who speaks or makes speeches **2** the person who serves as chairman of a group of lawmakers, especially ☆**Speaker,** the chairman of the U.S. House of Representatives: *the full name is* **Speaker of the House 3** a device that changes electric current into sound waves, used as part of a hi-fi system, radio, etc.

spe·cies (spē′shēz *or* spē′sēz) *n.* **1** a group of plants or animals that are alike in certain ways [The lion and tiger are two different *species* of cat.] **2** a kind or sort [a *species* of bravery] —*pl.* **spe′cies** —**the species,** the human race

speech (spēch) *n.* **1** the act or way of speaking [We knew from their *speech* that they were from the South.] **2** the power to speak [She lost her *speech* from a stroke.] **3** something spoken; remark, utterance, etc. **4** a talk given in public [political *speeches* on TV]

spell·bound (spel′bound) *adj.* held fast as if by a spell; fascinated; enchanted

spin (spin) *v.* **1** to draw out the fibers of and twist into thread [to *spin* cotton, wool, flax, etc.] **2** to make from a thread given out by the body [Spiders *spin* webs.] **3** to tell slowly, with many details [to *spin* out a story] **4** to whirl around swiftly [The earth *spins* in space. *Spin* the wheel.] —**spun, spin′ning** —**spin′ner** *n.*

spi·ral (spī′rəl) *adj.* circling around a center in a flat or rising curve that keeps growing larger or smaller, as the thread of a screw, or that stays the same, as the thread of a bolt ➤*n.* a spiral curve or coil [The mainspring of a watch is a *spiral.*] ➤*v.* to move in or form into a spiral —**spi′raled** or **spi′ralled, spi′ral·ing** or **spi′ral·ling** —**spi′ral·ly** *adv.*

splen·did (splen′did) *adj.* **1** very bright, brilliant, showy, magnificent, etc. [a *splended* display; a *splendid* gown] **2** deserving high praise; glorious; grand [your *splendid* courage] **3** very good; excellent; fine; *used only in everyday talk* [a *splended* trip] —**splen′did·ly** *adv.*

spoil (spoil) **v.** to make or become useless, worthless or rotten; to damage; to ruin [Meat *spoils* fast in warm weather.] —**spoiled** or **spoilt, spoil´ing**

spo·ken (spō´kən) **v.** *past participle of* **speak** ◆**adj.** said aloud; oral [a *spoken* order]

sprawl (sprôl) **v.** to sit or lie with the arms and legs spread out in a relaxed or awkward way [He *sprawled* on the grass.] —**sprawled, sprawl´ing**

squawk (skwôk *or* skwäk) **n.** a loud, harsh cry such as a chicken or parrot makes ◆**v.** ☆to complain loudly: *used only in everyday talk* —**squawk´er n.**

sta·di·um (stā´dē əm) **n.** a place for outdoor games, meetings, etc., with rising rows of seats around the open field

stain (stān) **v.** to spoil with dirt or a patch of color; to soil or spot [The rug was *stained* with ink.] —**stained, stain´ing** ◆**n.** a dirty or colored spot [grass *stain*]

sta·men (stā´mən) **n.** the part of a flower in which the pollen grows, including the anther and its stem

state·ment (stāt´mənt) **n.** **1** the act of stating **2** something stated or said [May we quote your *statement*?] **3** a report or record, as of money owed [The customers receive monthly *statements*.]

sta·tion·ar·y (stā´shə ner´ē) **adj.** **1** not to be moved; fixed [*stationary* seats] **2** not changing in condition, value, etc. [*stationary* prices]

stat·ue (stach´ōō) **n.** the form or likeness of a person or animal carved in wood, stone, etc., modeled in clay, or cast in plaster or a metal

stead·y (sted´ē) **adj.** **1** firm; not shaky [a *steady* chair] **2** not changing or letting up; regular [a *steady* gaze; a *steady* worker] **3** not easily excited; calm [*steady* nerves] **4** serious and sensible; reliable [a *steady* young person] —**stead´i·er, stead´i·est** —**stead´ied, stead´y·ing v.** —**stead´i·ly adv.** —**stead´i·ness n.**

stick·y (stik´ē) **adj.** **1** that sticks; gluey; clinging [His fingers were *sticky* with candy.] **2** hot and damp; humid; *used only in everyday talk* [a *sticky* August day] —**stick´i·er, stick´i·est** —**stick´i·ness n.**

stiff·ness (stif´nəs) **n.** the condition of being hard to bend or stretch

stom·ach (stum´ək) **n.** **1** the large, hollow organ into which food goes after it is swallowed: food is partly digested in the stomach **2** the belly, or abdomen [The fighter was hit in the *stomach*.]

strange (strānj) **adj.** **1** not known, seen, or heard before; not familiar [I saw a *strange* person at the door.] **2** different from what is usual; peculiar; odd [wearing a *strange* costume] **3** not familiar; without experience [She is *strange* to this job.] —**strang´er, strang´est** —**strange´ly adv.**

straw·ber·ry (strô´ber´ē *or* strä´ber´ē) **n.** **1** the small, red, juicy fruit of a low plant of the rose family **2** this plant —*pl.* **straw´ber´ries**

strut (strut) **v.** to walk in a self-confident way, usually as if to attract attention [The famous singer *strutted* across the stage.] —**strut´ted, strut´ting**

stur·dy (stur´dē) **adj.** **1** strong and hardy [a *sturdy* oak] **2** not giving in; firm [*sturdy* defiance] —**stur´di·er, stur´di·est** —**stur´di·ly adv.** —**stur´di·ness n.**

sub·due (səb dōō´ *or* səb dyōō´) **v.** **1** to conquer or overcome; get control over [to *subdue* an invading army; to *subdue* a bad habit] **2** to make less strong or harsh; soften [*subdued* anger; *subdued* light; *subdued* colors] —**sub·dued´, sub·du´ing**

sub·ject (sub´jekt) **adj.** **1** under the power or control of another [The *subject* peoples in colonies often revolt.] **2** likely to have; liable [He is *subject* to fits of anger.] ◆**n.** **1** a person under the power or control of a ruler, government, etc. **2** a course of study, as in a school [What is your favorite *subject*?] —**sub·jec´tion n.**

sub·ma·rine (sub´mə rēn) **n.** a kind of ship that can travel underwater

sub·merge (sub murj´) **v.** to put, go, or stay underwater [Whales can *submerge* for as long as half an hour.] —**sub·merged´, sub·merg´ing**

sub·mit (sub mit´) **v.** **1** to give or offer to others for them to look over, decide about, etc.; refer [A new tax law was *submitted* to the voters.] **2** to give in to the power or control of another; surrender [We will never *submit* to the enemy.] —**sub·mit´ted, sub·mit´ting**

sub·scribe (səb skrīb´) **v.** **1** to agree to take and pay for [We *subscribed* to the magazine for a year.] **2** to promise to give [She *subscribed* $100 to the campaign for a new museum.] **3** to agree with or approve of [I *subscribe* to the principles in the Constitution.] —**sub·scribed´, sub·scrib´ing** —**sub·scrib´er n.**

sub·side (səb sīd´) **v.** **1** to sink to a lower level; go down [In June the river began to *subside*.] **2** to become quiet or less active [The angry waves *subsided*. The teacher's temper *subsided*.] —**sub·sid´ed, sub·sid´ing**

sub·sti·tute (sub´stə tōōt *or* sub´stə tyōōt) **n.** a person or thing that takes the place of another [He is a *substitute* for the regular teacher.] ◆**v.** to use as or be a substitute [to *substitute* vinegar for lemon juice; to *substitute* for an injured player] —**sub´sti·tut·ed, sub´sti·tut·ing** —**sub´sti·tu´tion n.**

sub·tract (səb trakt´) **v.** to take away, as a part from a whole or one number from another [If 3 is *subtracted* from 5, the remainder is 2.]

a	ask, fat
ā	ape, date
ä	car, lot
e	elf, ten
ē	even, meet
i	is, hit
ī	ice, fire
ō	open, go
ô	law, horn
oi	oil, point
oo	look, pull
ōō	ooze, tool
ou	out, crowd
u	up, cut
u	fur, fern
ə	a in ago
	e in agent
	e in father
	i in unity
	o in collect
	u in focus
ch	chin, arch
ŋ	ring, singer
sh	she, dash
th	thin, truth
th	then, father
zh	s in pleasure

suc·ceed (sək sēd′) *v.* **1** to manage to do or be what was planned; do or go well [I *succeeded* in convincing them to come with us.] **2** to come next after; follow [Carter *succeeded* Ford as president.]

suc·cess (sək ses′) *n.* **1** the result that was hoped for; satisfactory outcome [Did you have *success* in training your dog?] **2** the fact of becoming rich, famous, etc. [Her *success* did not change her.] **3** a successful person or thing [Our play was a *success*.]

suf·fer (suf′ər) *v.* **1** to feel or have pain, discomfort, etc. [to *suffer* from a headache] **2** to experience or undergo [The team *suffered* a loss when Sal was hurt.] **3** to become worse or go from good to bad [Her grades *suffered* when she didn't study.] **4** to put up with; bear [He won't *suffer* criticism.]

sug·gest (səg jest′) *v.* **1** to mention as something to think over, act on, etc. [I *suggest* we meet again.] **2** to bring to mind as something similar or in some way connected [The white dunes *suggested* snow-covered hills. Clouds *suggest* rain.]

sun·ny (sun′ē) *adj.* **1** bright with sunlight [Today is a *sunny* day.] **2** like or from the sun [A *sunny* beam shone through.] **3** cheerful; bright [Lynn has a *sunny* smile.] —**sun′ni·er, sun′ni·est**

sun·shine (sun′shīn) *n.* **1** the shining of sun **2** the light and heat from the sun **3** cheerfulness, happiness, etc. —**sun′shin·y** *adj.*

sup·ply (sə plī′) *v.* **1** to give what is needed; furnish [The camp *supplies* sheets and towels. The book *supplied* us with the facts.] **2** to take care of the needs of [to *supply* workers with tools] **3** to make up for; fill [These pills *supply* a deficiency of iron.] —**sup·plied′, sup·ply′ing**

sup·port (sə pôrt′) *v.* **1** to carry the weight or burden of; hold up [Will that old ladder *support* you?] **2** to take the side of; uphold or help **3** to earn a living for; provide for [He *supports* a large family.] **4** to help prove [Use examples to *support* your argument.] —**sup·port′er** *n.*

sur·prise (sər prīz′) *v.* **1** to cause to feel wonder by being unexpected [Her sudden anger *surprised* us.] **2** to come upon suddenly or unexpectedly [I *surprised* him in the act of stealing the watch.] **3** to attack or capture suddenly —**sur·prised′, sur·pris′ing**

sur·round (sər round′) *v.* to form or arrange around on all or nearly all sides; enclose [The police *surrounded* the criminals. The house is *surrounded* with trees.]

sur·vey (sər vā′ *for v.*; sur′vā *for n.*) *v.* to look over in a careful way; examine; inspect [The lookout *surveyed* the horizon.] —**sur·veyed′, sur·vey′ing** *n.* a detailed study or inspection made from gathering and analyzing evidence [We made a *survey* of the class's favorite hobbies.]

sur·vive (sər vīv′) *v.* **1** to continue to live or exist [Thanksgiving is a Pilgrim custom that *survives* today.] **2** to live or last longer than; outlive [Most people *survive* their parents.] **3** to continue to live or exist in spite of [We *survived* the fire.] —**sur·vived′, sur·viv′ing**

swal·low (swä′lō) *v.* **1** to let food, drink, etc. go through the throat into the stomach **2** to move the muscles of the throat as in swallowing something [I *swallowed* hard to keep from crying.] **3** to take in; engulf [The waters of the lake *swallowed* him up.] **4** to put up with; bear with patience [We refused to *swallow* their insults.]

sweat·er (swet′ər) *n.* a knitted outer garment for the upper part of the body

Swed·ish (swēd′ish) *adj.* of Sweden or the Swedes ◆*n.* the language of the Swedes

sweep (swēp) *v.* **1** to clean as by brushing with a broom [to *sweep* a floor] **2** to clear away as with a broom [*Sweep* the dirt from the porch.] **3** to carry away or destroy with a quick, strong motion [The tornado *swept* the shed away.] —**swept, sweep′ing** ◆*n.* the act of sweeping, as with a broom

sweep·er (swēp′ər) *n.* **1** a person or thing that sweeps **2** a device for cleaning floors

sweet (swēt) *adj.* **1** having the taste of sugar; having sugar in it [a *sweet* apple] **2** pleasant in taste, smell, sound, manner, etc. [*sweet* perfume; *sweet* music; a *sweet* child] ◆*adv.* in a sweet manner —**sweet′er, sweet′est** —**sweet′ish** *adj.* —**sweet′ly** *adv.* —**sweet′ness** *n.*

sym·bol (sim′bəl) *n.* an object, mark, sign, etc. that stands for another object, or for an idea, quality, etc. [The dove is a *symbol* of peace. The mark $ is the *symbol* for dollar or dollars.]

sym·pho·ny (sim′fə nē) *n.* **1** a long piece of music for a full orchestra, usually divided into four movements with different rhythms and themes **2** a large orchestra for playing such works: *its full name is* **symphony orchestra 3** harmony, as of sounds, color, etc. [The dance was a *symphony* in motion.] —*pl.* **sym′pho·nies** —**sym·phon·ic** (sim fän′ik) *adj.* —**sym·phon′i·cal·ly** *adv.*

tar·dy (tär′dē) *adj.* not on time; late; delayed [to be *tardy* for class] —**tar′di·er, tar′di·est**

tel·e·graph (tel′ə graf) *n.* a device or system for sending messages by a code of electrical signals that are sent over a wire, by radio or by microwave

tel·e·phone (tel′ə fōn) *n.* **1** a way of sending sounds over distances by changing them into electric signals which are sent through a wire and then changed back into sounds **2** a device for sending and receiving sounds in this way —**tel′e·phoned, tel′e·phon·ing** *v.* —**tel·e·phon·ic** (tel′ə fän′ ik) *adj.*

tem·per·a·ture (tem′prə chər *or* tem′pər ə chər) *n.* **1** the degree of hotness or coldness, as of air, liquids, the body, etc., usually as measured by a thermometer **2** a body heat above the normal, which is about 37°C or 98.6°F; fever

ter·ri·ble (ter′ə bəl) *adj.* **1** causing great fear or terror; dreadful [a *terrible* flood] **2** very great; severe [*terrible* suffering] **3** very bad or unpleasant: *used only in everyday talk* [Our guest had *terrible* manners.] —**ter′ri·bly** *adv.*

Tex·as (teks′əs) a state in the south central part of the U.S.: abbreviated **Tex., TX** —**Tex′an** *adj., n.*

thaw (thô *or* thä) *v.* to melt [The snow *thawed.*] —**thawed, thaw′ing**

the·o·ry (thē′e rē *or* thir′ē) *n.* an explanation of how or why something happens, especially one based on scientific study and reasoning [Einstein's *theory* of relativity] —*pl.* **the′o·ries**

they've (thāv) *contraction* they have

thick·en (thik′ən) *v.* to make or become thick or thicker [Adding flour will *thicken* the gravy.] —**thick′ened, thick′en·ing**

thief (thēf) *n.* a person who steals, especially one who steals secretly —*pl.* **thieves** (thēvz)

throb (thräb) *v.* to beat or vibrate hard or fast, as the heart does when one is excited —**throbbed, throb′bing** ◆*n.* the act of throbbing; a strong beat

throw (thrō) *v.* **1** to send through the air by a fast motion of the arm; hurl, toss, etc. [to *throw* a ball] **2** to make fall down; upset [to *throw* someone in wrestling] **3** to send or cast in a certain direction, as a glance, light, shadow, etc. **4** to put suddenly into some condition or place [to *throw* into confusion; to throw into prison] —**threw, thrown, throw′ing**

tick·le (tik′əl) *v.* **1** to touch or stroke lightly, as with a finger or feather, so as to cause twitching, laughter, etc. **2** to have such a scratching or twitching feeling [The dust makes my nose *tickle.*] **3** to give pleasure to; amuse; delight [The joke really *tickled* her.] —**tick′led, tick′ling** —**tick′ler** *n.*

tight (tīt) *adj.* **1** made so that water, air, etc. cannot pass through [a *tight* boat] **2** put together firmly or closely [a *tight* knot] **3** fitting too closely [a *tight* shirt] **4** stretched and strained; taut [a *tight* wire; *tight* nerves] —**tight′ly** *adv.* —**tight′ness** *n.*

tight·en (tīt′n) *v.* to make or become tight or tighter

toad·stool (tōd′stool) *n.* a mushroom, especially one that is poisonous

toast (tōst) *v.* **1** to brown the surface of by heating, as bread **2** to warm [*Toast* yourself by the fire.] ◆*n.* toasted bread —**toast′er**

toil (toil) *v.* **1** to work hard; labor **2** to go slowly with pain or effort [to *toil* up a hill] ◆*n.* hard work —**toil′er**

to·ma·to (tə māt′ō *or* tə mät′ō) *n.* **1** a red or yellow, round fruit, with a juicy pulp, used as a vegetable **2** the plant it grows on —*pl.* **to·ma′toes**

to·mor·row (tə′ mär′ō) *adv.* on the day after today ◆*n.* **1** the day after today **2** some future time

tor·na·do (tôr nā′ dō) *n.* a high, narrow column of air that is whirling very fast: it is often seen as a slender cloud shaped like a funnel, that usually destroys everything in its narrow path —*pl.* **tor·na′does** or **tor·na′dos**

tor·pe·do (tôr pē′ dō) *n.* a large, exploding missile shaped like a cigar: it moves under water under its own power to blow up enemy ships —*pl.* **tor·pe′does**

tor·rent (tôr′ənt) *n.* **1** a swift, rushing stream of water **2** any wild, rushing flow [a *torrent* of insults] **3** a heavy fall of rain

tough (tuf) *adj.* **1** that will bend or twist without tearing or breaking [*tough* rubber] **2** that cannot be cut or chewed easily [*tough* meat] **3** strong and healthy; robust [a *tough* pioneer] **4** very difficult or hard [a *tough* job] —**tough′ness** *n.*

tour·ist (toor′ist) *n.* a person who tours or travels for pleasure ◆*adj.* of or for tourists

tow·el (tou′əl *or* toul) *n.* a piece of soft paper or cloth for drying things by wiping

trans·fer (trans fur′ *or* trans′fər) *v.* **1** to move, carry, send, or change from one person or place to another [He *transferred* his notes to another notebook. Jill has *transferred* to a new school.] **2** to move a picture, design, etc. from one surface to another, as by making wet and pressing ☆**3** to change from one bus, train, etc. to another —**trans·ferred′, trans·fer′ring**

trans·late (trans lāt′ *or* tranz lāt′) *v.* **1** to put into words of a different language [to *translate* a Latin poem into English] **2** to change into another form [to *translate* ideas into action] **3** to change from one place or condition to another; especially, to carry up to heaven —**trans·lat′ed, trans·lat′ing**

trans·mit (trans mit′ *or* tranz mit′) *v.* to send from one person, place, or thing to another; pass on; transfer [to *transmit* a disease] —**trans·mit′ted, trans·mit′ting**

trans·par·ent (trans per′ənt) *adj.* so clear or so fine that objects on the other side can be easily seen [*transparent* glass]

a	ask, fat
ā	ape, date
ä	car, lot
e	elf, ten
ē	even, meet
i	is, hit
ī	ice, fire
ō	open, go
ô	law, horn
oi	oil, point
oo	look, pull
oo	ooze, tool
ou	out, crowd
u	up, cut
u	fur, fern
ə	a in ago
	e in agent
	e in father
	i in unity
	o in collect
	u in focus
ch	chin, arch
ŋ	ring, singer
sh	she, dash
th	thin, truth
th	then, father
zh	s in pleasure

trans·plant (trans plant′) **v. 1** to dig up from one place and plant in another **2** to move tissue or an organ by surgery from one person or part of the body to another; graft ◆**n.** (trans′plant) something transplanted, as a body organ or seedling

trans·port (trans pôrt′) **v. 1** to carry from one place to another [to *transport* goods by train or truck] **2** to cause strong feelings in [*transported* with delight] **3** to send to a place far away as a punishment

treas·ure (trezh′ər) **n. 1** money, jewels, etc. collected and stored up **2** a person or thing that is loved or held dear ◆**v. 1** to love or hold dear; cherish [I *treasure* their friendship.] **2** to store away or save up, as money; hoard —**treas′ured, treas′ur·ing**

tri·an·gle (trī′aŋ′ gəl) **n. 1** a flat figure with three sides and three angles **2** anything shaped like this **3** a musical instrument that is a steel rod bent in a triangle: it makes a high, tinkling sound when struck with a metal rod

tri·o (trē′ō) **n. 1** a piece of music for three voices or three instruments **2** the three people who sing or play it **3** any group of three —pl. **tri′os**

tri·ple (trip′əl) **adj. 1** made up of three [A *triple* cone has three dips of ice cream.] **2** three times as much or as many ◆**n. 1** an amount three times as much or as many ☆**2** a hit in baseball on which the batter gets to third base —**tri′pled, tri′pling v.**

tri·plet (trip′lət) **n. 1** any one of three children born at the same time to the same mother **2** any group of three

tri·pod (trī′päd) **n.** a stand, frame, etc. with three legs: cameras and small telescopes are often held up by tripods

tri·umph (trī′əmf) **n. 1** a victory, as in a battle; success [His *triumph* over illness inspired us.] **2** great joy over a victory or success [She grinned in *triumph* when she won the race.] ◆**v.** to be the winner; win victory or success [to *triumph* over an enemy] —**tri·um·phal** (trī um′f'l) **adj.**

trout (trout) **n.** a small food fish of the salmon family, found mainly in fresh water

trudge (truj) **v.** to walk, especially in a tired way or with effort —**trudged, trudg′ing** ◆**n.** a long or tiring walk

☆**type·writ·er** (tīp′rīt′ ər) **n.** a machine with a keyboard for making printed letters or figures on paper

ty·phoid (tī′ foid) **n.** a serious disease that is spread as by infected food or drinking water, and causing fever, sores in the intestines, etc.: *the full name is* **typhoid fever**

ty·phoon (tī foon′) **n.** any violent tropical cyclone that starts in the western Pacific

un- **1** *a prefix meaning* not *or* the opposite of [An *unhappy* person is one who is not happy, but sad.] **2** *a prefix meaning* to reverse or undo the action of [To *untie* a shoelace is to reverse the action of tying it.]

un·a·vail·a·ble (un′ə vēl′ə bəl) **adj.** not able to be gotten, used, or reached [This book is now *unavailable*.]

un·cooked (un kookt′) **adj.** not cooked; raw

un·cov·er (un kuv′ər) **v. 1** to remove the cover or covering from **2** to make known; disclose, as a hidden fact **3** to take off one's hat, as in showing respect

un·der·neath (un′der neth′) **adv., prep.** under; below; beneath

un·der·sea (un′dər sē′) **adj., adv.** beneath the surface of the sea

un·der·wa·ter (un′dər wôt′ər *or* un′dər wät′ər) **adj., adv.** under the surface of the water

un·for·giv·a·ble (un′fər giv′ə bəl) **adj.** not deserving to be pardoned; inexcusable

u·nit (yoon′it) **n. 1** a single person or group, especially as a part of a whole [an army *unit*] **2** a single part with some special use [the lens *unit* of a camera] **3** a fixed amount or measure used as a standard [The ounce is a *unit* of weight.] **4** the smallest whole number; one

un·just (un just′) **adj.** not just or right; unfair [an *unjust* rule] —**un·just′ly adv.**

un·law·ful (un lô′fəl *or* un lä′fəl) **adj.** against the law; illegal —**un·law′ful·ly adv.** —**un·law′ful·ness n.**

un·like·ly (un līk′lē) **adj. 1** not likely to happen or be true [an *unlikely* story] **2** not likely to be right or successful [an *unlikely* place to dig for gold]

un·sel·fish (un sel′fish) **adj.** not selfish; putting the good of others above one's own interests —**un·self′ish·ly adv.** —**un·self′ish·ness n.**

un·u·su·al (un yoo′zhoo əl) **adj.** not usual or common; rare; remarkable —**un·u′su·al·ly adv.**

us·a·ble *or* **use·a·ble** (yoo′zə bəl) **adj.** that can be used; fit or ready for use

va·ca·tion (vā kā′shən) **n.** a period of time when one stops working, going to school, etc. in order to rest and have recreation ◆**v.** to take one's vacation

val·u·a·ble (val′y͞o͝o ə bəl *or* val′yə bəl) *adj.* **1** having value or worth; especially, worth much money **2** thought of as precious, useful, worthy, etc. ✦*n.* something of value, as a piece of jewelry

valve (valv) *n.* **1** a device, as in a pipe, that controls the flow of a gas or liquid by means of a flap, lid, or plug that closes off the pipe **2** a membrane in the body that acts in this way [The *valves* of the heart let the blood flow in one direction only.] **3** a device, as in a trumpet, that opens a branch to the main tube so as to change the pitch **4** one of the parts making up the shell of a clam, oyster, etc.

va·por (va′pər) *n.* **1** a thick mist or mass of tiny drops of water floating in the air, as steam or fog **2** the gas formed when a substance that is usually liquid or solid is heated [Mercury *vapor* is used in some lamps.]

vault (vôlt) *n.* **1** an arched ceiling or roof **2** a room with such a ceiling, or a space that seems to have an arch [the *vault* of the sky] ☆**3** a room for keeping money, valuable papers, etc. safe, as in a bank

ve·hi·cle (vē′i kəl *or* vē′hi kəl) *n.* **1** a means of carrying persons or things, especially over land or in space, as an automobile, bicycle, spacecraft, etc. **2** a means by which something is expressed, passed along, etc. [TV is a *vehicle* for advertising.] **3** a liquid, as oil or water, with which pigments are mixed to make paint

vein (vān) *n.* **1** any blood vessel that carries blood back to the heart from some part of the body **2** any of the fine lines, or ribs, in a leaf or in an insect's wing **3** a layer of mineral, rock, etc. formed in a crack in different rock [a *vein* of silver or of coal]

ver·dict (vur′dikt) *n.* **1** the decision reached by a jury in a law case [a *verdict* of "not guilty"] **2** any decision or opinion

vet·er·an (vet′ər ən *or* ve′trən) *n.* **1** a person who has served in the armed forces **2** a person with much experience in some kind of work ✦*adj.* having had long experience in some work or service [*veteran* troops; a *veteran* diplomat]

vic·tim (vik′tim) *n.* **1** someone or something killed, hurt, sacrificed, etc. [a *victim* of the storm; the *victims* of prejudice] **2** a person who is cheated or tricked [a *victim* of swindlers]

vic·to·ry (vik′tər ē) *n.* the winning of a battle, struggle, or contest; success in defeating an enemy or rival —*pl.* **vic′to·ries**

vil·lage (vil′ij) *n.* **1** a group of houses in the country, smaller than a town **2** the people of a village —**vil′lag·er**

vi·o·lence (vī′ə ləns) *n.* great strength or force [the *violence* of a tornado]

vi·o·lent (vī′ə lənt) *adj.* showing or acting with great force that causes damage or injury [*violent* winds] —**vi′o·lent·ly** *adv.*

vis·i·ble (viz′ə bəl) *adj.* that can be seen or noticed; evident [a barely *visible* scar; a *visible* increase in crime] —**vis′i·bly** *adv.*

vo·cal·ist (vō′kəl ist) *n.* a person who sings; singer

vol·ca·no (vôl kā nō *or* väl kā′nō) *n.* **1** an opening in the earth's surface through which molten rock from inside the earth is thrown up **2** a hill or mountain of ash and molten rock built up around such an opening —*pl.* **vol·ca′noes** or **vol·ca′nos**

vol·ume (väl′y͞o͞om) *n.* **1** a book [You may borrow four *volumes* at a time.] **2** one of the books of a set [*Volume* III of the encyclopedia] **3** the amount of space inside something, measured in cubic inches, feet, etc. [The *volume* of this box is 27 cubic feet, or .756 cubic meter.]

vol·un·teer (väl ən tir′) *n.* a person who offers to do something of his or her own free will, as one who enlists in the armed forces by choice ✦*adj.* of or done by volunteers [a *volunteer* regiment; *volunteer* help]

vot·er (vōt′ər) *n.* a person who votes or has the right to vote

voy·age (voi′ij) *n.* **1** a journey by water [an ocean *voyage*] **2** a journey through the air or through outer space [a *voyage* by rocket] ✦*v.* to make a voyage —**voy′aged, voy′ag·ing** —**voy′ag·er** *n.*

waf·fle (wäf′əl) *n.* a crisp cake with small, square hollows, cooked in a waffle iron

walk·way (wôk′wā) *n.* a passage for walking

war·ri·or (wôr′ē ər) *n.* a soldier: not often used today

wash·a·ble (wôsh′ə b'əl *or* wäsh′ə bəl) *adj.* able to be washed without being damaged

wa·ter·mel·on (wôt′ər mel ən *or* wät′ər mel ən) *n.* a large melon with a green rind and juicy, red pulp with many seeds

wealth (welth) *n.* **1** much money or property; riches **2** a large amount [a *wealth* of ideas] **3** any valuable thing or things [the *wealth* of the oceans]

weath·er (we*th*′er) *n.* the conditions outside at any particular time with regard to temperature, sunshine, rainfall, etc. [We have good *weather* today for a picnic.] ✦*v.* to pass through safely [to *weather* a storm]

weird (wird) *adj.* **1** strange or mysterious in a ghostly way [*Weird* sounds came from the cave.] **2** very odd, strange, etc. [What a *weird* hat! What *weird* behavior!] —**weird′ly** *adv.* —**weird′ness** *n.*

wheel·bar·row (hwēl′bar ō *or* wēl′ber ō) *n.* a small kind of cart pushed or pulled by hand and having a single wheel

a	ask, fat
ā	ape, date
ä	car, lot
e	elf, ten
ē	even, meet
i	is, hit
ī	ice, fire
ō	open, go
ô	law, horn
oi	oil, point
o͝o	look, pull
o͞o	ooze, tool
ou	out, crowd
u	up, cut
ʉ	fur, fern
ə	a in ago
	e in agent
	e in father
	i in unity
	o in collect
	u in focus
ch	chin, arch
ŋ	ring, singer
sh	she, dash
th	thin, truth
th	then, father
zh	s in pleasure

whis·tle (hwis′əl *or* wis′əl) *v.* **1** to make a high, shrill sound as by forcing breath through puckered lips or by sending steam through a small opening **2** to move with a high, shrill sound [The arrow *whistled* past her ear.] **3** to blow a whistle **4** to produce by whistling [to *whistle* a tune] —**whis′tled, whis′tling** ◆*n.* a device for making whistling sounds —**whis′tler**

whole·sale (hōl′sāl) *n.* the sale of goods in large amounts, especially to retail stores that resell them to actual users ◆*adj.* **1** of or having to do with such sale of goods [a *wholesale* dealer; a *wholesale* price] **2** widespread or general [*wholesale* destruction by the volcano] ◆*adv.* **1** in wholesale amounts or at wholesale prices [We are buying the clothes *wholesale.*] **2** in a widespread or general way [The members refused to obey the new rules *wholesale.*] ◆*v.* to sell or be sold in large amounts, usually at lower prices —**whole′saled, whole′sal·ing** —**whole′sal·er** *n.*

who'll (hōōl) *contraction* **1** who shall **2** who will

wil·der·ness (wil′dər nəs) *n.* a wild region; wasteland or overgrown land with no settlers

wis·dom (wiz′dəm) *n.* **1** the quality of being wise; good judgment, that comes from knowledge and experience in life [She had the *wisdom* to save money for her old age.] **2** learning; knowledge [a book filled with the *wisdom* of India]

with·draw (with drô′ *or* with drô′) *v.* **1** to take or pull out; remove [to *withdraw* one's hand from a pocket] **2** to move back; go away; retreat [She *withdrew* behind the curtain.] **3** to leave; retire or resign [to *withdraw* from school] **4** to take back; recall [I *withdraw* my statement.] —**with·drew′, with·drawn′, with·draw′ing**

wolf (woolf) *n.* **1** a wild animal that looks like a dog: it kills other animals for food **2** a person who is fierce, cruel, greedy, etc. —*pl.* **wolves**

wolves (woolvz) *n.* *plural of* **wolf**

wom·an (woom′ən) *n.* **1** an adult, female human being **2** women as a group **3** a female servant —*pl.* **wom′en**

wom·en (wim′ən) *n.* *plural of* **woman**

won·der·ful (wun′dər fəl) *adj.* **1** that causes wonder; marvelous; amazing **2** very good; excellent: *used only in everyday talk* —**won′der·ful·ly** *adv.*

wor·ry (wur′ē) *v.* **1** to be or make troubled in mind; feel or make uneasy or anxious [Don't *worry.* Her absence *worried* us.] **2** to annoy, bother, etc. [Stop *worrying* me with such unimportant matters.] **3** to bite at and shake about with the teeth [The dog *worried* an old shoe.] —**wor′ried, wor′ry·ing** ◆*n.* a troubled feeling; anxiety; care —*pl.* **wor′ries**

wrap·per (rap′ər) *n.* **1** a person or thing that wraps **2** a covering or cover [a newspaper mailed in a paper *wrapper*] **3** a woman's dressing gown

wrath (rath) *n.* great anger; rage; fury

wreath (rēth) *n.* **1** a ring of leaves, flowers, etc. twisted together **2** something like this [*wreaths* of smoke] —*pl.* **wreaths** (rēthz)

wres·tle (res′əl) *v.* **1** to struggle with, trying to throw or force to the ground without striking blows with the fists **2** to struggle hard, as with a problem; contend —**wres′tled, wres′tling** ◆*n.* **1** the action or a bout of wrestling **2** a struggle or contest —**wres′tler**

wrin·kle (riŋ′kəl) *n.* a small or uneven crease or fold [*wrinkles* in a coat; *wrinkles* in skin] ◆*v.* **1** to make wrinkles in [a brow *wrinkled* with care] **2** to form wrinkles [This cloth *wrinkles* easily.] —**wrin′kled, wrin′kling**

write (rīt) *v.* **1** to form words, letters, etc., as with a pen or pencil **2** to form the words, letters, etc. of [*Write* your address here.] **3** to be the author or composer of [Dickens *wrote* novels. Mozart *wrote* symphonies.] —**wrote, writ′ten, writ′ing**

writ·ten (rit′n) *past participle of* **write**

yes·ter·day (yes′tər dā) *adv.* on the day before today ◆*n.* **1** the day before today **2** some time in the past

yield (yēld) *v.* **1** to give up; surrender [to *yield* to a demand; to *yield* a city] **2** to give or grant [to *yield* the right of way; to *yield* a point] **3** to give way [The gate would not *yield* to our pushing.] **4** to bring forth or bring about; produce; give [The orchard *yielded* a good crop. The business *yielded* high profits.]

yolk (yōk) *n.* the yellow part of an egg

you'd (yōōd) *contraction* **1** you had **2** you would

you've (yōōv) *contraction* you have

zo·ol·o·gy (zō äl′ə jē) *n.* the science that studies animals and animal life —**zo·ol′o·gist**

Spelling Notebook

Spelling Notebook